D1631500

At Home with Michaela

By the same author

LEOPARD IN MY LAP

RIDE A RHINO

MAID OF MONEY

THE VOICE OF THE LARK

frontispiece Michaela feeds the ostrich chicks with lucerne, which is one of their favourite foods

Michaela Denis

At Home with Michaela

HUTCHINSON OF LONDON

HUTCHINSON & CO (*Publishers*) LTD
178–202 Great Portland Street, London, W.1

London Melbourne Sydney
Auckland Bombay Toronto
Johannesburg New York

First published 1965

This book has been set in Baskerville, printed in Great Britain on Antique Wove paper by The Anchor Press, Ltd., and bound by Wm. Brendon & Son Ltd., both of Tiptree, Essex.

To

Armand with Love

Contents

Illustrations

Colour frontispiece and pictures 1–4, 6, 8, 9, 20, 26–30, 34, 36 *Des Bartlett, Armand Denis Productions*

Pictures 7, 10–19
Bob Campbell, Armand Denis Productions

Pictures 23, 24, 25, 35
Akhtar Hussein of 'Nation Newspapers', Nairobi

Pictures 5, 21, 22, 31–33
Michaela Denis

PROLOGUE

Why Live in Africa?

IT WAS a sunny day in Bond Street. The two young girls who passed me gave me that meaningful stare which shows that I have been recognised. When I was barely past them, one said, 'You know who that was?' Her friend answered, 'Michaela Denis.'

I automatically looked behind me when I heard my name. They looked embarrassed, but I smiled at them. Encouraged they stopped and spoke to me.

'Where's your leopard?'

'The management of the hotel is a little narrow-minded, so I left him in Kenya.'

'Aren't you pleased to be over here and aren't you sorry when you have to go back?' asked the girl, looking down at my smart footwear and possibly mentally comparing them with my sensible safari shoes.

I was astounded. The girl was in the minority. Many of our correspondents begged us to tell them how they could go to Kenya to live.

It seemed rude to say as vehemently as I felt that I hated leaving Kenya. I said good-bye to the young girls after giving them autographs, and our conversation echoed in my mind.

The girl who asked me about our house in Kenya obviously would not have enjoyed living in the country, for she was a true product of the city. There is a vast mass of people who would do anything to live in natural surroundings with plenty of space and trees around them. I cannot guess what proportion these two different schools of thought represent, but I do know that we are flooded with letters from people all over the world begging us to take them to Kenya. Some ask for jobs, but some even plead to come at their own expense, or ask us what we would charge to accept them into our units. I feel sad at having to refuse them, because the writers of these letters so often betray the fact that they have given a great deal of thought to their decision to reject a 'civilisation'.

I was in love with Kenya. This love affair had started from the day I first stepped off the plane so many years ago. It had made of me, the veteran traveller, a stay-at-home. I, who had always been so foot-loose, dreaded now to leave the object of my infatuation.

Armand, of course, teased me about it. With phrases such as: 'You, of all people, a gardener', or 'Building again?' 'Making new curtains?'

Kenya is an extraordinarily comfortable place to live. Its climate is second to none in the world. It has every kind of landscape for every kind of taste. The desert lover will find what he wants as easily as the lover of the lush forests or even those conservative people who want to find another Europe so far from their home. The more you crave for Europe, the higher you go, for Kenya's climate is governed by altitude.

Armand and I live near the Equator, but the altitude of Langata, where we built our house, is round about 6,000 feet. Most of the year the temperature is in the eighties, and for only one brief period in August do we shiver in a morning temperature which can be as low as fifty-five degrees.

'Do you live in a house?' the girl had asked.

Yes, we did indeed live in a house, and when I met Armand that day for lunch I immediately suggested that we should include some scenes of our house in our television films. 'People wouldn't be interested,' Armand said. But I insisted. 'She asked me if we live in a tent when we are in Kenya.' I could see Armand was impressed. We both looked at one another and laughed. Armand said, 'Did you tell her we live in a museum?' But he said it proudly. Mysterious objects frequently appeared at the house, for I am a born collector. I love the beautiful and the rare, the ancient, and even the new if it has good lines.

Armand designed the house and to this day he still says that he would not change it. Except for a flat roof . . . but more of that later.

I

The Sun, the Forest—even Kilimanjaro

IT WAS Armand's task to find the site of our home. It had to be near Nairobi, because our films had to be sent off by air to be processed, and had to be in a non-claustrophobic place.

'What do you mean by a non-claustrophobic place?' asked Armand.

'Oh, somewhere where you can't see other houses from yours.'

We once couldn't find our house when it was first built and we had been on safari for a few weeks. It had rained in our absence. The vegetation was so luxuriant the house was hidden. We wandered round for half an hour where we thought it should be. We found the British Legion House, which we knew was above us on the hill. They were astounded when we told them that there was another house near them.

Yes, Armand had found the perfect site. It was at Langata, eleven miles from Nairobi. We had seen only one or two alternatives before the final choice. One was a large coffee farm beyond Limuru. It was overgrown, neglected. But the coffee trees were in full flower, giving promise of a bumper crop. A persuasive friend of ours tried to sell us on the idea of starting a company, in which he would also share and act as manager for the plantation. Coffee is an ornamental crop. Its white waxy blooms would not look amiss in a drawing-room. We were tempted, but common sense prevailed.

The second place we viewed lay deep in a wood of wattle. We could have been in Australia. When the estate agent heard of our plans he said: 'I know just the place for you. It could be England.'

'No!' we cried. 'It must be African. As African as possible.'

The agent looked shocked. He suggested no more properties for us to view. We drove back to our hotel in silence through the back streets of Eastleigh—which looked for all the world like Bombay.

Armand and I wanted a typically African location for our home. Neither of us could see the point in living in an exciting place like Africa and turning it into a second-rate Europe. A few afternoons later Armand said to me, 'Come for a drive, Michaela.' He didn't tell me why we were going in that direction, although I guessed when the car stopped and we went on foot through the bush. I followed Armand's broad-shouldered figure knowing that there must be something special to see. Even his back betrayed pent-up excitement. Abruptly we came to a stop. At our feet was a steep drop. We were on the edge of a quarry. In front of us was a ravine. Indigenous trees of unmistakable African appearance crowded thickly on the steep banks. From the valley's depths came the gurgle of water. A river!

'Like it?'

'It's breathtaking.'

And so it was. Armand managed to manœuvre our Land Rover back to the quarry's edge on an almost obliterated track which had been used by the quarry workers. Large ruts from the heavily loaded lorries made our ride a rough one. The coarse vegetation on the track which we crushed had a curious, almost minty, smell.

We stopped the truck where we had gone on foot. Armand scrambled on top of the roof. I followed him. He put his arm round my waist, and for a few seconds we were silent, as we might have been in homage before a great work of art. This was indeed a work of art, formed by nature and devised after centuries of a river's carving, of planting the slow-growing forest trees. Sunbirds thrust their curved beaks into blossoms of mauve and honey-coloured flowers which decked the trees.

From our vantage point on top of the truck we looked across the Masai Reserve. The plain had the purple irregular bulk of Ngong Hills on the far right of the landscape. The hills resembled a giant's knuckles. On the left was a snow-capped mountain in the distance.

'Look, Michaela,' Armand tightened his grip around my waist, 'Kilimanjaro.'

'Armand, you promised me an African home. But you never mentioned we should have a view of Kilimanjaro.'

'What makes you think that this will be our home?' he asked, but he was only teasing.

We hugged each other in sheer ecstasy. Such a perfect place was unique. Could it really be so near those horrible but useful innovations—aeroplanes, shops, cars and other modern conveniences?

'I am going to design our house,' Armand said as he stopped hugging me. 'I have always wondered why architects when given a view insist on having the bedrooms upstairs. You can't look at a view when you're asleep. You can never have as good a view on the ground floor as you can on the second.'

I agreed wholeheartedly with Armand. We had one thing in common. We liked things because we liked them, regardless of established custom. Tradition was all right if it was backed up by common sense. But what kind of a maniac would want to make our living-rooms on the ground floor?

Our beauty spot was part of the Hardy Estate. The land had recently been acquired by Remy Martin, a wiry aristocratic-looking Englishman. 'No relation to the cognac Remy Martins,' he ruefully replied to our unspoken question.

I was curious about the Hardys. Who were they, what did they do? I could discover nothing about Mr. Hardy, but Mrs. Hardy had become a legend. She was dark, beautiful and often wore a sari. She was a faith healer. She built herself a little sanctuary-cum-chapel some two or three miles from our land. It was while she was visiting South Africa that she became ill and was sent to hospital. Although not Jewish herself, she became a patient at the Jewish hospital.

She quarrelled with her heir, and, as a consequence, when she was on her death bed she left the whole of the Hardy Estate to the hospital. Although at her death's door, she decided to alter her will. It was only the old lady's fury which kept her alive long enough for her to see her lawyer. She died peacefully as soon as the will had been altered. Remy bought the estate from the representatives of the Jewish hospital.

We were nearly the first people to buy a plot in this area. Armand set up camp on what was the site many years later of my second goldfish pond.

Our African servants stood armed with pangas when they heard us come home at night after going to a movie in Nairobi.

'Why are you afraid?' I asked.

'Very bad men come here to hide,' Gitau answered.

He was right. Even murderers in those days had been known to go into hiding in the densely wooded valley.

Armand bought some squared paper, the type that children use in schools for sums. On this he drew plans of the house, using the squares as representing feet. From these plans the house was built exactly to scale, and without modification. After all these years I still think it is the most beautiful house I know.

I still remember how our house was conceived in Armand's head. When I close my eyes I can see him bending over that squared paper at the camp table, his khaki shirtsleeves rolled up above his elbows. I remember how I put my arms around him as he explained where each room would be. The house meant very much to me. I had been so poor as a child. Life had been kind to me, for I had lifted myself from a harsh ugliness of overcrowded, squalid, narrow streets, to the paradise of unspoiled nature.

I had found, besides, a husband who was not only my lover, but, in a mystic way, teacher and father. My father had died when I was three months old. Life in the back streets was not easy.

Luckily I won scholarships. But often I longed for someone of my own. I had to be tough to climb from the misery of cities, which even today make me slightly uneasy.

Armand had a first-class education. I find endless pleasure in talking to him. He looks benign. On the rare occasions when he is not benign I hate him with the passion of the betrayed. This is not his fault. Neither is it entirely mine. It is the result of my early deprivation, my fatherless state. For it is terribly dangerous to force another human being to assume the duties of a father, and to protect you, even sometimes from your own fears.

My fears, however, were not the kind that girls usually have. I wasn't afraid of insects, the creepy crawlies which abound in the tropics and which have often been our star performers in 'On Safari'. I wasn't afraid of snakes, only wary of them. I have had a machine gun stuck in my chest during a revolution in South America. Surely even the most unskilled marksman with such a weapon couldn't miss. Especially when that marksman was primed with coca, the raw material of cocaine. I'm not afraid of death. I'm not dogmatic about an after-life, but it helps to be psychic. I am certainly not afraid of other human beings with different customs to those I am used to.

No, my fears were within. Outwardly I was fearless. My only fear was of being separated from the man I loved. Fear not so much of losing him but of not belonging together. I was too proud to confess such girlish weakness. In those first wonderful years together we were as one.

Armand and I continued to go on safari as our house was being built. Each time we returned the house was never in completion. There was a long period when our home was a mere rectangle on the ground. The first really exciting moment came on the day we returned from a filming trip to find that we had a first floor.

There seemed to be an army of people working on the house on that golden day. It was in the days before the term 'multi-racial' became fashionable. The building of our house was a perfect forerunner of the harmonious building together of different races into one society. Our house was to be multi-racial from the beginning, at a time when it was considered both unfashionable and undesirable to fraternise with other races.

Around us sat Luo tribesmen, shaping stones, which they did skilfully with a steel chisel and mallet. They held the stones between their knees and they hammered. Bearded Sikhs worked on the woodwork, squatting on their heels. They talked animatedly amongst themselves in Punjabi, or occasionally shouted to the Luo in Swahili. There was, besides, a European plumber, whom we stopped from installing half-inch pipes just in time. He and his mate, a Kamba tribesman, plainly thought Armand and I were unreasonable in insisting on having wider pipes.

After the tussle with the plumber Armand and I went for the first time up our stairs. Concrete was being poured between the floors before the second-floor walls were built. I had a stick in my hand, and with this I wrote in the wet concrete: 'Armand loves Michaela. Michaela loves Armand.' I then felt shy and hoped that none of the fundis (experts, or in this sense workmen, in Swahili) read English.

'What if they do?' said Armand. 'It's very proper for husbands and wives to love one another.'

Our tame leopard often accompanied us when we went to see how the building was progressing. Tshui was always very good except when he frightened the plumber by leaping on his shoulders. Tshui was handsome, and always commanded an admiring court, over which he presided in regal fashion. His admirers amongst the

African workmen had never seen a live leopard at close quarters. Many may not have seen a leopard even at a distance, for most urban Africans are as unfamiliar with wild animals as their European or American counterparts. A new generation of African is emerging, which is beginning to realise the cultural gold mine on its doorstep. These are the people who will save the wild life if it can be saved from the apathy of the less educated.

I sometimes stroked Tshui as I passed the tree where he was tethered on a long lead. Then he would roll over on his back and show the silken expanse of his stomach, paws loosely flopping, eyes closed ecstatically. There would be a chorus of 'EEs and OOoohs'.

On our third visit to the house Armand discovered that the numbers of true angles were limited. Although this would everlastingly present problems in lining the carpets up straight, it gave the home a certain makeshift charm which those in more conventional settings lacked.

There was only one thing which we both regretted being talked out of, and that was having a flat roof. Our builder insisted that a flat roof would give endless trouble. 'It will always leak,' he said. We had *his* sloping roof, and it has always leaked! He didn't mention that bees would find *his* roof irresistible and that we would wage total war for many years against hordes of intransigent invaders. We are still waging that war! Every season I wonder whether we should resign ourselves to the discomfort and expense of having a flat roof put on when in between expeditions we visit our home. We have spent a small fortune on the roof already. Nothing discourages either bees or the rain. . . .

'Armand, darling,' I cried, 'we shall soon be able to move in.'

Neither of us thought at the time when I uttered these words that it would be five long years before we spent the first night in our house. A whole series of events caused this sad state of affairs. We made three films in Australia and New Guinea. We went to New York to cut and edit the films. We became famous overnight on TV and changed from film making for the cinema to film making for the new medium. The Mau-Mau rebellion compelled us to let the house, while we journeyed around Africa making our programmes. An empty house was an open invitation to the amateur gunsmiths, who raided it to rip out the water-pipes for the manufacture of home-made weapons.

Once we took tenants it would be difficult for us to get back into the house, because no one would take it unless it was on a long lease. There were times when I wondered if we ever would occupy our dream house ourselves.

One of our tenants must have been friendly with Clark Gable, because suddenly people in Nairobi began to ask us whether we were going to sell our house to him. We heard he had fallen in love with our beautiful house, which did not surprise us, and that he wanted to buy it.

We didn't want to sell, not even to Clark Gable, even though we were both fans of his. We were in a painful dilemma. We had our dream house, and we were homeless. It was quite difficult to book accommodation in Nairobi. Already Kenya was becoming known as a tourist's and sightseer's paradise. It had always been a top priority on the list of the wealthy. But now from the affluent societies of Western Europe came those who could afford to go further abroad than Europe, and arrive in the same amount of hours as it used to take days. Our own local people were still not geared to this new situation. In those days there was not enough hotel accommodation. Wild-life management was the Cinderella of the administration. Tourism was in its infancy. There was little or no attempt to save or preserve the unique assets which made East Africa the potential tourist treasure house it so obviously could be. Obvious at least to the sophisticated traveller.

It was necessary to book accommodation well in advance, and this was anathema to Armand. I have often teased him about his being unable to give his plans in advance. A direct question such as 'Where shall we be on the 20th?' will produce an evasive reply, as if the security of the world depended on the answer. Is it because Armand's boyhood was spent in a legalistic background, for his father was a judge? Perhaps he had said to Armand as a boy, 'Do not commit yourself!'

This could not go on in Nairobi any longer, and the day came when I suggested that we should move back into our house. The way I made this suggestion was typical of my requests for a definite plan of action. I looked diffident, even hesitant. I left the rest to the natural telepathy which exists between husband and wife. If Armand himself brought up whatever I wanted to ask him, and which I thought he might refuse, he might be likely to say 'Yes' instead of 'Perhaps'!

One day we came back to Nairobi from a filming safari and it was impossible to fit us into the over-full hotels. When Armand consented to moving into the house my joy was overwhelming. I suppose each person has private landmarks of significant events in his life which far outweigh the far more important landmarks of history. Such a one was the day we moved into our house.

Our house is furnished with antiques which have taken many years to collect. To furnish a house in this way is a continual adventure. There comes a time, too, when each purchase has to be followed by a sale, because saturation point is reached. Our house was not only our home but it was also a place of business.

In spite of its size we had only one bedroom. Armand had three workrooms downstairs. Our films for television were cut and edited and recorded, too, in these rooms. My writing-room led off the lounge and was particularly suited to the task of performing two jobs at once—of writing and being able to watch the household. It was almost a gallery overlooking the main part of the house and had four windows which overlooked the garden. It had only one blind side.

The crises of our household could be anything from Brucie Denis, our male half ridgeback alsatian dog, biting someone, to one of the gardeners finding a spitting cobra in the garden! The problems added to the fascination of our household rather than detracted from it.

Gradually other houses were built near ours. We still had the illusion that we were completely isolated from the world. We could go for quite long walks without seeing a single house or building. Neighbours moved into the houses they built; often they would have lived for a year or two in a shack. We ourselves had lived in a tent on our land. Many people practically built their houses themselves, working at weekends and doing a job during the week. We saw many dream houses rise from nothing.

In a few years' time there were many beautiful villas and gardens at Langata which did credit to their owners. After the houses were built there was followed a way of life which reminded me often of the stories about pre-1914 Europe I had heard from older people. Children and adults could be seen bobbing along on horses. All these people kept a syce, sometimes two or three. Life was prosperous and gracious. The emigrants worked hard for this luxury. Nearly every wife around Nairobi was a working woman and divided her time between working in an office and living the life of a country gentlewoman. It was a happy, prosperous state of affairs, or so it seemed. If there was any fault at all it was that the people lived in a state of myopia with regard to the other races of Kenya.

I was often puzzled by the fact that many of our European friends, whom we had known for years, did not seem to possess a single African friend. There seemed to be absolutely no contact between the three races inhabiting Kenya—the Asians, the Africans and Europeans. Only in our house, and undoubtedly there were one or two others whom we didn't know, was there the likelihood of finding Africans, Asians and Europeans.

Our own friends have always been chosen entirely because they interested us. It would be as unthinkable for me to choose my friends because of their outward appearance as it would be for me to refuse to know someone because their blood group might be 'A' or 'O'.

I well remember my first contact with an African. After my father died, Mother, with tremendous stubbornness, refused to take any money either from my father's relations or her own. She preferred to live in poverty and bring me up herself to the best of her ability. Until I was at least eight years old I had never had a new dress. My clothes were all made from grown-ups' old ones. My undies were made from my uncle's evening shirts. Luckily my mother was a good needlewoman. When I was four years old I had a slight eye defect. My mother thought I needed glasses and took me to the eye hospital. We naturally could not afford to go to a private oculist. We waited on long hard benches for hours, gradually moving up to the doctor's ante-room. I remember the other patients, some with bandages over their eyes, all awaiting their turn.

Finally we entered the ante-room outside the consulting-room. Here only two sets of patients sat—another mother with a child about six years old and my own mother and myself. Out came a patient. As she passed us she hissed, 'The doctor's black,' and then disappeared. Before we could assimilate this information the nurse beckoned to the six-year-old and her mother to enter the room.

My mother immediately started preparing me even before we heard the screams from the next room. I had never seen an African, and my mother, who was excessively sensitive about hurting other people's feelings, was already nerving me for the meeting. 'The doctor doesn't look like you. He has a black skin and you must not be rude, stare at him or pass remarks. He is exactly the same as ourselves, except for this difference in his colour.'

The door opened again, the six-year-old was red-faced and wet with tears. Her mother mopped the child's damp face. The doctor himself appeared at the door. He was black. He was the blackest man I had ever seen. His white coat emphasised his onyx hue. He beckoned me. I ran across to him without any prompting on my mother's part, and gazed up adoringly at his face.

'You're not afraid of me?' he asked.

'Of course not,' I replied. 'Why should I be afraid?'

My mother followed in behind us. The other child stopped snuffling and looked at us—mouth open. The doctor left the door ajar. I tried not to stare, as my mother directed. The doctor examined my eyes expertly. When he had finished he beckoned to the other little girl, who came forward hesitantly. 'Now why did you cry?' he said chidingly.

'Because you're black,' said the child candidly.

He turned to me. 'But you did not cry because I am black. Why was that?'

'Because you are beautiful,' I answered with equal candour. As he had brought up the subject himself, I avoided my mother's eye and started to question him.

'Are you black all over?'

The doctor said, 'Yes.'

'Can I be black too?' I asked.

'I am afraid you can't,' said the doctor, laughing.

I was examining his hand in fascination. 'Come along,' said my mother in an agony of embarrassment.

The doctor laughed. 'It's quite all right—I have a little girl the same age as your daughter.'

'May I come and play with her?' I asked.

'I would love you to, but she is far away in our own country.'

2

Top Dog and Other Pets

IN THOSE early days there was only one dark cloud on our horizon. It was all so perfect, so idyllic, that we asked ourselves, inevitably, could it last? It is a very human quandary to find oneself in, and it must have happened to us all at some time or other. It may be something which is connected with love itself, the fear that all is so perfect that it cannot possibly last. Whether it is love for human beings or love for a place, or even love for the work you do, there is always the nagging doubt, the fear that it will not last.

So it was with us, we were in love with Kenya and our house and our valley. In those days there was no cause to be alarmed. One would have thought the British rule would have gone on for several hundred years. Then, overnight, or so it seemed to those ordinary people who were not in the administration, the whole peaceful scene exploded. We are now told that the ominous signs had been obvious but had been hushed up. But to Armand and myself and the many thousands of others it was a sudden, unheralded disaster. One minute everything was gaiety and sunshine, and the next there were ambushes and military operations.

Most of you will know something about Mau-Mau. You will not have forgotten the horrid and sometimes gory details of that movement.

If we had hoped for complete peace we were mistaken. The basic problem of people who had not adjusted to a new mode of life was still there. The people still talked of their land hunger. There was no denying that the multiplication of many tribes who lived by agriculture had reached a point where there was just not enough good land to divide.

If anyone had thought of putting to these people the idea that modern people were not all land-owners, and that they made their living at jobs other than tilling the soil, the transition would have been easier. The transition would have been easier, too, if modern medicines had not upset the balance of nature by causing a population explosion. Fertility in tropical climates is high. When all the progeny survive it is overwhelming, as India shows. Semi-urbanisation poisons the souls of people whose roots are in the cleanliness of the country. Crime follows on the frustration. In Kenya robbery, often with violence, became more and more frequent.

Our beautiful house and garden were isolated enough for us to wonder whether we would escape the attentions of the gangsters. What we needed was a dog. At that time we had a South American ant-eater, two chimpanzees, four cheetahs, six mongooses, two Asian bears, an Indian ratel, a secretary bird, a hornbill and several other kinds of animals, numbering, in all, over 200, but no dog!

Brucie was not quite the first dog to belong to our household. Two dogs had been left to us by our tenants. Both had been killed by leopards. At that time a leopard roamed our valley and was responsible for killing over thirty dogs. This had discouraged us from owning dogs.

'Armand, let us have a dog.'

'But what about our other pets, Michaela?'

'He will accept them if he knows they are part of our household.'

'That's what you think, but supposing he doesn't?'

'We must find a good home for him before we get fond of him. We shall soon know if he is a good mixer. Certainly not a puppy.'

'What I would like, Michaela, is a half ridgeback, half alsatian.'

'But where could we find such a mixture?'

'Let's look in today's paper and see whether there is an advertisement for a dog searching for a good home.'

People were leaving Kenya and every day kind-hearted animal lovers were advertising for a good home for the pets they had to leave behind. Armand picked up the paper. We were sitting having our coffee on our verandah on the first floor. We looked down on to the tops of the trees where the sunbirds glided and shimmered as they took the nectar from flowers.

'Finished your coffee? Let's go,' Armand said. He gave me time to read the paragraph which stated: 'Wanted good home for half alsatian, half ridgeback, good watchdog.' We raced down the stairs together to collect 'our dog'. Armand tried to curb my enthusiasm. 'We'd better wait until we see him, Michaela.' But it was useless. I knew, I absolutely knew, that this was 'our dog'. I even reminded Armand to bring a rope with us for a lead.

We arrived at the address which had been given in the paper. A neat house with a well-kept garden, the approach only marred by a small girl who stuck out her tongue at us! We went to the front door and tapped on it. It was opened by a small bright-eyed woman.

'Good afternoon,' said Armand. 'Did you advertise for a home for your dog?' After she had got over her surprise at seeing us she laughed.

'Wait until I write home to tell my mother that Armand and Michaela have come for one of my animals.' Then she added in a serious tone: 'He is a wonderful dog, I would love you to have him. As a matter of fact we have only had him for a week. We gave him a home when some friends of ours left for the U.K.'

She answered our unspoken question in the next sentence. 'He is a splendid watchdog, but unhappily he doesn't like my little daughter.'

'I don't blame him,' I whispered behind my hand to Armand as we followed the lady into the house.

Loud barking came from the living-room and when the door was opened we caught the first glimpse of 'our dog'. He advanced upon us stiff-legged, the ridge along his backbone bristling, teeth bared. I let him smell my hand. Slowly, his attitude changed. His tail began to wag, at first sluggishly and then accelerating rapidly. When Armand stroked him it was obvious that this massive brute was going to be a new addition to our household.

'He has never behaved like that with anyone before,' said the lady.

'What's his name?' asked Armand.

'Bruce.' I was secretly disappointed. It sounded uncompromisingly un-African. Surely it should have been a Swahili word. We took Bruce off with us, having thanked the lady, who looked tremendously relieved, as did her servant, who appeared as soon as Bruce was on his lead. The servant said, as we clambered into the car, '*Mbwa kali sana*,' which means in Kiswahili, 'Dog, very fierce.'

'Well, that is what we wanted,' I said to Armand, who was beginning to look a little doubtfully at our newly acquired pet.

'Could he be too fierce, do you suppose?'

'Oh, no, Armand. Look at him. How could he be too fierce?'

Bruce was lying with his heels firmly wedged against my leg, his head pillowed on Armand's lap. He rolled his eyes first at me and then at Armand, lovingly, as though he had worshipped us from the day he was born.

'Yes, perhaps you're right,' said Armand guardedly. 'Now, Michaela, if this doesn't work out we must find him another home.' I ignored this remark and changed the subject.

'A pity his name is Bruce.' Bruce pricked up his ears at the sound of his name.

'We can't change his name, he knows it too well. Let's change it to Brucie. Swahili-ise it, in other words,' I suggested.

We arrived back at the house. Our servant Tshikadi opened the front gate for us. Brucie bared his fangs and when we held him back howled in rage. He slavered like a mad dog. Tshikadi prudently kept his distance as we led Brucie into the house. Tshikadi shook his head. '*Mbwa kali sana*,' he said. It was an understatement if ever there was one!

I will never forget the first meal which was served to us on the evening of Brucie's arrival. He stalked Tshikadi as he passed round the table serving first me, then Armand. What was even more alarming, he gripped Tshikadi by the heel and held him. Tshikadi is not afraid of animals. With great presence of mind, he stood stock-still. I disengaged Brucie's jaws from Tshikadi's foot. He hadn't hurt him, but I nevertheless had to escort Tshikadi to the kitchen door, putting myself between him and Brucie.

'If this goes on,' said Armand, 'we won't be able to keep a servant in the house!'

I obliterated the memories of the time I had done all the housework plus writing a book and being filmed for television. The house had never looked so clean and I had never been so tired!

'He will make friends with Tshikadi.' But the words were barely out of my mouth when Tshikadi, carrying a bowl of fruit, was again molested by Brucie. Tshikadi shook his head. It was obvious that his patience had been sorely tried. I went to the kitchen and brought back with me a handful of biscuits. Brucie showed immediate interest. It was extraordinary what expressions the dog seemed capable of, mainly, I think, because he had a good deal of white in his eyes. This gave him an almost human look.

'Tshikadi, give him the biscuits,' I said.

Brucie watched the transfer of the biscuits to Tshikadi's hand, and although he growled, and bared his teeth, he accepted the food.

It took three days for Brucie to become completely friendly. When he had finally given his trust to Tshikadi it was amusing to see that Tshikadi had to act as escort to our other servants. Tshikadi was elevated to the role of major-domo. Gradually Brucie sorted out who was permitted to enter our house and who was not. He took an unreasonable dislike to the man who delivered the meat to the house. We could never understand why Brucie should dislike him. Possibly the man had threatened Brucie with a stick. Whatever happened on their first encounter Brucie never forgave him

This same employee was in charge of the motor-mower. As things get broken very easily in Africa it is a good idea to put anything mechanical in the charge of only one person. You can then find out, roughly, why, if there is a post mortem.

While Mbogwa mowed the lawn, Brucie had to be locked up. Mbogwa was attached to the staff of our other house, where our chief assistant, Des Bartlett, and his wife lived. When our part of the land was mowed, Brucie had to be locked up in my bedroom. If anyone forgot that he was there, and let him out inadvertently, he would dash into the garden bristling with fury. Often I saw Mbogwa keeping Brucie at bay with the lawn-mower.

Brucie was completely multi-racial. He bit everybody who dared to set foot across our threshold. He tore a policeman's trousers. He bit a European, who complained to the police. He chased an Asian inspector of electricity meters to his car. One of his more villainous exploits was to chase a European lady who was mounted on a horse. It was Sunday. Tom, the other man who worked in our house (it was Tshikadi's day off), came to talk to me in the kitchen where I was preparing a meal for myself. He was doubled up with mirth.

'Brucie has just chased a memsahib on her horse and she is very angry and swearing. She wants to see you.'

I feared for Brucie's safety. It was just after the incident of biting the European. I went down to see the lady on her horse. She was very angry. I let her talk.

'Why don't you control that bloody dog?' she shouted. 'My horse bolted. Not a single horse and rider can pass this house without being annoyed. It's a disgrace.'

'I will make arrangements to have the dog shot tonight,' I said, acting on the assumption that horse lovers are almost invariably dog lovers.

'Oh, no,' said the lady. 'Don't do that.'

'It is rather awkward. I didn't train Brucie. He came to us as a grown-up dog when his former owners had to leave for the U.K. I will shut him up all day in a cage and not let him out.'

'Oh, no, please don't, please, please don't do that.'

'I had better advertise for another home for him, then. It must be very unsettling for him to be moved. As fast as he gets used to one set of people, then he's moved to another. That probably explains why he is apt to be difficult. Poor old boy.'

I patted his great head. Brucie was now behaving like an angel because the lady was engaged in conversation with me, and rolled over on his back. His paws were elevated to heaven, his tongue lolling out, looking for all the world a picture of docility and innocence.

'Don't send him away,' said the lady earnestly. 'You never know what kind of home he will find himself in.'

'That is one of the reasons why I cannot bear to part with him. I am so very sorry that he is annoying everybody.'

The lady said something under her breath quietly to Brucie, in his ear. She seized my hand and mounted her horse. 'Good-bye.'

In the late afternoon the lady came by again. 'Please forgive me for being so angry.'

'Not at all, you had every right to be.' Brucie had achieved a victory.

It was soon after this that Armand and I decided that Brucie ought to have a wife. We acquired Suska, a pure-bred ridgeback bitch. Her former owner, obviously an ex-cavalryman, wrote a cryptic letter extolling Suska's charms. 'Good little bitch. Bit short in the neck. Used to two hours' horse exercise daily.'

'Do we have to provide her with a horse and jodhpurs?' asked Armand.

Suska arrived early one morning. We went to Nairobi station to collect her. No one seemed to know which platform the train would be expected. The station was crowded with tanned Europeans coming back from the coast. Asians as colourful as butterflies, in their graceful saris, surrounded by incredibly lively dark-eyed children, who raced happily in and out of the crowds. Africans going on leave, with large bundles on which they sat, containing bedding and lumpy objects, probably saucepans, shoes and clothes. Many had wooden suitcases besides the bundles. They said loud good-byes to friends. Among East Africans only a sly dishonest man will talk in a quiet voice, because he has something to hide.

Everyone was in high spirits but no one could tell us on which platform Suska's train was expected. We finally located it. Dogs in East Africa travel in small compartments underneath the train. We looked through the window of Suska's compartment. She looked back at us with gentle eyes. We opened the door and the first thing that Suska did was to fall heavily on the line. It was an omen of Suska's personality. She was an accident-prone dog!

She fell downstairs once, over an invisible obstacle, a thing which I thought only human beings could be clumsy enough to do. She has survived being spat upon by a spitting cobra. Spitting cobras are in great abundance in our garden.

The spitting cobra is a dark-skinned snake which spits its venom with uncanny accuracy into the eyes of its victim, who is blinded for several days. It has front fangs and can also inject its venom, which is mainly neuro-toxic and can cause death.

Although Suska was always referred to as 'Brucie's wife', she was a wife in name only. Suska's first litter was sired by the champion ridgeback of Kenya.

I agreed to this betrayal when Armand pointed out that Brucie himself had not been a very good husband to Suska. We soon discovered that Brucie was a great Don Juan. It was rare for him not to be recuperating from his wounds. His upstanding ears had been marred by the right-hand one sagging. The other ear had a triangular piece removed from its edge. Brucie's face was often bloated with bites which had gone septic. He was narrow-minded, he couldn't bear other dogs to exist.

We tried to keep Suska's puppies, all seven of them, but had to give up. We were warned that the family would grow into a dangerous pack which would hunt down and kill the residents of Langata who were brave enough to pass our house. As the personalities of our delightful puppies developed, we decided not to take chances on this dismal prophecy being false.

There were six dogs and one bitch in the litter. We called them

'Moja, Mbili, Tatu, Eeni, Tanu, Sita, Saba', which in Kiswahili is 'One, two, three, four, five, six, seven'. As the dogs grew large, first one and then the other challenged the position of Brucie as top dog. We could see that we must save Brucie embarrassment, and possibly his life, because Suska's puppies were obviously going to be larger and more powerful than Brucie.

A Swede took one of the young dogs, which was flown to Sweden to join his bride, the first female registered ridgeback in that country. He was the first male registered and obviously destined for a long and glorious life founding a new breed in Sweden. The other puppies found local homes and many have won prizes at dog shows.

Ridgeback owners are proud of their extraordinary pets. Extraordinary because of the ridge of hair which runs in the opposite direction from the rest of the coat, along the back, ending in a rosette between the shoulder blades.

The dogs can be any shade between wheaten and darkest copper. The ridgeback is a truly African dog. It's ancestors were the companions of the bush-men. They are known in modern times as 'Rhodesian ridgebacks'. Armand had first seen the ridgebacks at the home of Errol Flynn. Errol referred to them as his 'lion dogs'.

Our fence had to be made higher and higher to keep the dogs inside our grounds. We ended up with a six-foot fence, and I grew spiky vegetation along its base.

Brucie was quite good with our cats.

The Denis cats joined our household many years before Brucie arrived. They therefore regarded Brucie as an interloper and would not tolerate cat chasing. We acquired our first cat when we had to find a foster mother for Gwak and Gwok, white-tailed mongooses born at our home. The mother of the mongooses was brought in by a neighbour. She had been found injured in their garden. Perhaps she had been caught by a dog and managed to make her escape. We put her into a large and airy cage to recuperate, intending to let her loose when she recovered. One morning we saw that she had given birth to twins. Mother mongoose was still disturbed mentally by her fortunate escape from death.

She didn't look after the twins too well. After she had bitten one severely we thought it was better to remove the babies and try to rear them ourselves. We tried to feed the babies with milk from a doll's bottle. The babies didn't seem to thrive. Armand decided we ought to have a foster-mother. I called the E.A.S.P.C.A. 'Do you know where we could borrow a mother cat with kittens? We need her to nurse two baby white-tailed mongooses.'

'We have just taken in a mother cat with two kittens who is looking for a home,' said the lady from the E.A.S.P.C.A. in Nairobi. 'Do you think you could keep her?'

'Of course, it would be wonderful to have our own cats in the house.'

The mother cat and her two kittens were fetched from Nairobi and installed in our bedroom. She was a beautiful long-haired tortoise-shell cat, with pale green eyes the colour of grapes.

One of the kittens was ginger, the other was near-Siamese with a black streak on the side of its nose.

We removed the kittens from the cat basket after a few hours. We took them into another room and put them into a box lined with a blanket, then we placed the mongoose twins in the same box. All snuggled up and slept together. The mother cat called plaintively to the kittens outside the locked room. After an hour we returned her kittens and the two small mongooses, which we hoped had acquired a feline scent! Mother cat made little noises of welcome to her children. She gave a perfunctory sniff to the mongooses and then began to lick them. In a few minutes all four babies were suckling, and mother cat was purring loudly with contentment. After that the mongooses never looked back. They grew up faster than the kittens, but all four were perfectly friendly and played prettily together.

Gwak and Gwok were so named because that was the noise they made. It was almost impossible to tell them apart, especially when the bite from mother mongoose healed completely. They were finally known collectively as the Gwoks.

The Gwoks were much heavier animals than their foster-brothers, and soon outstripped their foster-mother in size. She still licked them energetically, and they allowed these liberties with obvious pleasure. They seemed to enjoy our stroking them and they were especially fond of being stroked under the chin. The Gwoks would close their eyes with every sign of pleasure. They would not allow themselves to be picked up and put on the lap. The Gwoks had one very bad habit. They enjoyed creeping up and biting your toes quite hard. Armand often wears sandals at home. His unprotected toes were irresistible to the Gwoks!

We finally found a good home for the Gwoks when they were

grown up. We discovered also that they were male and female after they had incestuously produced their own family.

The near-Siamese cat, Smudge, died in mysterious circumstances. I have always thought he was attacked by a snake or perhaps the snake had defended himself against an attack by Smudge! Ginger, happily, is with us still. He is the father, grandfather, or great, or great-great, etc., of all our cats except one. The exception is a foundling.

One morning Armand called me. 'Michaela, there is a small wild kitten on the roof of the guest house.' I left my writing-room and went into the garden. There are cages which adjoin the guest house, used only for segregating our pets at feeding time so that all may get their share of food. On top of the cage, a small round object, not much bigger than a snowball, glared ferociously down. The kitten, a grubby white, resembled the dingy colour of 'Before you use our detergent'. It was certainly wild. It spat and arched its tiny back—its four-inch tail fluffing out like a bottle brush.

Armand reached up to attempt to take it down. It retreated sideways, and, when Armand persisted, lashed out with its small paws. 'I don't know what we can do about it,' said Armand. 'It is obviously in need of care and protection, but I doubt whether it could ever be tamed. Where on earth has it come from?' When Armand went into the house I took a step-ladder and propped it against the cage. I got on to the roof of the cage with a saucer of milk. The little kitten went through the same performance as with Armand. I wondered if it was too small to have learned to drink by itself. Anyway, I kept trying to tempt it. Finally it came towards the saucer, sniffing, but still timid. It started to drink. I put forward my hand and stroked its head. To my surprise it began to purr. I picked it up and carried the kitten in one hand and the saucer in the other into the house. It was less than an hour after Armand had said he doubted whether it could ever be tamed!

She gave promise of the way she would look when she grew up after I had washed her in the hand basin and taken the burrs out of her fur. Armand named her Kitty-Kat. Kitty-Kat developed into a truly beautiful cat.

Shortly after Kitty-Kat had joined our household we had a telephone call from the Kenya Broadcasting Company at Langata. The rains had started. Most of the day the sky was blue, with large white luminous clouds. It was sunny, but the mood of the day would change fast. The sky would become dramatically overcast. There might be thunder. The rain pelted down as though it wanted to pound us into the earth. This fury would only last a short time usually and then out came the sun again. Sometimes during the night it would rain on and off for several hours. The call from the K.B.C. came to us after such a night.

A man's voice said: 'We have found some small animals in a culvert. We heard them calling for three or four days before we rescued them. We were hoping their mother might come back, but she seems to have disappeared. Last night we thought they would surely get drowned. We managed to extricate them and now we have them at the radio station. Could you or your husband manage to come and identify them?'

'What are they like?' I asked.

'They have upstanding ears and are greyish. They look not unlike a fox.'

'Have they very large ears?' I asked.

'Not particularly.'

'Then they are probably jackals.'

'Do you think you could adopt them?'

'I will ask Armand. I am sure he will say yes. We can at least look after them until we have found a home for them.'

Armand and I went to collect the animals from the K.B.C. building, only a short drive from our house. They *were* jackals. One of the men who worked at K.B.C., and who had rescued the cubs, kept one and we took the others.

'We had better take them to David Roberts,' Armand suggested as we drove home. David Roberts and his family lived at Lake Baringo. They already had some tame jackals.

When we arrived home we lifted out the box.

'Armand, how many jackals were there supposed to be? There are only two.'

'I am sure there were three.'

'That's funny. I thought there were three too. Could we be mistaken?'

'We can call K.B.C.'

Armand went into the house to make the phone call. I stayed outside looking under and around the car, quite convinced that there had been three cubs in the car when we had left K.B.C.

'We have lost a jackal, Michaela.'

'What a sad business.'

'It is. It will have a poor chance of survival. It's much too small to be able to survive by itself.'

'Let's retrace our steps. We might find it on the road.'

'There's not much hope of finding it again, Michaela.'

I was obstinate. I could not resign myself to the fact that the jackal cub should be abandoned to its fate. Common sense told me that Armand was right in his assumption. It is just part of my character not to give up. I clambered back into the car. 'I won't be long.' I cruised slowly back to K.B.C. There was a group of men looking on the ground at the entrance. 'No news?' I called.

'We were just looking to see whether it could have gone back to the culvert. We haven't found any sign of it yet.'

'I am sure we put three jackals in the car,' said the man who had adopted one of them. 'Perhaps it fell out of the car.'

'It couldn't climb out of the box. The sides were too steep.'

'I'll call you tomorrow if it is found.' I waved good-bye and drove home.

We continued searching the next day. Our two gardeners were alerted to look out for the jackal. The remaining jackals thrived. I kept them in the cutting-room at night and left them outside during the day in a specially constructed play-pen with one part shaded so that our charges could have sunshine or not, whichever they preferred.

Three days after the installation of the jackals in the Denis ménage our night watchman asked me why the cats made such a weird noise at night. He imitated the sound. 'It must be a wild animal,' I said.

'No,' he insisted. 'It must be the cats. It comes from there.' He pointed in the general direction of my garage.

I walked to the garage and looked inside and underneath the car. There was no sign of a cat. The next day the watchman again asked me about the weird noise. I was just getting into my car when I heard a scratching from inside. Ngugi and I heard the scratching at the same time. 'It must be the jackal. Perhaps that is the weird cry you heard in the night, Ngugi.'

I backed the car out. We took out the seats and searched the car. There was no repetition of movements from the car. When we had put the seats back I drove to the MacRae Service Station near our house. I was certain now that the jackal had somehow wedged itself between the inner and outer walls of the car. It was a convertible and had a small space where the folding roof could fit in snugly when it was down. When the hood was up there was a space large enough possibly for a small animal to squeeze inside. I remembered the hood had been up when we had gone to collect the jackals, as it had been raining. Since then I had put the hood down, and we had not thought of looking into the space.

Frank MacRae took off some of the inner panelling.

'Look, Michaela.'

I looked inside, his wife Phil looking over my shoulder. There inside was an emaciated little body, all eyes. It was featherweight and its bones were sticking out, but it was alive. I took her home, but was afraid she would not get enough food if put with her sisters. They would be almost certain to bully her. I gave her glucose and water. Within a short time she was eating normally and had put on weight. Jackie became very attached to me and I decided we should keep her.

I didn't want to keep Jackie in a cage. I wanted her to live as freely as possible. Making such a decision could involve me in much anxiety. An animal with not much experience of danger might not be able to look after itself, but undoubtedly would be happier if allowed to wander in the woods. I fed the cats and dogs in the late afternoon, and hoped that by giving Jackie her main meal in the evening she would learn to come back to the house at night. For three days she disappeared altogether, but again we heard her strange keening call. I discovered her on the top of the cages next to the guest house. She had obviously climbed up the expanded metal of the cages and couldn't get down by herself. I got the step ladder and coaxed her to me. I carried her down. She had lost a great deal of weight but she seemed happy to see me. Jackie disappeared once more before she settled down completely. This time I knew where to look for her. I got her down from the guest-house roof again. After that she decided to come home every night.

Her sisters were sent to Lake Baringo, but Jackie was not lonely. She was about the same size and age as Kitty-Kat. They became inseparable. Jackie stayed outside during the daytime with Kitty-Kat, at night she slept on my dressing-table. Before Kitty-Kat and Jackie went to sleep they played for at least half an hour, running after one another, stalking, pouncing from behind furniture, leaping on to my bed and off again, before finally settling down.

Jackie enjoyed being stroked, although she wouldn't allow strangers to touch her. When we took the dogs for a walk she would join us as quietly as a ghost. She was pathetically in love with Brucie. She wagged her tail when she saw him and lay on the ground, paws up, but he hardly recognised her existence. Wherever she was if I called her she would come out of the woods, usually in the company of Kitty-Kat.

Marie Clare Sandys, the wife of Duncan Sandys, and Mrs. MacDonald, the wife of Kenya's governor, came to see us and I called Jackie out of the woods. I had told them about her and was hoping that she would behave as usual, for they were both very fond of animals. I hoped that she would not be too shy in front of visitors. She was not. I stood on the edge of our woods and called to her. After a minute or two she came out of the shade and trotted to me. She took a dog biscuit from my hand.

I often sat in the evening with Suska at my back. She always managed to insinuate herself in my chair. Jackie sat on top of Suska and Kitty-Kat and Ginger sat on my lap. We would watch television together.

Jackie often refused to come into the house at night. She sat outside, near the front-door light. She reminded me of the jackals of ancient Egypt in her quiet alert dignity. She was dainty and aristocratic, and it was easy to imagine her as the companion of the gods.

Unhappily I had to go to London on business. When I returned Jackie had gone, but I heard what had happened to her. One of our neighbours had a male jackal. Jackie grew up in my absence and male and female met. She didn't come back to us, but stayed in our neighbour's garden with her mate. The jackals have now moved on elsewhere. I like to think of them living happily ever after. It was a perfect ending to the story of Jackie.

Our South American ant-eater was lucky in that he joined our household at an early age. When anyone asked us where he came from Armand always astonished them by answering truthfully, 'Russell Road, Birmingham.' Our South American ant-eater had been bought from a pet-shop there, and shortly after he had joined our household in Africa the shop had been burnt to the ground. The ant-eater would undoubtedly have lost his life if he had stayed in England.

I talked to him every day. He grew rapidly. It seemed to me he gained an inch or two every day. He had a long thin head with a tiny mouth, his tongue was several inches long. One of the difficulties of having wild animals as pets is to know what to give them to eat. Their natural food often has to be substituted for practical reasons.

Occasionally we have had the difficult feeder who will not accept a substitute. Then one or other of the employees of Armand Denis Productions can be seen with butterfly net in hand, pacing slowly up and down the roadway, swiping at invisible prey. Such a feeder was an elephant shrew which Des Bartlett and his wife Jen kept in perfect health for years, although everybody said it was impossible to keep it alive, even for days.

The giant ant-eater whom Armand and I feared would prove to be fussy about taking anything except ants and termites, as he grew older and had to be weaned, gave us a pleasant surprise. At first we had given him egg, milk and chopped meat, with a little formic acid to improve the taste. Des or Jen gave him his food without formic acid in it and he ate it with the same evidence of enjoyment.

He was friendly, but you always had to be careful of his large claws, used in the wild state to rip open ants' nests. When he reared up on his back legs it was advisible to back away. He never harmed any of us, but that was because we knew our ant-eaters.

Armand and I tried to give every homeless animal in need of care and protection a home until it could be rehabilitated. Animals were always being brought to us by people who had found some victim to the ruthlessness of nature. Baby animals are often found in the wilds, after heavy rains or even after drought, abandoned or lost by their mothers. Most people who find such animals will attempt to rescue them.

Armand answered the phone one morning. I heard only one side of the conversation, which ran like this.

'Yes, Armand Denis speaking.

'You have found some wild cats? You want me and Michaela to adopt them?' Armand made a face at me. I knew his views on wild cats. He had made several abortive attempts at taming them, and the last time even Armand had to admit when he was beaten. 'Have you tried the S.P.C.A.? But . . . But . . . Oh, all right. Where? Quite near? I'll write it down.'

Armand's expression became doleful as he noted the long and

complicated directions. I could tell he was on the point of refusing to pick up the kittens when the voice on the line obviously sensed the same thing. 'Wait. Oh damn. Michaela, stop laughing. It's not funny. What a waste of time. You know I want to finish cutting the spider sequence today.'

Armand went off, disgruntled, to pick up the wild cats.

He arrived back at dusk tired but triumphant.

'Michaela, you'll never guess what I've got here.'

'Wild cats with halos on their heads?'

'Wild cats indeed! Look.'

Armand lifted back the blanket which covered the large basket he carried. Four dark furry bodies lay close together. I put in my hand cautiously, ready to withdraw it instantly if the babies showed hostility. I put my hand under the chin of the nearest one and lifted its head to see it better.

'Oh, Armand. How wonderful. Are they all all right?'

The kittens had a black line from inner eye corner to corner of mouth. We had acquired four baby cheetahs.

3

Shadows in the Sunlight

ARMAND and I had never imagined we would have the good fortune to possess four cheetah kittens. They were quite adorable. Everybody wanted to see them, including our neighbours, both African and European. The baby cheetahs were brownish beige. The golden spotted coat of the adult cheetah would gradually develop. It was no wonder that the farmer's daughter who had called us up had mistaken them for wild cats, for they looked quite different from grown cheetahs in colour. Their fur is much fluffier and softer than the adult animal. When they are half grown cheetahs keep a fluffy mane-like ruffle on the backs of their necks. When the cheetah is fully grown this small mane disappears.

Cheetahs are sometimes mistaken for leopards by newcomers to East Africa. Seen side by side there are several differences. The cheetahs have a spotted coat and there the similarity ends. The leopard is a much heavier-looking animal, with shorter, thicker legs and softer fur. The cheetah's legs are long and slim, which help to make him the swiftest animal on earth. He has been clocked over short distances at sixty miles an hour. His head is small in comparison with his body. The face of the cheetah has two black marks which run from the inner part of the eyes to the corners of its mouth. The cheetah is a true feline and is unrelated to the dog. It is a mistake to think that the cheetah is canine because it has unsheathed claws. It is a true feline, as an examination of its teeth will confirm. Cheetahs have another un-cat-like characterstic. All the large cats breed well in captivity. Until three years ago the cheetahs had never been known to breed in any of the zoos of the world. Recently when the cheetahs' enclosure was being cleaned out in a Czech zoo the keeper found the still-born bodies of cheetah cubs. Since then another case has been recorded in America of a little one being born, but that also died soon after. Many people have endeavoured to give captive cheetahs privacy in ideal conditions but have not succeeded in having them breed.

As with all animals in Africa, cheetahs are in need of protection. Luckily for them their fur has not the soft luxuriant quality of the leopard. A president's wife wore a leopard-skin coat; immediately millions of foolish, thoughtless women copied the lead and there was an enormous demand for leopard skins. This vogue has been responsible for nearly wiping out the leopard population. The leopards are most cruelly trapped, and if the ladies who wore their skins knew of the bloody agony and misery which has preceded the ownership of such a coat they would be both ashamed and horrified to own one. What makes it even more unjustifiable is that nylon or orlon coats of leopard design are in every way superior to the animal fur and untainted by cruelty. Fortunately the cheetah has a wiry coat.

Cheetahs are reasonably easy to domesticate. Unlike Armand, who thinks cheetahs are stupid, I have the highest regard for them. Naturally, individual animals vary a great deal in personality, just as human beings do. I find cheetahs affectionate, especially if you give them plenty of time and attention. We gave one of our cheetahs to a friend as a companion for his tame cheetah. Wherever possible two of a species should be kept so that loneliness is avoided.

Our cheetahs were kept in a large enclosure with natural rock on one side. It had to be fenced in to protect the other animals we kept. The area fenced was large and the cheetahs thrived. They had the security of captivity with an illusion of freedom. The big cats had plenty of exercise too, for besides being able to run on the flat ground, they could bound up and down on the rocks. They became quite tame. We should still have them now but for the fact that they learned to escape from their comfortable quarters. Every few weeks one or the other would leap over the high fence which curved inwards at the top. The others followed our first escape.

The men who looked after the animals found it more and more difficult to get them back into their enclosure and one or two of them were actually afraid of our cheetahs.

Armand and I were due to go on safari. It was on Sunday that our cheetahs, all three of them, escaped from their enclosure. Sunday is the day that most of our African staff have off. The Bartletts were on safari. At this time, too, we had Moja, the last of Suska's male puppies, at home. He had grown into a fine, strong russet-red dog. Armand and I had hoped that we should be able to keep Brucie and Moja, the two dogs, and Suska and Mbili, the two bitches. All went well until Brucie and Moja took a dislike to one another. It was impossible to have them in the house together, or even in the garden at the same time. When Brucie was in, Moja would be out, and vice-versa.

The cheetahs escaped five minutes after Brucie and Moja met face to face in the garden. I don't remember who let Moja out, it was so easy to do. If you heard the phone ringing you would go into the house to answer it. One of the dogs would be ready to dash out and engage his enemy. As we were endeavouring to part the two snarling, biting antagonists one of the animal men came running to us. 'The cheetahs have escaped,' he panted. Thirty seconds later we saw our cheetahs in our part of the grounds, wide-eyed but suspicious at the strange smell in the unfamiliar surroundings. Two of the cheetahs came straight up the drive. They were obviously awaiting an opportunity to enter into the scrap now taking place between Brucie and Moja. They were deterred by the fierce sounds coming from the dogs. Another cheetah was examining our hedge, presumably to see whether it was possible to leap over it into the roadway.

I could also see a young Masai, whom I have known since his boyhood, just about to enter the gate. When he saw what was happening he wisely decided to keep away from the house. The Masai instinctively do the right thing in such an emergency. He didn't run, as so many people would have done, until he was some distance from the house.

There was only Armand and me, one animal man, and one of our servants to cope with the emergency, but to act promptly to deal with such a situation at least six people were needed. Our man who worked in the house was unfamiliar with handling animals, but he had courage. He and I managed to get two of the cheetahs into the cages where our cats were fed. Armand left us to go to the store in the house. He came back with a large piece of meat. Tom and I surprised Armand by managing to get two of the animals into the cages. The third was still hovering around the dogs, hoping to get into the fight but not having quite sufficient courage. Armand waved the meat under the nose of the preoccupied cheetah. He followed Armand, who held the meat invitingly to the threshold of another cage. There he refused to move. Armand threw the meat into the cage but the cheetah spat. Finally, all three of us converged on to him and picked him up bodily and put him into the cage. We then parted the dogs, who were by this time exhausted and bleeding.

Sadly we decided it would be unfair to leave anybody else the responsibility of looking after the cheetahs. Although they were reasonably good with us, we could not be sure how they would react if they saw a running child or a strange dog. We called up John Seago, who is an animal collector, who would see that our cheetahs had a good home.

Moja was found a home with a newly married neighbour, who gave him the love and attention he deserved, and would ensure that he would be top dog in her household.

There was another reason why we decided to find homes for the cheetahs. We were not sure of what was going to happen in Kenya. We ourselves had no fear for our safety, although the security situation had deteriorated.

We were sad that Brucie could not see eye to eye with other dogs. This regrettable trait had, however, done some good. Brucie was responsible for our cutting the little paths through our valley. When he had first joined our household we discovered that the dogs of Langata were as narrow-minded as he was. It was virtually impossible to take him for a walk outside our own grounds without being involved in fights. Armand decided we should cut little paths through our forest, so that we could take Brucie for walks on our own land with no fear of his getting into fights. The little paths opened a new world to us.

We discovered that our trees often contained wild orchids a stone's throw from the house. It was impossible to see another house. It was easy to forget that there was a city only eleven miles away. We walked often in our beautiful valley, on the winding paths we had cut through the woods. There was always something to look at, to observe, which was new even though these paths were so familiar to us. We would be astonished by the flight of a radiant bird, radiant because its plumage glowed in iridescent colours. We would find something of interest on all levels. Even beneath our feet. The tiny dainty hoof-prints of a Dik Dik, an antelope not bigger than a dog, would be imprinted in the dust of the path. Sometimes a bird's track or even an undulating snake-print would give us something to discuss.

At eye-level we might find a mysterious cocoon—was it moth or mantis? Only time could tell us. We often hatched these mysterious objects and photographed them for television. We might sometimes, too, find a chameleon making its way ponderously on a twig, with its eyes rolling independently of one another, in search of victims. A chameleon resembles those ancient lizards who ruled the earth centuries ago in the Jurassic Age. But in miniature, of course! The chameleon is in many ways an intriguing little creature. It is well known for its ability to change its colour and its pattern in minutes, according to the surroundings. Another strange feature is its eyes. The eyes of the chameleon are set in a protruding circle of flesh. These organs behave like independent gyroscopes, the right eye perhaps glancing backwards without the head being turned as the left eye looks in front. The chameleon then is able to survey all around it with the minimum movement of its head. Its tongue is its weapon for finding food.

It is carnivorous, and its method of catching its prey is unique. Having ear-marked some juicy fly as victim, it shoots out its tongue, which is almost the length of the chameleon's body, and the fly is imprisoned on the sticky surface. Then the tongue is withdrawn into the chameleon's mouth. This operation is swift as lightning, as we have found to our discomfiture when trying to film the chameleon in the act of eating. The tongue action reminds me of those Christmas squeakers which blow out and roll up at Christmas parties.

The grounds were a timeless world, a paradise, peaceful, logical.

Outside this secret world things were very different.

Mau-Mau had been stamped out. What came next?

There was an interim period of getting back to normal, but the mood of the people had become hopeful. Kenya was like a saucepan on the stove. It had boiled over once, the pressure had been turned down and now the country simmered. But like the simmering saucepan the country might boil over again. The calm was only on the surface, and a thousand currents pulsed beneath the calm.

There must have been many who feared the worst. There were many who left the country in blind panic, selling their homes at rock-bottom prices. There were some, even, who abandoned their homes and the farms which they had won from the wilderness.

My African friends reassured me.

'Don't go, Michaela,' they said. I had no intention of going.

At last the time came for a constitutional conference to be held at Lancaster House, London.

One of my African friends was married to a delegate.

'Let us go and see him off. Do come with us,' they asked me. I went off to the airport. It was evening. There was singing, excitement and much good humour.

'What do you think will happen?' I was asked. I found my voice answering as though my words came from another person. 'You will get what you want, even more than you ask for.'

'But, Michaela, the British will never give up Kenya without a struggle.' Again I heard my voice answering as though a stranger had taken possession of my body. 'You will get everything.' They shook their heads disbelievingly.

Finally it was time for the delegates to go. We stood on the large terrace overlooking the runway. We looked down on the delegates. The crowd went wild. I stood next to the mother of a Kikuyu friend. She ululated shrilly. The crowd around us took it up, it was the pulsating voice of Africa. Ancient and mysterious, primeval. Nairobi, with its supermarket, its cinemas, its theatres and modern hotels, could have been on another planet, light years away from the soul of a people who swayed and moved and murmured in unison. A plane took off, the crowd dispersed.

I took some of my friends home. We passed hundreds of others going on foot towards Nairobi. We passed bicycles which had not only the cyclist but a companion teetering on the back of the bicycle as a passenger. Many stood jam-packed on the back of trucks. They roared *Uhuru* slogans as we passed them.

After taking my friends home I journeyed back to Langata. Armand met me at the door.

'Did they get off all right?' he asked me.

'Yes,' I told him about the departure of the delegates. I told him what had happened at the airport.

'When do you think they will be back?' he asked.

'It's hard to say. Perhaps in two weeks.'

It was not two weeks. It was more like two months!

There were endless arguments. Finally the delegates returned.

They had everything. Internal self-govenment and a constitution which virtually meant that the country would be run entirely by Africans. To most people, who had envisaged the changeover taking five years at the minimum, it was staggering. It was the cause of anxiety, also, because the decision to give self-government came directly after the collapse of the Congo. Nairobi had seen the fleeing refugees. The tales of horror, of rape, murder, and worse, were still fresh in everybody's mind. Instantly all building stopped. Many businesses went into bankruptcy.

I even remember going into one shop to buy Christmas presents. The owner apoligised because there was not a very great choice of merchandise. 'I simply haven't dared to order anything for the last few months,' he told me.

There were small signs of human sorrow to be seen every day. There are several auction rooms in Nairobi, and one of the oldest was Muter & Oswald. Muter's was stacked with household possessions, some well worn and some new, but all obviously well looked after. These were the possessions of the people who were abandoning their homes to go to other countries, who either feared the change or could not adapt themselves to it. I remember seeing an elderly, well-dressed woman at an antique sale. I was sitting near her. I couldn't help watching her and thinking that the British should be proud of producing such people. She was tall and slim. Her hair was brown, streaked with white. She had clear grey eyes which gazed candidly at the world. She wore a blue linen suit and had a single strand of pearls round her throat. I wondered what she was interested in buying.

The bidding was fairly slow. The auctioneer said, 'Come, ladies and gentlemen, I am not going to sell it at that price.'

The woman in blue touched her companion's arm. 'I don't think I can bear to watch it go,' she said, 'I remember when my husband bought it.'

The auctioneer had started selling. It was too late for her to get out of the room without causing some disturbance, so she sat there. She was obviously selling up her home. Probably a widow on some lonely farm somewhere out in the bush. I watched with a horrible feeling of guilt, as though I was seeing something of an intimate nature which should have been private, with the woman sitting so near. To see her emotional suffering was somehow indecent.

I nearly bid for the sideboard myself, so that I could say to her,

'Your piece of furniture has a good home.' But I already had a house full of furniture, and had come in to the auction to buy a table lamp only. The sideboard fetched only seven pounds. It was far too big obviously for people to risk buying something which they could not transport easily if Kenya had to be evacuated. The calmness was gone—the woman was sobbing without any attempt to hide her grief. The two women left the showroom immediately after the sale of the piece of furniture. It was tragic to think of their treasures being given away.

The ordinary sales in Nairobi were also pitiful—well-worn, very clean saucepans and other kitchen utensils which hinted of a lifetime of use were also being auctioned. It was almost symbolic of their owners, who, after a lifetime of service to the country, found themselves through no fault of their own discarded.

At the time the keynote was one of bewilderment. It was also the time of heady, weekend rallies. Large open trucks careered along the roadways, crammed with Africans who shouted political slogans and gave Mr. Churchill's famous 'V' sign. Although the passengers of these crowded vehicles seemed elated, it was somehow not a natural elation but rather the excitement of fever. The whole country was running a temperature.

At this time there were many robberies with violence, some of them quite shocking. It was distressing to the whole community of whichever race. Perhaps it was most disturbing to the Africans.

My African friends told me many tales. The Africans often didn't dare to go to the police. There were dark tales of people being kidnapped; whether this was true or sheer rumour it is hard to say.

At this time I went off to Nairobi one evening. I was by myself and was visiting some Asian friends. Armand had gone to a Kenya Wildlife Society meeting; he was on the executive council. My friends had given me reasonably careful instructions to get to their house. Unhappily many parts of Nairobi have no street lighting. I got completely lost. I was in a side street and had that well-known feeling of motorists—that they are almost at their destination, but that one is in a sort of maze. It might be hours before the distance of only a few yards to one's destination could be covered. At the end house I got out of the car and knocked on a wooden door. A murmuring there was instantly silenced. I knocked again impatiently, anxious to be on my way. The door swung open and there stood an

Asian man, a head shorter than myself. Around him clustered three children, a small elderly lady, his mother probably, and a beautiful young Asian girl. All were wide-eyed and obviously frightened. The man carried a hockey stick in his hand ready to use it to defend himself and his family. I apologised to them and asked the way. They were smiling and relieved, and even tried to persuade me to come in and take some tea with them, to make up for being slow at opening the door.

'I had better not stop,' I apologised. 'My friends will wonder where I am unless I arrive soon. I am late already.'

'Are you all by yourself? Are you not afraid?' asked the young Asian wife gazing up at me.

'No, I'm not really afraid,' I said. I didn't like to tell such a dainty little creature why I didn't fear to go out by myself at night. It seemed too crude to mention it. At that time I always carried a panga under the seat of the car, well sharpened, and a small pot of pepper in my handbag. If I found myself in an ambush my plan would be to open my handbag, shake the pepper into the face of anyone who tried to get me out of the car, and then in the other hand I would knock them on the head with the panga. I had some lessons from my gardener in panga wielding. Luckily, I never had to defend myself in this way, but I felt that if I were going to be a victim of a hold-up at least the terrorists would take a few blows too.

I have always believed that even when outnumbered your reaction can often save you. I remember once I went for a walk on our land when the dogs flushed something in some thick bush near our rubbish dump. It wasn't the healthiest place in the world to hide. I took a large stone and hurled it into the bushes, and up stood two men (heaven knows what they could have been doing there), but that they had no right to be there was obvious by their guilty manner. One had a panga and one was unarmed. They ran off in opposite directions and I chased the one with the weapon. He ran down into the valley. I ran after him and would have caught him if I had been wearing different shoes, but the soles of my shoes were plastic and it was terribly slippery on the sloping ground. I had not intended to run down into our valley. I shouted to him to come back, but he refused. My dogs were with me. How I envied them running on four feet! The man ran to the river and crossed it, wading up to his waist. I had no desire to risk bilharzia by going into the water after him. He scrambled across to the other side and without looking back at me ran for dear life up the bank.

The word must have gone round that I and my dogs were very *kali* (or fierce in Kiswahili). We had no more uninvited visitors for quite a considerable time!

Besides despondency over the political situation, nature itself seemed to be punishing Kenya.

There had been nearly a century of chopping down trees. Although dead wood had been used by the Africans as firewood, there can be no doubt that urbanisation and settlement had accelerated the destruction of the forests. I remember that Professor Pearsall had once said to me, 'Why do we find the ruins of the cities of antiquity standing in desert?' Geologists give us the answer, which is written for eternity in the soil. There were rivers where the cities stand. Where there are rivers there is lush vegetation. The answer is, of course, that man has destroyed the trees and where tree cover is lost the desert takes over. Without trees there is nothing to bind the soil and when the rains do come the water rushes down the slopes and the soil is lost for ever.

Without the shade of the trees, water evaporates quickly and is lost.

The destruction of the trees in Kenya had been speeded up through several causes. One was for fuel for the railway. The trains consumed vast quantities of wood. The early settlers, too, had destroyed trees wantonly without giving much thought to the part trees played in helping climatic conditions in the tropics. Perhaps they did not even know that trees create humidity. All the settlers could think of was planting familiar plants.

The Africans, also, speeded up the disappearance of tree cover. When the British came they brought peace to Kenya. The formerly warring tribes could circulate in larger areas. This had a destructive influence on the wild life and its habitat. In the old days the African's requirements, of necessity, had to be near his own village, otherwise there were hostile neighbours who could attack him, or he might fall a victim to kidnapping by slave traders.

The British had an active Forest Department which tried bravely to teach the benefits of reforestation. The peasants resisted such practices, and who could blame them for their ignorance? Until recently few countries in the world knew the havoc they were causing. Man-made deserts are everywhere, but so few people seek the cause. We now know that trees take 100 litres of moisture from the soil and will transpire 150 litres back.

To chop a tree and not to plant one in its place is a crime not only against one's own generation but to the many generations to follow. To destroy trees on a steep slope is suicidal, especially in the tropics. The soil without its natural cover has no protection from the sun. When the next rains come there is no seepage of the water into the soil, and no transpiration or storage of water. The water table is lowered when tree cover is removed. The rain washes away the top soil into the valley below, and in no time at all a gully is formed. In most of the little valleys there is a river or stream, but when the trees go, the river goes. On the slopes of hills when the tree cover is destroyed the rains remove the top soil and the wind does the rest.

In many places in Kenya there was heavy over-grazing by goats and cattle. Wild animals do not cause such disintegration through their feeding habits. The indigenous animals feed at different levels. The giraffe browsing from the top of small thorn trees, and other antelope species eating at different levels. The population of the herbivores is kept down by predators. If man could have fitted into this perfect harmony all would have been well. Man has caused untold damage all over the world by introducing animals from one country into another, where they have not evolved. These animals are usually most destructive to the local animals. They also destroy the habitat. A century ago the early explorers had no respect whatsoever for wild life in other countries, but massacred right, left and centre. To read some of these early journals makes men and women of today quite sick. Everything which moved had to be destroyed compulsively. How is it that these early travellers were unmoved by so much beauty?

But it was not only the beauty of the animals and birds which left them unmoved, but they were also indifferent to the exotic splendour of the forests, which they chopped and destroyed ruthlessly.

In their place, if at all, were planted Australian gum trees, because of the rapid growth of this species. Very good in Australia but quite unsuited to some other countries. It was certainly not a good example to give to the indigenous people.

I first became aware of the big drought when we drove to Arusha in Tanganyika. Our journey took us right through the heart of

Masai-land. The Masai are in both Kenya and Tanganyika. The earth was bare, and baked red, the colour of old Flemish tiles. On the roadway the vehicles ploughed through fine powdery dust which followed the car behind like a red and vengeful phantom. Red phantoms followed behind the hoofs of the weary Masai cattle, as the herds plodded across the plains in search of nearly non-existent grazing. We passed three Masai who were endeavouring to raise a cow to its feet. The cow was a living skeleton. Its mournful eyes pleaded with the men to let it lie down and die. The men could not bear to leave it there. For while it was on its feet there was the very slightest hope that grazing and water might be found. It was a terrible sight, and one which we were to see repeated several times during our journey.

Once we saw a whole herd standing still and mournfully gazing at us as we passed. They were waiting for one of their companions to die. The Masai who stared at us looked just as parched and thirsty as his beasts. His fine bones seemed as if they would burst from his skin. We stopped counting the number of dead animals we passed, both wild and domesticated ones. Amongst the casualties were zebra, wildebeest and giraffe. It was a terrible sight to see the corpses, which were often covered with maggots; and the stench was unbearable. Only the vultures looked plump and reasonably well fed.

When we returned to Nairobi we found that the animals from the National Park had in several places broken through the fences. There were heavy casualties amongst these animals. Some were shot by farmers, others were hacked to death by the outlaw element, who sold the meat on the black market in Nairobi. Whole bands of animals wandered across the roadway at night, desperately looking for water. The British Army was stationed in Kenya at this time. Greatly to their credit, the Army gave its services freely to help get the animals back into the park. There was a large drive, which was a military operation in itself, and which, undoubtedly, saved the lives of countless animals. The Army and the Air Force helped too, in distributing food to the stricken population. If the Army had not been in Kenya at this time many human as well as animal lives would have been lost.

In the midst of these tragic days, which lasted on and off for nearly three years, came another scourge. I was going to our other house. I looked at the ground. Could I be dreaming? The earth itself seemed to be moving. I bent down to look and then came back to our house.

'Come quickly, Armand.'

'What is it, Michaela?'

'The ground is alive with caterpillars.' It was army worm.

The army worm is a yellow and black caterpillar. Singly it is not unattractive—a living, moving carpet of them is a frightening and repellent sight. The worms had spread in the time it had taken me to get back to the house. They had advanced to the other side of the driveway and were now near the servants' house. What little grass had been left was being eaten by the rapacious larvae. The invasion was on such a scale that we couldn't cope with it. I was thankful we didn't keep horses or cattle. There was strong evidence to suggest that grazing animals died after army worm had crossed their pasture. Many people thought the worms left some harmful organic residue in their wake which caused death to animals who ate the grass.

There were masses of orphaned animals in the National Park and elsewhere. We often adopted these animals ourselves. Some discretion had to be used so that a trade did not start up in wild animals. We looked after two or three wildebeest and returned them to the wilds when we thought they were able to live by themselves. We hoped they would join a herd.

One morning Armand and I went into Nairobi. We were passing the New Stanley Hotel when a voice called to us. We stopped and a man introduced himself to us.

'You are Armand and Michaela Denis?' We nodded.

'I farm just past Athi River. We found a baby zebra on our farm. Its mother had probably died in the drought and it got left behind by the herd. My wife and I have adopted it. We would like you to have it. We hate the thought of parting with Little Bella, as we call her, but she follows my wife everywhere, and we are unable to cope with looking after a baby.'

'We would love to have your zebra,' I said. The farmer gave us exact instructions as to how to get to his farm. We went in the Land Rover the next day. The road was not too difficult, but we thought that my Buick convertible would not be quite a suitable vehicle to transport a young zebra.

At last we arrived. The farmer's wife and her husband were there to greet us. The farm overlooked a rugged landscape, with lava rocks jaggedly pointing to the sky. The farmhouse stood on a hill. Directly around the house was a garden, which made decorative use of the rocky outcrops. It was planted with indigenous plants, succulents and aloes. Another section of the garden was devoted to roses. It was here we found the farmer and his wife. As I was shaking hands I heard a little noise behind them, almost like a dog. From behind the farmer's wife a head appeared. It was not much higher than her hip. It belonged to the smallest zebra we had seen for a long time.

Bella looked most appealing, even to two people as un-horsy as Armand and myself. She had long, straight eyelashes which shaded dark bright eyes. Her ears were round and furry and proudly up-standing. She was symmetrically striped in that most elegant colour combination of black and white. It would be an insult to describe her little feet as hoofs, that most ugly word! She nuzzled the farmer's wife and when she didn't respond she gave her a little push.

'She wants to play,' explained the farmer's wife. 'This is our little game, do you want to watch?'

The farmer's wife ran off and hid behind one of her rose bushes. The little zebra waited deliberately a few seconds and then galloped along in pursuit. It was an amazing sight to see woman and zebra play hide-and-seek.

After the game Bella was given a carrot which she eagerly gobbled. I stroked Bella's velvety nose and was completely captivated.

When the time came for Bella to be loaded into the Land Rover the farmer's wife disappeared. She couldn't bear to see the little animal she had grown so fond of, in a few days, leaving the farm. I could have cried with her, I knew exactly how she felt.

We drove back safely to Nairobi. Bella looked round at the garden, decided she liked the look of it and without any help from us sprang from the back of the Land Rover. She galloped round five or six times, then trotted over to me and whinnied. I kissed the top of her head and went into the house to get some milk for our new pet.

4
A Timeless World

IF ANYONE had peeped through our large gates three weeks later he would have seen a strange sight. Every day I walked on our paths accompanied by my pets—Brucie, Suska and Mbili, the ridgeback dogs, one ginger cat and a zebra. I hadn't realised that it looked extraordinary until Armand commented on it. Bella followed like a dog, sometimes running ahead, sometimes finding a piece of vegetation interesting to a zebra, and then she lagged behind. I needn't have worried about her getting lost. Her pounding hoofs broke the silence of our forest as she rushed by to get ahead, pushing unceremoniously past Ginger (who always lagged behind) and myself.

Sometimes Armand would accompany us on these walks, then Bella would be unable to resist giving him a little kick as she passed. Bella had only once tried to kick me. I gave her a smart tap on her rump. She had accepted this admonition with good grace and had never attempted to kick me again. She was not so good with other people. A friend, who particularly loved animals, was visiting our house. She had no fear of animals whatsoever. When she saw Bella she wanted to caress her.

'Don't go too near her,' I warned. My friend ignored the advice, because Bella was a tempting little animal to stroke. Bella turned her back on my friend stood sturdily on her front legs and kicked with both back ones, simultaneously. Down went the poor animal lover on the grass. Bella ran off, kicking her heels up and behaving like a miniature rodeo performer. The poor lady was marked with black bruises for several days.

Bella hated me to stop petting her and constantly wanted to be paid attention. This was one of the reasons why I kept her in her paddock. There was nothing I would have liked doing more than spending my life making a fuss of Bella, but I had work to do. She always gave me a tremendous welcome when we had our daily hour or so together.

Our house was a hub of activity; the cutting and editing of the film went on downstairs. We were often recording our T.V. programmes. It is quite an event even when a car passes our house, so we had imagined that sound recording in the house would be easy. It is strange how human ears mask out the noises we don't want to hear. We hadn't been recording long before we began to wonder how many cockerels lived in Langata. Another painful discovery was that all our immediate neighbours owned motor-mowers. I often wondered if they owned two per household!

Besides all these outside distractions Brucie Denis cannot bear to be parted from me. Whenever I record he tries to sneak into the recording-room. Often a whole recording has been made with Brucie in the room. At other times he has ruined a recording by scratching, a sound which resembles the gnawing of rats, three inches from one's ear. During recording sessions he often has one of his mercifully infrequent barking fits, which I have always suspected as being a duet with some other canine friend whose voice is beyond reach of our sound range.

The best method when recording is to ask Armand if he would mind taking Brucie, Suska and Mbili for a long walk, well away from the house.

When not recording I am working on a book, as Armand does his cutting and editing. The animals are looked after by Mbogwa, who has been with us for many years. We have in the past employed various European young men to help look after the animals when we are on safari. Although I love our journeys, I always worry about the animals. Only occasionally did we take our pets on safari with us. It is always hard on animals to be transported, and this is one of the many objections I have against circuses. Animals are like human beings in that they can be victims of boredom and monotony. The more animals' natural environment can be reproduced when they are in captivity, or domesticated, the more they will thrive and be happy.

Because of the cutting and editing of the film, and the other administrative jobs connected with producing a half-hour television film every three weeks, Armand and I have usually at least two, or possibly three, units in the field somewhere in the world. I have, wryly, often joked that our employees were more often on safari than ourselves. In the early days of our marriage Armand and I could be nearly a year on an expedition, now we had to divide our life between production and filming. We were compensated by enjoying some home life, which in our case was as exciting as being on safari. There are not many homes where you can see a lion or leopard in your garden! Fortunately Langata is one of the few places where you may have a chance of still doing so.

Des Bartlett, our chief assistant in Africa, and his wife Jen had gone on an assignment to film the work of the palaeontologists Dr. Leakey and his wife Mary, at Olduvai Gorge. The Leakeys were neighbours. Armand had long wanted to make a film of their work. Such work, quite apart from its scientific interest, gives modern man a sense of perspective. He has come a long way from his remote ancestors. If he manages to conquer his greed and superstition he may still have his descendants travelling even higher in the scale of evolution. The man of the future may be as different from the man of today as he was from his prehistoric counterpart. The Leakeys in those days managed to do good work on very slender funds. Armand in wanting to make the film of the Leakeys' work had in mind that it might be helpful to their work, besides making a most interesting programme. We had no idea just how interesting it was going to be.

Des Bartlett had been late in going up to Olduvai. The Leakeys had started work on a new site.

Olduvai Gorge is surely one of the greatest wonders of the world. It ends at the Balbal Depression, which is part of the Great Rift Valley and stretches from the Jordan Valley to Mozambique, a distance of approximately 4,000 miles. At one time Olduvai was the site of a great lake. Violent earthquakes changed the land and formed the great chasm known as the Great Rift Valley. Olduvai Gorge is a side valley created by erosion.

In 1911 a German entomologist named Kattwinkel discovered Olduvai Gorge. He was chasing a butterfly when he almost fell over the steep bank. When he had recovered from the shock of his near accident he climbed down over the edge to explore. In the gorge he found fossil bones which he took back with him to Berlin. In 1913 German scientists made an expedition to Olduvai. Professor Hans Reck was its leader. Work went on until World War I. After the war Reck wrote to Dr. Leakey asking him if he would take over the exploration. Reck and Leakey were not ready to carry on with the work until 1931, due mainly to lack of money.

The gorge was in exciting country. It lay past the Ngorongoro Crater, past the Balbal Depression, at the edge of the Serengeti Plain. Wild life abounded. The Leakeys had many adventures during their excavations at Olduvai.

One of the great difficulties was lack of water, all of which had to be carried by trailer thirty-five miles away. Every year the Leakeys went back to Olduvai, although during most of these years Dr. Leakey was curator of the Coryndon Museum. Mary Leakey was, and is, often in charge of the excavation by herself when Dr. Leakey is elsewhere. She is a competent palaeontologist.

Dr. Leakey was convinced that Olduvai was a likely site to find early man. In Leakey's own words, 'The gorge was one vast storehouse of Stone Age relics, a fossil museum such as existed perhaps nowhere else in the world.'

The Leakeys uncovered fossil remains of over a hundred different extinct species. The prehistoric animals were gigantic in size. Sheep towered six foot at the shoulder with a horn span between four and five yards. Baboons dwarfed a gorilla. A member of the ostrich family was over twelve foot high.

The Leakeys divided their excavations into different beds. The work was hard and arduous. It needed much patience to scan the ground on the slopes of the gorge, with eyes a few inches from the ground. On hands and knees the Leakeys would pause for every small clue, whether it was fossil bone or stone implement. Their favourite tools were a fine brush and dental pick.

Over the years they searched, but still early man's remains eluded them. The Leakeys' faith was unshaken. Somewhere in the tons of rock would be found man. On July 17th, 1959, Leakey awakened with a slight fever. Mary went out alone to the digging. At camp Leakey dozed fitfully. He awakened to hear the sound of the Land Rover coming up the slope to the camp. Mary called excitedly, 'I've got him, I've got him,' over and over again. She had found a piece of bone lodged in a rockslide. Her trained eyes realised that it was part of a skull. It was not an animal's remains.

She searched higher. She saw two enormous human teeth in the rock above. She marked the spot with a pyramid of stones and hastened back to tell her husband the good news.

Leakey's fever was forgotten. Together they retraced Mary's footsteps back to the small stone pyramid. The find was uncovered. Dr. Leakey at once confirmed that Mary's find was indeed human. The teeth were premolars and nearly twice the width of those of modern man. No one can ever know the elation that Mary and Louis Leakey felt as they gazed down at the culmination of their many years' work. Their early intuition had been right. Showing tremendous will-power, they waited until the next day, when Des Bartlett arrived from Langata, to begin their work of uncovering the find.

Working with dental picks and brushes it took them nineteen days to unearth the skull. It was nearly complete, minus only the lower jaw, but in hundreds of fragments. Tons of scree had to be removed and sifted below the finds. Leakey deduced from the teeth that *Zinjanthropus* was mainly a vegetarian, yet there were several broken bones around the site of his home. He probably ate animals small enough for him to kill, including rodents, reptiles and birds.

The Leakeys had been finding crude stone tools for many years in the gorge, which also indicated that *Zinjanthropus* was a meat eater. He would have used the tools to cut up his meat.

Des Bartlett sent a radio message to us in Langata.

'Urgent, come to Olduvai.' He dared not give us any details, as the Leakeys wished to keep their discovery secret until they had a carbon dating for their discovery.

Armand and I rendezvoused with Des at Ngorongoro Crater and he guided us to the Leakey camp. Armand and I had no idea until we reached Ngorongoro that we would be seeing a record of ancient human history being made. Des told us the momentous news as soon as we got there. He had photographed the uncovering of the skull step by step, thus making the Leakey discovery the most completely documented in the history of science. Des and Jen Bartlett were as excited as I have ever seen them. Their enthusiasm was infectious and Armand and I were eager to put the miles behind us to join the Leakeys in their camp.

The roughness of the terrain had not been exaggerated. It *was* hard going.

Armand decided that we should photograph any animals if they presented themselves in our way. We got a good sequence of rhino, and further on we saw hyena. Because of the isolation of Olduvai the hyenas did not appear to be shy. Des called Armand from our Land Rover, 'Take some shots of us in the background with the hyenas in the foreground.'

Armand looked approvingly at me after Des had shouted these directions: 'You look fine, Michaela. Look in the mirror.'

I looked in my small compact mirror and laughed. We were in an open Land Rover, as we had planned to be photographed. I was covered with dust, or rather caked with it. It was impossible to see an inch of skin exposed. Armand was just as dusty as I was, but it looked worse on me because of my fair hair.

Armand drove off the rough track. I hung on to my seat. Armand had refused to allow me to have a safety belt in the open Land Rover. He thought it looked sissy. (One year I had broken a rib because it was not always possible to hang on to one's seat.) Armand was looking over his shoulder at Des trying to manœuvre our Land Rover into position, with the hyenas between us and the other car. Without warning the car tipped up and I shot through the air straight on to the iron bar on the windscreen. Des and Jen laughed when they saw the crazy angle of the Land Rover, but they stopped laughing when we didn't move. Des continued filming, nevertheless. He came over for his close-up. They found Armand most distressed, the Land Rover covered with blood.

Armand was mopping my face as fast as I bled. There was a deep cut on my forehead. 'Are you all right, Michaela?' Armand said. I opened my eyes and closed them again as the blood ran into them.

'Did Des get it?' I said finally.

'Was he filming?'

'I got the whole sequence. We didn't know you were hurt, Mrs. Denis, otherwise I would have come across straight away.'

'A good job you didn't know,' I mumbled.

'We had better turn back and get you to hospital,' Armand said.

This made me fight the dizziness.

'Oh, no, we don't, Armand. We can't go back now. Is it very much further, Des?'

'It's about ten miles.'

'I'm quite all right now, Armand. Please let's go on.' I knew Armand wanted to see the skull and where it was found, and so did

I. If my injuries had been greater I would still have insisted on going on. I saw Armand weakening.

'It's only a superficial wound. You know how the forehead bleeds,' I said. 'Have you any band-aids, Des?' Des unearthed a roll of medicated tape. Armand pushed the two sides of the wound together and stuck it with tape.

'Are you sure we shouldn't go back, Michaela?'

'No, we must go on. I feel fine.' I didn't, but I would have felt worse if we hadn't continued our journey. We arrived at the Leakey camp looking like soldiers returning from a battlefield. The Leakeys were most concerned about us. I felt weak, but the excitement of reaching our destination gave me strength.

'Where is he?' I demanded.

Mary Leakey took us to a table outside the dining tent. There on the table was the giant skull. She had already started to assemble it. I marvelled at her patience. There were literally hundreds of little fragments of human bone, which she was still piecing together like a jigsaw puzzle. How did she know which were fragments of human bone and which might be fragments of some other creature altogether? I felt too weak and muddled to be able to ask any intelligent questions and then after a drink the Leakeys took us to Bed One. The men were still using their gigantic sieves sifting the scree. The Leakeys took the opportunity of looking through what the men had found. These fragments they took back to camp to add to the other pile on the table.

The next morning was devoted to photography. I had a black eye and my face was swollen. We photographed the Leakeys at work in the morning. In the afternoon Armand decided it would be a good plan to photograph our Land Rover traversing difficult country. It was certainly an ideal place to show the capabilities of this vehicle. This footage would be most useful in giving the atmosphere of the camp. It would also be useful for a film we were making for Land Rover.

At any other time I would not have been concerned. I got into the seat. Armand took the wheel. He chose the steepest, toughest way he could into the gorge. I was terrified. It was almost impossible not to fall out of the Land Rover unless one hung on. Even then it was likely that a hole in the road would make the vehicle bounce so much that my fingers would lose their grip. How I cursed to myself at not having a safety belt. Armand had just completed a really hair-raising piece of driving when he stopped the vehicle to call to Des.

'How did that look, Des?'

'It looked fine, but could Mrs. Denis open her eyes?'

'Did you have your eyes shut, Michaela?'

I nodded, ashamed at being caught out in this piece of cowardice.

'Why on earth did you close them? We will have to do it again.'

'I am sorry, Armand. I was afraid. I thought if I closed my eyes I wouldn't see what was happening. I suppose it is because of yesterday's accident. I've lost my nerve. Do you think I could have a safety belt when I get back to Nairobi?'

'Don't be absurd. You are supposed to be a tough explorer.' Then he relented.

'Let's talk about it when we get back to Nairobi.'

We finished the shots. Mercifully I was used only for the close-ups. There were several long shots of the two vehicles travelling one after the other, in which I was not needed.

It is now a standard practice to have safety belts on vehicles. It is a most sensible idea. Armand is won over to allowing me to wear a safety belt when we are working in rough country. It is especially necessary for the passenger to wear a safety belt, because the driver can cling on to the steering wheel.

We drove back to Ngorongoro after we had been in camp for a few days, leaving Des to complete the photography. We were urgently needed in Nairobi to record one of our programmes. I was quite light-headed. I must have had a slight concussion. I remember dimly that June Wright, a fully qualified commercial pilot who worked for Campling Brothers & Vanderwal, picked us up at the landing field at Seronera. I don't remember much of the journey, but I was told afterwards that I attempted to open the door of the plane, thinking we had arrived in Nairobi when we were still in flight.

A good rest soon put me right. The cut on my forehead was deep. I had to be filmed for our television programme in extreme close-up. We stuck a neat patch of sticking-plaster on my forehead. Before we showed the accident we would have to wait until the film was developed, cut and edited. Afterwards several of our fans wrote to me to ask what had happened, because this sequence had to be used before the scenes at Olduvai. I am always grateful to the kind people who watch our programmes and really seem to take an interest in what happens to us.

Michael Wood, an eminent plastic surgeon in Nairobi, decided that I should not have an operation to remove the scar. Armand had done a good job in pressing the two edges of the wound together. After a few years it hardly shows at all except when I'm tired.

Armand is a close friend of Melville Grosvenor, President of the National Geographic Society. We had met the Grosvenors last in Japan. Armand had told them about Leakey and had urged that his work was worthy of financial support.

After the discovery of the skull, Armand wrote to the National Geographic Society giving details of the find and again pressing for help for the Leakeys' work. We were delighted that the outcome of these recommendations was that the National Geographic Society, after careful investigation, enabled Leakey to give his entire time to his palaentological research.

Dr Leakey was able to give up his curatorship at the museum and buy the vehicles he needed, and Mary was able to spend even more time at the dig.

Armand lent all our services to making Leakey's lecture film. The Bartletts stayed, in all, five weeks at the gorge. We came dangerously near to deadlines on our television schedule, but I agreed with Armand that the Leakeys' work deserved priority.

Nairobi seemed a dangerous place after our journey to the gorge, discounting the accident. A new and annoying type of theft became a daily occurrence. Cars would be found with all their tyres taken. This crime was an especially usual one at Langata. It was surprising how the operation of removing a tyre was performed so soundlessly —even the dogs of the stricken households were not awakened. It was most mysterious.

It was rumoured that the thieves smeared themselves with leopard grease and the dogs were cowed in consequence. My own dogs always bark when there is a leopard around, so this story seems unlikely to be true. Shortly after our return from Olduvai two Masai arrived at the house. I recognised one of them as having a Kikuyu wife. He lived not very far away. Masai and Kikuyu intermarry because both Masai and Kikuyu women practise female circumcision.

'Can you give my brother a job?' asked the Masai I knew. It was an unusual request. Masai are usually cattle-men only. It is rare that they seek other work.

'Why does he want work?' I asked.

'Many of my cattle have died and I have school fees to pay for my children.'

I wanted to help. 'What can you do?' I asked.

'My brother can be an askari,' interposed the brother. 'He was a soldier once.'

'Has he any documents?'

'Yes.'

I was given a card which said the bearer had done some military service and that his character was good. We needed a watchman. I went into the house to ask Armand if he thought it was a good idea to employ the Masai ex-soldier.

'Now, Michaela, are you sure you haven't fallen in love with his ear-rings or something. Do you really think he will make a good askari?'

'Of course. Come outside and see for yourself. He looks strong and is carrying a formidable-looking club.'

'It would certainly be a good idea to have an askari, there is no doubt about it,' Armand mused.

My own car tyres on the Buick convertible were reasonably safe because they were special. The Buick convertible was the only one of its kind in Nairobi. There was, however, one other Buick convertible—a black one which was a year younger than mine.

Our vehicles most in danger from the tyre thieves were the Land Rovers. The Land Rover is a most popular car in Kenya, perfect for safari, and the tyres could be sold very easily.

Armand came out to see the two men. I explained that I knew one of them and I was friendly with his wife. Armand examined the documents.

'When could he start?'

I translated.

'He says tomorrow, but could he have an army overcoat and a torch?'

'It could be arranged. You had better hire him.'

The next day I went to Nairobi to buy the promised torch and overcoat. There was a shop near the bazaar which sold second-hand army clothing. I found a magnificent greatcoat which looked as though it had belonged to a major at least, perhaps even a major-general. It had epaulettes on which a few marks still remained from the owner's insignia of rank. I myself would have preferred to see our guard in the national costume of the Masai, called a shuka. This is a rectangular garment which is now usually a blanket, reddish in colour. In low altitudes it is a rectangle of cotton. In the old days the same garment used to be made of skins. It is nearly always red because of the red ochre with which the Masai paint themselves.

Our Masai was delighted with the garment. He tried it on proudly and marched backwards and forwards to show it off to his brother. He switched the torch on and off several times.

'The batteries won't last long if he doesn't stop playing with it,' Armand laughed. After the first half-hour he got used to the torch. His brother said good-bye to him and left him with us.

Our new askari arrived every evening as an askari should do. There is no more awful situation than imagining you are safe from a surprise attack when you are not. He often told me about his army exploits, which I recounted to Armand in the evenings. We considered ourselves lucky to have found such a first-rate employee.

He had been working for us for two months. One evening very late the dogs began to bark.

'I had better go to see what is happening,' I said to Armand.

'Call the askari, Michaela. Find out where he is. Ask him if he has seen anything suspicious.'

I went outside and called the askari. There was no answer. Could he have been waylaid by thieves and knocked unconscious? I took the stick which I kept by my front door and called up the stairs to Armand.

'I am going to find him. He doesn't seem to be here. I am going over to the servants' house to find out what has happened to him.'

'Wait for me,' said Armand.

I waited and together we walked across the garden to the other house.

'Tshikadi,' I called. 'Have you seen the askari?'

Tshikadi came to the door of his house. 'No,' he replied.

The next day there was no news of the missing man. Three days and four Langata robberies later the askari's brother paid us a visit. He looked worried. 'Have you seen my brother?' he asked.

'I have not.'

He sighed heavily. 'Then he has been killed, it is certain. My wife told me to come and see you. She said you would help us to find him, but I am sure he is dead.'

'Have you now news of him?'

'Yes, you know there is a school near my maniatta? The children were walking across the plains to their classes early this morning when they saw a mass of cloth on the ground. They went up to examine it. It was an army overcoat. Underneath the coat was a torch.'

'Oh, how dreadful!' I exclaimed, unable to hide my fears. Armand came out to join us.

'What is he saying, Michaela?'

I repeated the story of finding the coat and torch.

'It is so typical of him to have guarded his overcoat and torch. He was so proud of them. He wouldn't have allowed anything to harm them,' I said, with a lump in my throat.

'He must have been attacked by a lion, or perhaps he was killed by gangsters.'

I was rather inclined towards the view that the askari had been beaten up and robbed, possibly murdered, because he had been paid his wages the night before. It was quite a considerable sum of money. I feared that the robbers had seen some of the notes in his pocket.

'It certainly looks like it,' said Armand gravely. 'You had better go straight to the police.'

I took the askari's brother in the car and together we drove to Hardy police post. The African policemen were most sympathetic. They found chairs for me and the bereaved brother, and as other policemen joined us in the room we told them our story. A fifth policeman entered. I was halfway through the story to the fourth policeman. When he heard the name of the askari the newcomer asked, 'What did you say his name was?'

The brother gave our askari's full name, including who he was the son of.

'Is he tall and good-looking?' The policeman continued to describe our askari. The body must have been found!

'Have you found the . . .?' began the brother. Before he could say 'body' the policeman nodded.

'We found him, but he won't be returning with you tonight, or for many nights to come. You had better find yourself another askari, madam,' he said to me.

'Why, what happened? Is he injured?'

'He is not, but several other men are,' said the policeman with a chuckle.

'We've arrested him for being drunk and causing a public disturbance. He is jailed for a month.'

I decided to take the policeman's advice, much as I liked our askari. It was too dangerous to employ someone who might get drunk and leave our home unguarded. I engaged a Kikuyu who had been employed as a watchman by a company which was closing down the branch at which he had been working for the last eleven years. I called his former employers and they told me he was highly satisfactory, had worked for them during the Emergency and had no criminal record. We engaged Ngugi on the spot.

We received a pitiful letter from our ex-askari, who was still in jail. It had been written by one of his educated nephews. It begged forgiveness. I felt really sad that we couldn't hold his job for him. I answered his letter, saying that I thought he was a very good man, but that we had to have an askari straight away because our house couldn't be left unguarded. I also said that drinking too much was a terrible thing. It was as bad as over-eating and could ruin the health. Nevertheless, he should always consider us his friends. This he has done. After his jail sentence he has several times come back to visit us.

After my many years in Africa I have made a host of friends of all races. I have never felt the slightest feeling of unease because I am of a different race from them. I can truthfully say that I am as much at home with Africans and Asians as Europeans. For this reason I am often consulted for advice. There are so many problems when a country has adopted another culture, as the Africans have done. Often the leap is barely the span of a man's lifetime. In fact, I feel I am sometimes closer to the one who has made his leap than his own parents.

A Masai schoolboy of fifteen years, whom I have known since he was some three feet high, asked me for advice about getting married.

'My father has asked me which I want to do next term. He will buy me a wife or I can have another year at school. What shall I do, Michaela?'

'You should have another year at school. Don't be in too much of a hurry to get married. If you are hoping to get a bursary to study abroad you don't want to leave a wife, possibly a child, behind, to fend for themselves. Preference is sometimes given to the student who has no responsibilities.'

I knew a young African teacher. I have known him many years from his very first job when he was barely out of school. He was a dedicated young man and a very good teacher. One afternoon Tshikadi told me, 'There is a man who wants to speak to you.' I looked down from my writing-room window. There was the young African teacher below.

I waved to him and he called, 'May I speak to you for a few minutes, or shall I call back later if you are busy?'

'Do come in,' I said. I went down the stairs to open the door. I had just finished writing for the day. 'Do come in. We will have some tea and you can tell me what's on your mind.'

When we were installed in my writing-room he began his story.

'I am very much in love with a girl. She has come to live with me in my house. She loves me very much.' He paused.

'But?' I asked.

'Her father will not let us marry without a bride price. The bride price for our tribe is very high. It will be many years before I can assemble so much money. The girl flatly refuses to go back to her father. I couldn't bear it if she went, either. Our situation was difficult enough, but two days ago I got this letter.' He handed it to me.

'We have heard you are living with a girl as your wife and yet you are not married according to the laws of the Church. If this is true this relationship must stop immediately. Unless you take action within the next week we shall terminate your employment.'

'What shall I do, Michaela?'

I sat and thought. Of course, I could lend him the money for the bride price, but I had made it an absolute rule not to lend money to friends. If I gave it to him I would be starting a precedent. I would make more enemies than friends in the long run. I would be inundated with requests for money, and the fact that I had given once, and refused to give it again, would be a mark against me. Besides, I didn't think the young African was asking for a loan, or even hinting for one. He genuinely wanted advice. After an interval I had the answer.

1 After the morning's work I stroll in the garden with the chimpanzees just before lunch

2 Jackie jackal was a lovely little puppy as a baby

3 Hy-hyena's early feed

4 Piggy, the warthog, loves to be petted

(*over*) 5 Elephants and egrets fraternise

6 Hy-hyena and Piggy grow up together and are the best of friends

(opposite) 7 Baba the duiker is as affectionate as a dog

(opposite) 8 Pardon me, your slip is showing! (Our pet hyena with Michaela)

9 A park warden's pets. Stephen and Eunice Ellis's lion cub and caracal are close friends

'What would happen if you are out of work and the girl has a baby?'

'We already have one child who is six months old.'

I hope I successfully suppressed my surprise.

'Does the father of the girl know about your child and he still won't give his consent?'

'Yes, he knows all about it. He has nothing against me except that I can't afford the bride price.'

'Have you been supporting the girl all this time?'

'Yes, I have. I buy her everything. She hasn't cost her father a penny for the last year and a half.'

'Go to him, tell him that you are going to lose your job and why you are going to. You could also tell him that you can no longer support his daughter and grandchild. How much do you think it has cost you to keep his daughter for a year and a half?'

The young teacher took a page from his notebook and jotted down some figures. The total came to a tidy sum.

'Did you ask this girl to come and live with you?'

'No, she came by herself. I wouldn't have dared to ask her such a thing. She just arrived with her baggage, and as it is eight hours' walk from my house, and it was evening, I couldn't send her back. Besides, I had no transportation, only my bicycle. The lamp was out of order and it was dangerous to use it, as there was no moon, even if I had taken her back without her baggage.' A human problem had arisen because a bicycle lamp had been out of order.

I looked down at the figure which the teacher had written in his notebook.

'Tell the girl's father that you did not ask his daughter to come and live with you, and that you want this sum from him. When he has recovered from the shock tell him that if he will waive the bride price you will not press for payment for his daughter's keep.'

The young man's serious expression changed. He smiled and then laughed.

'It might work, Michaela. If it does I shall be eternally grateful.' He said good-bye and left.

A few months later I was in my garden near our hedge of crimson bougainvillaea, its bracts, loaded with colour, mingled well with the tiny sky-blue flowers of our indigenous hedge plant. I peeped into the road. I could see but not be seen. A handsome young African couple were walking past. They looked very much in love, and it pleased me to see them. They turned into our drive and I recognised the young teacher.

'I want to introduce you to my wife, Michaela.'

I shook hands.

'As you see, your advice worked. I am most grateful.'

5
African Dances

ONE of the greatest joys in life is dancing, at least to me—and to millions of other people. Armand doesn't dance, but he has never objected to my interest in it. We enjoy most things together but dancing is not one of them.

Unless you have seen a country's dancing you cannot really know its soul, or its temperament. I have danced all over the world, with many different people. I have found it is one of the best ways of breaking down shyness. It is a good way if you can dance easily. I am rather like those people who can play music by ear.

When I was very small a man and woman had seen me dancing in the street. They asked me to take them to my mother. The couple had a dancing school and they proposed to my mother that they should take me as a pupil, entirely free of charge.

Although my mother knew the name of the dancing school, and that it was reputable, she decided against my having a career as a dancer. I was very disappointed at the time, but perhaps she made the right decision. Usually even today I can follow any dance step that I see if I watch closely. The pigmies, I discovered, have the same gift. On one visit to the little people I had introduced them to Hindu neck movements which they immediately copied.

I have been a guest at various sacred dances which are generally not revealed to foreigners. I believe that dancing stimulates one's telepathic and psychic faculties. This view, is an ancient one, I have discovered from a study of comparative religion. Many religions incorporate dancing in their ritual.

Many years ago, when I was in the Congo, Armand had wanted

to do some work at a certain village. For some reason there had been no co-operation. The administrator shrugged when we appealed to him for help.

'You are not the first, and neither will you be the last, film unit to find that you can't work with these people.'

They were photogenic and Armand lamented the bad luck of not being able to take advantage of it.

'May I try to get friendly with them?' I asked.

'You heard what the administrator said. Anyway, try and see what you can do. It would be wonderful if we could get some film.'

I wandered off by myself. I seemed to remember that I had seen a drum tucked away under the eaves of a hut. At the outskirts of the village I found what I was looking for.

An old wrinkled woman sat on the ground in front of her hut. Her skinny old legs were stretched straight out in front of her. She had a pile of grain in front of her which she was raking through with her fingers. A plump grandson, barely able to toddle, staggered into her and managed to retain his balance by hanging on to her pendulous old bosom. The child righted his balance and then after another step or two sat down suddenly in the dust.

There was a man of about forty-five leaning against the doorway of the hut who didn't think it necessary to greet me as I paused in front of the little group. The old woman gave me one dull incurious look and then bent down to her work.

I asked them in Kiswahili whether I could look at their drum. The man, ungraciously, uncoiled himself from his prop and passed me the drum. I examined it unhurriedly. It was about two and a half feet high, and looked not unlike the drums I am familiar with in Kenya. I tapped it lightly and then I went into the syncopated rhythm which I had been taught when visiting the Ituri Forest. Instantly the man and the old woman's attitude changed. They regarded me with interest, even the baby stopped trying to stuff the dusty grain into his mouth. Within three minutes we had a small crowd around us. It was a noisy crowd, very good-humoured. The women squealed with delight, amused to see a European lady play the drum African fashion. I varied the performance by demonstrating a rhythm I had been taught from the Embu District in Kenya.

The circle of bodies around me was getting thick. Other drums, and drummers, had appeared magically. There were five of us playing with gusto. The rhythm was irresistible. One of the women started to sing the usual question, with answering chorus from the crowd. Such traditional songs are centuries old, and never fail to grip me with excitement. Soon, first one, and then another, started to sway and shuffle in a dance. Their shoulders shaking, their feet barely moving, they formed two concentric circles. In the middle a man wearing a small loin-cloth made of raffia fabric and a woman wearing a brightly coloured print around her hips did an African *pas de deux* together. Their steps were far more complicated than the chorus which whirled around them, framing them on every side with dancing bodies.

I left my drum to watch. One of the women beckoned me to join in the circle of dancing women. I took my place amongst them and did exactly the same steps as they did. There were roars of approval. We now had a crowd of spectators. When the chief performers in the middle had tired each would choose his own successor to carry on with the dance. The woman performer who now had the centre came to me, and made signs that I should carry on with the dance. The roar of approval was even louder when I carried on with the intricate steps, as though I had been doing them since childhood. We danced for several hours.

I was quite unconscious of anything except the dance and was quite surprised when it ended to see that there were five Europeans, including my husband, all busy taking movies and still pictures of us. The dance was only broken up when the women went back to their homes to cook.

Armand was delighted with the film footage.

'One day I am going to write a book called *I Married an Extrovert*,' said Armand, 'and like it.'

'Then I am going to write a book called *I Married a Carnivore*,' I retaliated, as I took my tin of apricots from Armand's proffered hand. Armand always teases me and calls me his herbivore because I am a vegetarian.

We drove off from the village some few miles. We usually avoid eating in front of the various villagers because they crowd around breathing down one's neck and commenting loudly on the kind of food one is eating. Extrovert I may be, but not about food!

Armand opened the tin of apricots as I took out from my camera box my Japanese chopsticks, which are made of extremely light wood and not as heavy as the Chinese type. I always carry chopsticks on safari because not only are they light but they take up hardly any room at all. I dislike getting my fingers messed up with food, as I am often using a camera as well as being photographed, and hate stickiness on anything I possess. I find eating with chopsticks as easy as, if not easier than, eating with a knife and fork. Armand watched me as I ate my half-apricots straight from the tin with the chopsticks. I finished off the juice and felt fighting fit again. We took the tins off with us, for we never leave litter, however inaccessible the place. It is something drummed into me from childhood, and I would feel completely immoral if I left any debris about, even if no one was around to see. I collect all the rubbish, or tacka-tacka as it is called in Kiswahili, and bury it, carefully covering it so that there are no traces. The only time I have been thwarted was when a hyena unearthed everything to bear off the empty corned-beef tin which Armand had discarded.

I finished off my meal in the car with a handful of peanuts and an orange. I felt refreshed and said so. Armand said, 'If eating "cabbages" keeps you looking fresh after dancing for four hours, more people should try it.'

Armand, besides calling me his herbivore, calls me the cabbage eater, and although I had been eating apricots I knew exactly what he meant.

We drove off to the next village triumphantly, having succeeded in doing a good day's filming.

In a city like Nairobi it is rare to see tribal dancing except on some special occasion. It is a great pity, because East Africa has quite a variety of folk dances. Many dances are held, especially on Saturday nights. The dance bands are mostly African, and they are as good as, if not better than, those from anywhere else in the world. Africans are splendid dancers. I don't go out dancing often in Nairobi because I don't like leaving Armand alone.

It is boring for him to come with me, as he doesn't dance. He always has plenty to do with our work and I can usually persuade him to let me go for a few hours.

'Don't be long, and not too late,' are usually his last words.

We live eleven miles away from the city. I have often driven the whole distance from my house to Nairobi without passing another car. If the car broke down it would be a very long walk in between houses. For this reason the boot of the car, when I go dancing, always contains a pair of flat-heeled shoes and usually a raincoat, in addition to my panga and pepper pot on the front seat beside me.

I was preparing to go to a dance. Armand had gone on a six weeks' journey to the States. I was alone in the house. The animals looked miserable as they watched my preparations. They always knew when they were going to be left alone for the evening. Suska, especially, put on an expression of martyrdom.

'Why are you doing this to me?' her look seemed to suggest.

I was hurrying to go to a New Year's party which also happened to be a family anniversary of an African friend. Henry and Mary had met me two weeks before when I had been shopping in Nairobi.

'You know my cousin James?' said Mary.

'Yes, I have met him.'

'He wanted to invite you to his party, but he had heard that you were in the States.'

'My husband is in the States but I couldn't go. It is only going to be for six weeks and we can't afford it. Even if we could, we would think it was an extravagance.'

'It's not too late to get in touch with James to tell him you are in Nairobi, after all. I'll call him tonight to tell him that you are here and we will bring you along with us.'

'Where is the party?' I asked.

When I go out by myself at night I often get lost. It detracts from the joy of going out if you have to prowl up and down an unlit road, looking for name boards. We have no street numbers in most residential districts around Nairobi. Often your host and hostess will overlook the fact that the name board they so carefully erected several years ago has become overgrown.

I put on a lilac and silver jersey dress based on Kikuyu costume and was just slipping into my coat. I couldn't help being a little proud of making them myself. There was a rap on the door.

'What do you want?' I asked.

I opened the door.

'There are two Masai waiting for you. I told them they shouldn't come so late at night,' said my faithful servant. It was after dark already.

I went outside and there were the Masai, one of them carrying a very large spear.

'We have brought you a present.'

One of them produced a mugumu seedling a foot high. It looked healthy and strong. The mugumu is a lovely tree. It is the sacred Kikuyu fig. It is an evergreen and has glossy leaves.

'Thank you for your kindness. I shall treasure your gift. It is a symbol of our friendship. I will plant it near the house where I can go and see it every day.'

'Could you give us a lift?' the Masai with the spear asked. There was nothing for it—it would have seemed ungracious to have refused such a request after being presented with a gift.

'Hop in,' I said, being careful as I got into the driver's seat that the spear didn't pierce my shoulder blade. I drove them to the end of our road, where they got out.

'We won't come so late next time,' they said, flashing a smile.

I drove to Nairobi to Mary and Henry's house to pick them up, or, rather, to follow behind their car. I often make this arrangement with friends. If I am going to a place I don't know I follow behind them. It is too unnerving to try to be punctual and try to find one's way in unfamiliar surroundings.

We arrived at one of Nairobi's many dance halls. The rhythm poured out of the door and engulfed the people passing by. It was not tribal music, but it was the grandchild of it. From the folk dances of the past had been born a music resembling Latin American rhythm, itself owing much to Mother Africa. The dance floor seemed filled with professional dancers! Everyone was dancing with such skill, such verve, that it was good to watch. The girls were in short evening dresses, the men for the most part in dinner jackets. I was the only European, but I was surrounded instantly by friends. I saw my host, and, with difficulty, went to greet him, closely followed by Mary and Henry. The floor was packed. He was a handsome man. He had a look of prosperous authority about him.

I danced every dance. I don't think I sat down for more than five minutes, and that was when the band stopped playing to get some refreshments for themselves.

One of my partners was a Mkamba from Machakos District. We whirled into the dance and simultaneously fell into step with a wakamba tribal dance. There was applause on all sides and looking around I saw that three or four other couples had followed our example. My partner said, 'It is easy to see who is a Mkamba here, but you are the first Mkamba I have ever seen with yellow hair.'

'If only London, Paris and New York could see us we would start a new dance phase, the wakamba.'

'Where did you learn it?'

'We filmed the dancers at Kitui.'

'You filmed them?'

'Yes, we make television films.'

I tried to explain what television was to somebody who had never seen it. My partner had heard about it but didn't know how it operated. In those days we had no television in Kenya.

I danced several wakamba dances with the other people of that tribe who were in the room. Rumbas and sambas followed. Henry asked me for a dance. He said in a low voice, 'Michaela, do you feel the tension over in that corner?' I didn't, and said so. His words surprised me. He shook his head and I urged him to tell me why.

'What is it all about?'

'That group over there hate one another.'

I could see what he meant as we moved nearer. The young men were watching one another like wary cats who have not quite made up their mind to have a scrap.

I had had a truly wonderful evening which had a piquant ending. The last song but one someone in the band had slipped on a mask of a red-faced European. It was obviously a Halloween mask from the States, made of plastic, and extraordinarily lifelike. It didn't need a genius to know that a subversive song was being sung. The dancers united in an abandoned samba.

I drove back to Langata thoughtfully. It was quite obvious to me that everyone had completely forgotten that I was a European. I was highly flattered.

It was a beautiful night. The drought was still on. On my left was the road which led to the National Park. There was a scurry of hoofs—the animals had once again got out on that side and were making towards the dam. It was pathetic to see how thirst had made them lose their caution. Normally they stay happily in the park, but now few lost their torment of thirst. Their bodies looked ghostly in the moonlight, clothed in black and white stripes, making them appear like skeletons. There were several herds, some just crossing in front of my car, from left to right. Their sense of urgency contrasted with those who had already slaked their thirst, to the right of the road. These animals waited until my car had passed, but the others who had not drunk waited for nothing. Extreme care had to be taken not to run into them. There were often animal casualties those days on the roads. One zebra had got completely lost a little further up the hill. He was by himself trying unsuccessfully to jump over the large expanded metal fence which enclosed the barracks. I couldn't bear to see it. It was madness to get out of the car and I knew it. I stopped and got out, leaving the motor running. There wasn't time to change into flat-heeled shoes.

I chased the zebra down the road on foot, shouting and waving my hand. The zebra ran from me, as well he might. I wondered what an onlooker might have thought at seeing me running like a maniac in my evening clothes chasing a zebra. I managed to put him on the right road. I stopped out of breath at the bottom of the hill. It was a long walk back and it seemed to me that the solitary patch of light where my car stood was miles away.

After the excitement of the chase was over I realised that I had been dancing for several hours and that I was tired out. So tired that I could almost have fallen asleep on my feet. If it had not been such a dangerous time I would have taken a little nap when I got back to the car. As I came near to the car my heart missed a beat. A very drunken African, whose breath even at a distance of several yards was heavy with drink, stood between me and the car. I sniffed methylated spirit. He came towards me.

'I want a lift to Nairobi,' he said.

I wasn't afraid of him, because I knew I would be able to outrun him, but did he have companions with him, and was it an ambush? I was completely alone in a sleeping world and the sleepers were several miles from me. Although the barracks were to the left of me, the soldiers were a great distance away from the fence. If I was going to be chopped up or murdered there was no likelihood of having any witnesses to it, except the zebras and they wouldn't talk. The drunken man lurched towards me and I side-stepped just in time. He was looking for support as well as for a lift. He could be an old man of the sea, and once he was clinging to me, I would have to drag him back to the car and would never be rid of him.

'I am not going to Nairobi,' I said, which should have been

obvious to the most intoxicated, as the car pointed in the other direction.

'Help me,' said the drunk, but I was already galloping up the hill at a speed I would have thought was impossible a minute or two ago, when I felt so terribly sleepy. The strenuous exercise had awakened me completely, which was just as well. I had almost reached the car when I saw another two figures with their arms around one another's necks, slowly staggering in my direction. I just managed to reach the car in time, and leapt into it, thankful that I had left the motor running. The few seconds it would have taken to start the engine might well have been my undoing.

Safely home, I put the key into the lock, and stepped aside to let the stream of dogs come out. Their boisterous welcome was reassuring.

Three days later I was coming into the lounge. I looked through the window. Outside it seemed as though we were having a hail-storm—perhaps the weather had broken at last—but it was not rain or hail, it was bees. There was a terrible din. We had recently had the bees removed by a bearded expert. (Why are all bee experts in Kenya bearded?) He and his assistant had gone on to the roof, in itself a perilous adventure. The roof had a fairly large cavity for bees, but not for men. It was constructed with lathes of wood and on the room side the ceiling was composed of hardboard painted white to match the white walls. The front staircase has a length of about forty feet from floor to ceiling. If anyone were to fall through the hardboard at this point he could very easily break his neck. The only way to cross the house to where the bees had their favourite swarming point was to crawl along the wooden beams. One of our men had fallen through the roof at one time, but luckily only on the verandah, where the drop was shorter. They carried smoke bombs and buckets, and looked like a decontamination squad in their thick rubber knee-high boots and overalls. The youngest bee expert wore a hat with a net over his face, but the other man, his senior, scorned such protection. I asked him if he ever got stung. He shrugged. 'Not for a long time.'

'You will be careful, won't you?'

The men took out the remains of two gigantic hives. One swarm of bees had been removed without waging total warfare on them. The other had not been so lucky. They had to be smoked out. It was not a welcome sight to see that the bees were back. If only I had insisted on a flat roof we wouldn't have been the unwelcome hosts to the stubborn insects.

There was nothing we could do to discourage them. As I watched, I saw reinforcements had come through the window into the house. This was really too much. It was exasperating to have the intruders moving in on us. There were thousands of bees humming like a giant dynamo in the lounge—the air was thick with moving insects.

I called to Tshikadi to shut the kitchen door, but it was too late. Another swarm had entered through the kitchen window; the enemy had surrounded us.

Brucie and Mbili slunk downstairs, but Suska, poor accident-prone Suska, decided the bees were good to eat. It didn't take her long to find out that she had been mistaken. She ran round the room, knocking over a coffee-table and pushing up the carpet into untidy humps.

Tshikadi sprayed the room, the bees fell down in little heaps, miniature mountains of bodies. I felt terribly sad and left him to sweep them up.

Our roof has one good attribute. It gives shelter to a large population of creatures. Martins, owls, red-wing starlings nest under the eaves of the roof. Time would not be wasted in spending the morning looking at these families building, searching for food and occasionally quarrelling when one or other of their neighbours lands in the wrong place. On the verandah roof is a hole in the ceiling board with an opening of an inch and a half.

Swifts fly swiftly on to the verandah and without pausing fly straight into this narrow opening of an inch and a half, folding their wings to their body the second their heads enter the hole. Two other families of lesser striped-breasted swallows have constructed nests making use of the angle between wall and ceiling. The nests are comfortably round with a narrow entrance tunnel. They are made of hundreds of pieces of mud carefully cemented together.

There must be many more occupants there which we never see because of the roof's inaccessibility. Almost certainly there are many small mammals.

One evening I was in our store-room, which leads off the kitchen. It has shelves on which food is kept. I had some cooking chocolate bars piled one on top of the other. I wondered who had been gnawing them.

I picked up a packet of peanuts, which showered down on the floor from a hole in the bottom of the container. Suska obligingly gobbled them up. She is a great peanut eater.

I was soon to meet the uninvited guest; for on opening the door to the kitchen wing one day, something fell on my hand. There was a scurry of feet, and a mouse (or was it a rat?) climbed nimbly up the expanded metal wall of the store.

It had creamy-white fur on its stomach and pinkish-brown fur on its back. The feet were pink and dainty; the eyes were the typical large nocturnal eyes, bright and beady. It vanished.

Mystified I went into the store and peered upwards. Sure enough, there was a hole in the ceiling. After that I saw the little rodent nearly every evening.

It became quite tame, and wouldn't bother to move away when I took something from the shelf. If it saw one of the cats it seemed to sense danger, kept perfectly still and behaved in quite a different manner.

One evening Ginger followed me into my store. He leapt into the air and I caught him in midflight in my hands. The rodent was hiding behind a tin of cocoa, but had left its tail hanging over the edge of the shelf. It ran up the expanded metal like a sailor running up the ladder to look-out. It disappeared to safety. Ginger was annoyed with me and sulked the whole evening.

It is a great sorrow to find that animals don't get on together. The legend of the Garden of Eden is one dear to the hearts of all animal lovers. With some traditional enemies co-existence has been known to work out, but in most cases it is a risky business!

One evening Ginger lay asleep, paws neatly tucked under his chin, and by his side the little rodent. There are times when my love for cats is sorely tried and this was one of them.

'He has killed my friend, the murderer. He is well fed. He hasn't even bothered to eat the victim,' I thought to myself. The next evening I was happily surprised by seeing the rodent back. I realised then that I had not one individual but several under my roof. I wondered if I would be overrun with rodents. My worries about over-population were allayed when that very week an owl took up residence under the eaves.

Armand arrived back from the States. He told me that many of our friends in that country wanted us to set up house there, as they imagined us in deadly peril. They were astonished to hear that I was living in the house alone. The wife of one of our business friends said that she would not even stay in her New York apartment by herself, let alone in an isolated house miles from the city.

'I wouldn't do it for ten million dollars,' she said.

6

The Young Visitors

LIFE went on as usual after the initial excitement of Armand's homecoming. I love travelling, but I also enjoy home life to the full. After the first few months in our house, and before it was furnished fully, and as comfortable as it is now, I had been worried about Armand's attitude towards the house and home life generally.

'I prefer to live in a hotel or a tent,' he often said.

'But what about having pets, Armand? Hotels won't always accept pets, and most animals hate to travel.'

Now Armand is completely won over into liking home life, for there is no doubt a well-run home is hard to beat. To my delight he not only enjoys home life but he is actually proud of our home. The bird life, alone, is surely enough to put chains round one's ankles, which one wishes to remove only occasionally.

Our home was run efficiently enough for me to spend most of my time working. People were beginning to pay complimentary remarks about our garden, which, as a tropical garden should be, was filled with vibrant colours. Nothing was planted in straight lines, but mostly curves, making use of what nature had given us already, not unlike the Japanese system of garden architecture. I was still very ignorant about planting but, as with everything, it can be learnt by trial and error and by going to wiser people than one's self.

There was a marvellous old lady, Mrs. Crompton, who lived down the road. She was sprightly and could walk me off my feet when showing me round her garden. She was born not with a green thumb but with two green thumbs. She and Phil MacRae were my first teachers in gardening. Mrs. Crompton sent flowers to me once a week, which filled the house, because I was unable to bring myself to cut our own flowers, a trait which has been with me all my life.

When I was four years old my mother had given me a 'garden' in her own pocket-handkerchief-sized one. Mine was exactly one yard square. In it I grew pansies, mint and horse-radish. It was this strongly implanted love for the things I grew which forced my uncle to get up in the middle of the night and uproot my horse-radish. My mother had imagined that I would supply her with this root for Sunday dinners to go with her roast beef, but, alas, I flatly refused to murder my plant. The ubiquitous horse-radish threatened to take over the whole garden.

Phil MacRae was an ardent gardener. She was an energetic, well-built woman who not only ran a house without staff in those days but also helped in her husband's garages. Phil had the quick nervous energy of my half-French aunt who started in life as a two-pounds-ten-a-week typist (many years ago for that salary!) and has ended up as a director of her company, being only second to the owner in importance. She became a top sugar expert in England. During the war her recommendations were adopted by the Government. Her name appeared in *Hansard* in consequence. Phil was most generous in giving me plants, and between her and Mrs. Crompton my interest was stimulated to such an extent that I was in danger of becoming a gardening bore. For two or three months my favourite reading was seed catalogues and gardening books.

'You are unpredictable, Michaela,' Armand said. 'I would never have suspected that I was married to a latent gardener.'

I am always faithful to my interests. The fact that I had taken up gardening with such enthusiasm didn't mean that I had stopped covering furniture when required, writing and filming, and having some time to give to the pets. The busier one is, the more time one can seem to make to do other things.

Armand had been home for two days when Tshikadi told me the police would like a word with me. My first thought was that one of the servants had been up to something. Last time one enterprising man who has left our employment had been operating a still hidden away in our valley. He was found out when several servants who worked for neighbours were arrested for being drunk and incapable. Someone gave his little business enterprise away. Langata lost one of its bootleggers and we lost a good servant. The police inspector was with two other officers.

'We are not on duty today,' laughed the inspector, seeing my expression. 'May we come and look at your fish? We have heard all about them from our patrol.'

'Certainly.' I took them to the pools. My goldfish pools are large and irregular in shape, to simulate nature, and have stones around them. Yellow water lilies and papyrus give shade to the fish. I have a theory about gardening, which is to beautify the ugliest part of the garden. If this is done, the effect is remarkable. The whole garden is lifted out of the commonplace because ingenuity has to be used. When the soil is poor, pools are the solution to the beauty problem.

I had one place in our garden where nothing would grow, not even grass. The murram and stone at this spot discouraged any attempt at planting. I drew an irregular shape on this ground with white shoe cleaner, and hired some workmen. Armand said we looked like the builders of the pyramids. We dug it out, cemented it and turned it into one of the most successful places in the garden.

The earth we excavated I piled up into a winding terrace which looks down into the pool. It has been planted with poinsettias, crimson Mexican orchids, local succulents and golden shower. The flowers repeat the colours of the goldfish, who have thrived and bred.

After the police had seen my ponds the inspector asked me whether I could let him have two or three of my goldfish to start a pool of his own at the police post.

'Certainly; come back when you have your pond ready.'

I gave him directions as to its construction. I warned him to fill the pond completely with water, leave it for three or four days, then drain and refill it. There is something deadly in cement which kills the fish, and this procedure should always be done if any living things are being kept in a cement pond. I gave him water plants, water lilies, parrot's feather and papyrus.

'Plant them in tins, otherwise your whole pond will be overgrown in no time. The fish must have shade, and it is always a necessity to have vegetation in and around the water to provide a cool place for them.'

I also advised making a deeper place in the water, which would provide a different temperature level for them.

Fish are very sensitive to temperature changes. If taken from water of one temperature and put into water of another temperature, many will die.

As I was gazing at my fish I fell fully clothed with my handbag in my hand into the pond. Tom and Tshikadi came to my assistance faces grave. They helped me out of the pool dripping wet from head to foot. When I laughed they were convulsed. They had nobly refrained from laughing until they had found out whether I was hurt or not, which I thought showed a high level of good manners. I looked very absurd, my hair dripping down on to my shoulders.

A few weeks later the inspector arrived on his day off with two of his men, and he spent a vigorous half-hour capturing three fish. Some months later the inspector told me that other police posts had made fish ponds and that my goldfish had started a craze which had been written up in the police gazette. The police found, as I had, that watching goldfish after a strenuous day's work was a soothing and relaxing occupation.

There is always something going on around and in a pool. It wasn't long before platana frogs invaded the smaller of the goldfish ponds. The platana has claws. We had first met it in South Africa at the University of Cape Town, where tests were being made to determine its efficiency in diagnosing pregnancy.

The larger pond overlooks a sunken garden created from a rubbish dump. One of our tenants had kept horses and drain-pipes in the same spot to the detriment of the drain-pipes! Armand had bought the pipes for an engineering scheme which had not materialised.

The pipes were earthenware and in the two dozen there was not one whole piece. Each was broken in some part or other. We had taken over the house, and Armand, who is not usually a hoarder, clung to his drain-pipes. I was always itching to get my hands on them to throw them out or bury them. I caught Armand at a weak moment when he admired the goldfish pond.

'We should have a sunken garden shouldn't we?'

'A good idea, Michaela. What would you do with those stones in the middle?'

'I would dig them out and make them a feature of the garden. I could plant rock plants and succulents, cacti and aloes. Some of those wild white pelargoniums would look decorative and grow well in such a garden. May I do it, Armand?'

'Yes, of course,' said Armand, rather surprised. 'Go ahead.' The next morning I and my workmen were carrying off the drain-pipes!

'Michaela, what are you doing with those drain-pipes?'

'Putting them into a nice big hole and I shall then cover them up.'

I ran off with another one in my hands. Armand's voice trailed behind me.

'We may need them some time.'

I pretended to be out of earshot.

There had been one or two building hazards. We had removed the concrete where the former stable of our tenants had been and discovered a nest of young spitting cobras beneath the foundations. In one place we had been attacked by large voracious black ants. I and my workmen hopped about removing them from our persons for at least half an hour. Suska naturally got one on her and leapt two feet off the ground.

Armand forgave the loss of his drain-pipes when he saw the finished sunken garden.

The cats took a great interest in our goldfish. The interest was not reciprocated by the goldfish, who kept their distance. Kiki, our pastel tortoise-shell, spent many hours by the pool with her tail actually in the water. I presumed she was fishing. I have only found one half-eaten fish since we have had the pool, but perhaps she caught others whom she devoured, leaving no trace.

If we had not had our own dogs we might have had several other casualties from other sources. I was having tea with a friend. There was a mighty splash in the water and at first I thought Suska, the accident prone, must have fallen in, but no, it was a hammerkopf, a large brown bird with a head like a hammer (kopf meaning head in Afrikaans and German). The bird swooped down to the water and would have taken a fish if he hadn't been chased off by the dogs.

The platform formed by the sunken garden and which overlooked the pool became a favourite meeting place where I could sit with my friends and talk as we sipped coffee or tea. Even later a happier scene took place on this spot.

I am asked to serve on all sorts of committees. One I was on was the Junior Society for the Prevention of Cruelty to Animals.

The committee had organised a competition for schoolchildren, 'My Favourite Animal and Why'. Children of all three races had competed and their essays were refreshing. The majority of the African children were strictly utilitarian. Their favourite animal was usually a cow. The Asian children admired daintiness, the Europeans mostly cuteness. It was a hard job to judge the various competitors. Each member of the committee took a large batch of papers to judge at home. Finally they managed to weed out eleven children as the finalists. We gave silver cups, book tokens and shields for the school of the top two finalists. At a meeting of the committee of the Junior S.P.C.A. I asked, 'I wonder if all these children have been in the National Park?'

'I am sure they haven't,' answered Florrie Lyons. Florrie was one of the first to pioneer animal welfare in East Africa. She was truly dedicated.

I was told that she gave considerable sums of money to the cause, although she was not a millionairess by any means. She had also devoted many years of her life to furthering animal welfare.

I pondered Florrie's reply.

'May I suggest something and will the committee give their opinion on whether it could be done? I would like to invite the winners of the competition to come to the park with me. Then they could have lunch or tea at the house.'

The committee's reaction was evident before I had finished the sentence.

All that remained was to organise the details.

The children came from all over the country. A great deal of work had to be put in by committee members. All the principals of the schools involved had to be written to and parents' permission had to be sought.

Committee members insisted on coming earlier to my house to attend to the catering. My job was to arrange the hire of a bus.

The day of the outing was sunny. The children were meeting me at a central point in Nairobi, at the Touring Company's garage. The shining-eyed children were introduced to me. As many watched our programme it was exciting for them to meet a real person from television. There is always some kind of glamour attached to TV, radio, theatre or screen personalities. I have felt the same kind of pleasure mixed with wonder when I have met eminent scientists, writers or doctors and discovered they are indeed real.

Some of the children curtsied and all shook my hand. They were breathless with excitement. The parents had arranged to meet the children at the same rendezvous after our outing. We clambered into the bus, which was painted all over in a zebra pattern. We loaded on bottles of highly coloured red raspberry-flavoured liquids and a bag of sweets for each child. I was greatly touched that all the children offered their sweets to me on the journey.

We started off with a flourish, waving good-bye to parents and helpers from the Junior S.P.C.A. We came to the first hill, ten minutes' ride away from town, and the bus stopped halfway up. The driver tut-tutted and pulled and pushed various knobs on the dashboard like an organ player. The bus wouldn't budge. He finally put it into reverse and backed it down the hill. It was to our advantage that the vehicle was both large and forbidding. The other vehicles kept us at a distance!

I was weighed down with despondency. How disheartening it would be if something went wrong. I tried not to let the children sense my dejection. They were not in the least upset by this unfortunate start. If only we retained the elasticity of a child's mind which can find pleasure out of the mishaps of daily life.

The driver managed to start the bus. It lurched creakingly up the hill, protesting all the way. It stopped dead at the top. This time it really had stopped.

It was a hot and sunny day. The inside of the bus was becoming as hot as an oven. I suggested we should get out of the bus, which had stopped exactly beside a ditch, to get off the road as much as possible. A strong young African lad got out first and politely helped me down. He proceeded to help the other passengers. There was an exceptionally intelligent little girl called Martine Hunt whom two African teenagers were looking after in our expedition.

We had stopped near Wilson airport, which was the first airport in Nairobi, now used mostly for civilian and charter flying. We waited for ten minutes whilst the driver endeavoured to start the bus, but his old magic didn't work this time. Two or three drivers tried to help, but the bus was not co-operating. I was worried about the children getting sunstroke. How dreadful to have to tell their parents. I saw a large flat-topped thorn tree on the other side of the road, to which I shepherded the children, and then went off to telephone the garage for another bus.

'Don't separate,' I told them.

I walked to one of the offices in the airport and asked if I could use the telephone. 'Certainly,' said Mrs. Ellis, who was most sympathetic. The manager of the garage also was most concerned to hear of our plight.

'I will send a relief bus at once,' he said.

I went back to the children, who were in high spirits. This was really a great adventure.

'What a blessing it didn't happen in the park,' I said to one of the boys.

'We could perhaps have spent the night in the park.'

'It would be wonderful.'

The relief bus arrived. We climbed up into it and were on our way.

Our first stop was at the animal orphanage at the entrance to the National Park. The director of the National Parks, Mervyn Cowie, had started this new venture. Many animals for some reason or other became orphans. Their chances of survival are very small unless they are adopted by some kind-hearted human being. Usually these babies grow into large difficult-to-look-after animals. Unless someone is willing to dedicate their whole life to looking after them they are a real problem. Many of these animals have been sent to foreign zoos. The ideal solution for the animals is to keep them in their country of origin, where they have their natural food and habitat.

Mervyn and Stephen Ellis, also of National Parks, had long wanted an orphanage attached to the National Park. Not only would the animals be in perfect safety, and in ideal conditions, but visitors to the parks would be able to see the animals at close quarters. Mervyn had constructed large enclosures with plenty of trees, for shade, and enough sunlight if the animals wanted it. There was a lion which Stephen had looked after since it was a very small cub. Stephen's lion was now fully grown and had only just entered its new quarters.

When fully grown the lion would be introduced to the park itself, as many of the other animals would be. The lion always greeted Stephen with little affectionate grunts.

There was a herd of buffalo, so tame that I had seen them on my last visit taken from one enclosure to another, as if they had been a herd of Jerseys. They were calm and sedate. I thought of all the tales that people told of their ferocity. It was a good example of how kindness breeds gentleness and docility.

The orphanage was also used as a rehabilitation centre for animals which had been moved from outside the park to safety within the park. By using new methods of capture it was possible to remove the animals from the hazards of living in a cultivated area where they were unwanted, and might come to harm, to the park, where they were wanted.

One of the children was overwhelmed when she saw a baby elephant four foot six high. She could not believe that such an animal was real. It occurred to me that she probably didn't know how big it would grow. I pointed to the top of the eight-foot fence. It would be taller than this fence. She followed my eyes to where my finger pointed.

'Does it eat human beings?' she asked.

'No,' I smiled, 'but unless it is a tame elephant you know very well it is not advisable to go up and stroke it.'

Two or three of the children had brought cameras and were busy taking pictures. We said good-bye to the animal orphanage and then continued into the park.

Now we were back in the Africa of Rider Haggard, Stanley and Karen Blixen. This was the golden shimmering wonderland, filled with a huge variety of wild life, which had enthralled them. This was the Africa which drew the tourists of many lands. Such places are now sadly depleted, victims of the so-called 'progress' perpetrated by the despoiler and the philistine.

An African teenager sat in the front of the bus. He was very quick at spotting the animals and pointing them out to the other children. Martine, too, was very quick at seeing the animals. It was a good day. We saw ostriches flurrying their feathers flirtatiously because it was the time of their courtship. The males' legs were a vivid red, to attract the females, who were a demure brown. I caught a brief glimpse of a male sitting on his ankles, performing his ritualistic mating dance. His small stumpy wings, covered with long elegant feathers, waved first left, then right, rhythmically. The long serpentine neck dipped to the ground, first one side, then the other, in perfect harmony with the wing movements. The female gave only a cursory glance to her crouching suitor, and then continued with the serious business of eating. Was she playing hard to get? I wondered.

I didn't draw the attention of the children to the birds, because they were in turn looking at a herd of zebra. In the herd was a mother with a small foal. They were delighted at this toy-like creature. Its legs were almost the same length as its mother's, this being nature's way of ensuring that the foal would keep up with the herd when danger threatened.

One of my treasured memories concerning zebras was to see a

baby one born. Within minutes of freeing itself from the afterbirth it sprung to its feet, somehow keeping balance; and, after taking a few steps, sprung into the air. Half an hour later this baby was walking as easily as an adult zebra. By comparison, human babies seem extraordinarily backward, but then they do not have to fend for themselves as herbivores do. Nor do they face dangers from predators; they have a longer time in which to grow up.

We passed a herd of impala with their lyre-shaped horns and sleek russet bodies.

'Which are the ladies and which are the gentlemen?' Martine wanted to know.

I explained that these were all males and they were bachelors. The impala is a polygamous animal. The strongest male rounds up the females into a harem. He jealously guards his females until one of the young bachelors feels himself strong enough to challenge his ownership. Not all the antelopes are polygamous. The little dik-dik, smallest of the antelopes, who stands an average eighteen inches high, takes monogamy to extraordinary lengths. Not only does he have one mate, but if his mate dies it is said that he will not take another. He will remain a widower for the rest of his lifetime!

The bus driver took us to the hippo pool. Khaki-clad game scouts were waiting to receive visitors. Here it was permitted to leave the car under their escort, and to walk on the river bank to look for hippos.

Ahead of us were some American visitors. We followed them along the path. The thorn trees grew right to the edge of the steep banks of the river, concealing the visitors. Down below the hippos were at last discovered, lolling in luxurious ease like fat Roman matrons. Now one, and then the other, raised a voice in peevish protest—or so it seemed to our ears. Perhaps it was not protest at all but a way of passing the time of day!

The American visitors looked at our party with curiosity. 'A school, I suppose,' one of the visitors whispered.

'They're all different age groups. They can't be.'

Before I could enlighten them about us an Indian girl asked a European girl how many children belonged to the E.A.S.P.C.A. in her school.

Two of the ladies overheard.

'East African . . .'

'Society?' guessed the other lady.

I told them.

I was really proud of Kenya. The children were something to be proud of, good-looking, eager and enthusiastic about animals. The questions they asked me clearly showed their intelligence. The fact they had joined a society which was dedicated to the welfare of animals spoke well for Kenya. I was aware that this had not escaped the notice of the Americans.

'Do you think we shall see lions?' asked a girl with a camera.

'Perhaps.'

'If only we could.'

'I have never seen a lion except the young one we saw when we visited the animal orphanage,' a boy said.

'Have the animals lost their mummies and daddies?'

'Many of them, but they are being well looked after.'

We walked back to the bus. I saw with alarm that the vehicle was entirely surrounded by large baboons.

'What if the children became too excited and the baboons bit them?' I thought to myself, with visions of facing schoolteachers and parents. I have always considered the baboon the prima donna of creatures—one moment friendly, the next a raging fury. No light matter when his teeth rival a leopard's in sharpness and size. But I am fond of baboons and can forgive them their eccentricities.

I hoped I could get the children into the bus as fast as possible. They were extremely good children. I only had to tell them once not to feed the baboons. This was always the greatest danger. Baboons often get in an ungovernable temper when their feeding is stopped. Acting on my instructions, the children kept together and did not scatter. Neither were they noisy. The baboons looked up at us cheekily, but left us alone. When we had got in the bus we stayed for a minute to watch them in safety.

Baboons are vulgarians. Their walk, their expression, show this. But they have an unparalleled zest for life, as most vulgarians have. They are also inclined to look down their noses at non-vulgarians, much the same as their human counterparts. The children were enchanted with them. So was I.

We moved off. We soon saw a bevy of cars surrounding some high grass on another river bank. It could mean only one thing. Lions! The driver took the bus carefully to the spot. I told the children to hang on to their seats, as I had first-hand experience in falling into concealed holes when travelling in long grass. The grass was tawny.

Cradled in the thickest part of it was a magnificent lioness. We were almost on top of her before we saw the noble head and amber eyes. Our driver had driven with great skill to a distance only a yard away from her. I was annoyed at myself for not having brought my own cameras. I had purposely left them behind, the better to concentrate on the children, who were at fever-pitch of excitement. The camera boys and girls used their film at a fast rate, like veteran cameramen who knew that they were on to a good thing. I had to watch these proceedings closely, knowing that photography is an all-absorbing hobby.

'No heads out of the windows.' I rescued one young photographer. There was no selfish hogging of the best positions. Each one took his or her turn at the window that gave the best view of the lioness—she obligingly rolled on her back like a giant domestic cat. She then gave a great yawn, as though she wished to show the children her beautiful teeth.

We reluctantly left the park, already late, and drove homewards.

We swung into the drive, gates held open either side by Tom and Tshikadi. The ladies of the committee had a table spread like a banquet. After tea prizes and presentation shields were given. The little ceremony was performed on the terrace by the goldfish pond, with the majestic Ngong Hills in the background. They were already tinged pink by the sunset.

I returned to Nairobi with the elated children, where parents were collecting them, and arranged transportation for three of the bigger ones, who had forgotten that the bus which passed their school stopped running at six in the evening.

I got into my car, and I drove home, tired and happy. The children thanked me and their thanks still rang in my ears. I thanked them for coming. I had enjoyed the day as much as the children.

Was there or is there anywhere in the world where you could have taken a party of schoolchildren to see such wonders? Ostriches dancing, baboons begging, lions so close you could have leant out of the bus window and patted them on the head; all of these wonders against an out-of-this-world setting whose beauty has to be seen to be believed.

7
Phase of Violence

IN CONTRAST with myself, some of the settlers in Kenya lived in such fear of the changing times that they would not make repairs to their homes or even buy so much as a duster. Windows that became cracked remained cracked. Then people would not plant anything new in the garden. Once spick-and-span homes began to look shabby and seediness set in. Their cry was: 'Why should we spend time and money on our homes when we may have to leave them?'

It was distressing, especially when some of the couples had children. One couple had a son who had been born in Kenya, the mother was Kenya born, and the father was English. Both mother and father were anxious for the future of their son. The mother also would not hear of her child going to the same school as an African. I spoke to her about it, because I could see that her husband did not want to leave Kenya.

'It is absolutely out of the question, Michaela, and that is that.'

'If we are going to make an integrated country there is no better way of doing so than by starting in the schools.'

She gave me a bitter smile. 'I don't *want* an integrated country,' she said.

The last time I saw them was in Nairobi waiting outside a shop. I spoke to the mother. The child at the back was near to tears.

'We have sold our house, did you hear, Michaela?' Billy looked out of the opposite window to hide his face from me. The back of his neck, his whole person, expressed dejection. He was like a poor little animal put into a cage from which it knows it cannot escape, and longs for its lost freedom.

'We are going to Canada,' she said.

I didn't know what to say. I could hardly coegratulate her for giving up a lovely home, and for plunging her son and husband into such heartache, yet when he came back to the car he backed his wife up.

'It is a question of schools,' he said.

I said good-bye to them. How grossly stupid humanity could be. There is only one standard for judging people, and that is the standard of ability. Were they themselves afraid that their son would not be able to stand competition? A white skin is not enough today. If the Africans will learn from the mistakes of the Europeans they too will realise that a black skin is not enough either. Self-respect does not come from unearned honours and privileges.

I was waiting in the post office for a stamp. In front of me stood an African business man neatly dressed with brief-case under his arm. At the back of me was a Hindu woman resplendent in a sunset-coloured sari. The counter assistant was a bearded Sikh with that bandbox look they tend to have. I can't ever remember having seen an untidy Sikh. He wore a dark blue turban and had some kind of striped blue and white band on his forehead. Was it a cap underneath the turban? I wondered, and how did he get his beard so neatly knotted up in some sort of plait round his chin? Armand and I had often discussed it, and we just couldn't solve this mystery. It would be easy enough to ask one of our Sikh friends, but perhaps they would think it rude of us to pry.

The Sikh counter assistant wore a steel bangle on his right wrist. The Sikhs wear five k's. This is to distinguish themselves from their fellow men. The five k's or 'keshas' are the turban enclosing the long hair and the beard, the second symbol is the 'kunga' or comb, the third the steel bangle or 'kara', the fourth the 'kirpan' or short sword, the fifth the 'kachla' or pair of shorts. It is obligatory for Sikhs to wear these emblems. There are very few Sikhs who don't observe this tradition.

I enjoyed seeing all these people from different racial groups. It enriched Kenya, giving it far more interest than the countries which have basically one racial type. Much could be learned from the old people of the country who still remembered their early traditions. I often spent happy hours talking to these old people.

I once visited an Asian trade union leader's house with some African friends. Our hosts old great-grandmother had been the first Asian lady in Nairobi. She had lived in a tent and she had lived to be over 103 years of age. Her grandson told me that on her hundredth birthday Sir Arthur Kerby had presented her with a memento. He asked her, through an interpreter, to what did she contribute her longevity, and how could he emulate her. The old lady answered straight away, without pondering her reply, 'Not to worry.'

It was good advice and she could obviously speak with the voice of authority!

After I had bought my stamps I stood near the door to put them on the envelopes.

A European woman came in.

'Oh, Michaela, I am so happy I've bumped into you like this. I called you two days ago to try and get hold of you, and I was going to telephone you at the end of this week again. We are off, did you know?'

I looked at Mrs. Smith to see whether she was off to Mombasa, but no, she looked too sad for that. She had been a great advocate for multi-racialism. Her husband was a civil servant; Europeans, Asians and Africans could be met in her house at parties.

'Why on earth are you going?' I asked. 'I know how you love this country.'

'It's not a matter of choice, my husband's contract has not been renewed. He is at present training an African to take his place.'

'What qualifications has the African?'

'He is an African. That is his qualification. That is the one qualification my husband hasn't got,' she said without bitterness.

It was a loss to Kenya, not only of a skilled man but of his wife and family. They had given much to their country of adoption and if allowed to they would have given more, much more. To me that dreadful word 'Africanisation' smacks as much of discrimination as the very enemy liberal people all over the world are fighting against. It is a retrograde step and cannot be defended. Merit, and merit only, should be the yardstick for a job. It is to the ultimate benefit of the community that standards should always be maintained. Africans have as much intelligence and are as hard-working as any other race. They can, and will, catch up in every way. To take the easy way out is to their ultimate detriment.

I had barely said good-bye to Mrs. Smith when I met a couple who lived at Eldoret.

'What are you doing down here?' I asked.

'It's our last shopping expedition to Nairobi.'

'You're going too?' I asked.

'Yes, we're going too. My grandfather came up to this country by ox-waggon,' said the husband, in a strong South African accent. 'We are making the trek again in Land Rovers, all of us. I was born in this country and I never thought I'd live to see the day when I would leave the farm.'

'But why are you leaving, then? Aren't you going to try and stick it out?'

'We've got squatters on the farm,' his wife answered. 'Harry's had his pump house smashed twice by men with pangas because he tried to turn the squatters off the farm. Worse still, Harry was in hospital for six weeks. A gang of nearly thirty men attacked him when he tried to stop them destroying the crops. There is no future for me or my children in this country, and I am getting out while I am still active. My sister and her husband are coming too, with their children and grandma.'

'But what about the farm?' I asked.

'We've left it. We tried to sell it, but no one even answered the advertisements we put into the papers.'

'Besides, I don't want my wife to be afraid of moving a hundred yards away from the house,' Harry said.

I sympathised with them and wished them luck.

I thought of their farm the last time Armand and I had visited it. It was a beautiful place, with its spreading fever trees, like flat-topped umbrellas with yellow-stemmed handles, and its placid, well-fed cattle. Harry had employed a lot of labour. His workers seemed to like him. Many of them had been his companions as a child, and he spoke their language as easily, and fluently, as he did English and Afrikaans.

I wondered what would happen to all those older people who had worked for so many years for him and his father. I said good-bye to Harry and joined an African friend to have coffee in the Thorn Tree, an open-air restaurant in the New Stanley Hotel. The statue of Lord Delamere by Peter Scott's mother was exactly opposite, in the centre of the roundabout where several roads joined one another.

'I am worried,' said my friend. She too?

'Why are you worried?' I asked.

'I don't like my husband being in politics. It is too dangerous. The other day someone telephoned him and said they were going to kill him. Michaela, I am afraid. What is going to happen?'

That same day Armand too was grave-faced when I returned home. We took a long walk down to the river. I could see he had something on his mind.

'What is it, Armand? Something is worrying you. Has there been bad news from London?'

'No, Michaela, but I am seriously considering putting the house up for sale.'

'Oh, no,' I cried. 'You can't do that. We shall get nothing for it if we do. Besides, I think we could help this country. If people see us here they will think that there is still some hope in the situation. If we left they would know that things in Kenya were intolerable. Let's wait and see.'

'Perhaps you are right.'

'I am going to behave as though I am going to live here for ever and live to a very great age.'

I continued the next day with my construction work. Our guests who came to the house looked at me spending my hard-earned royalties on building a guest house. They must have thought I was mad. One man commented that it reminded him of the book *On the Beach* by Nevile Shute.

'You can't stop living and improving things just because the whole world is in a state of uncertainty. Life must go on,' I said.

Nairobi had always looked so beautiful, its people reasonably prosperous, and because of the planting in the city by a genius called Peter Greensmith was lovely to look at, with its flowering shrubs and trees. Visitors from abroad always remarked on the garden-like appearance of the city.

The buildings were handsome too, although I am not a great admirer of modern buildings. I like them in a city. Certainly we had some original-looking designs, which were often painted and decorated in light colours and gave a tropical gaiety to Nairobi.

I can't remember any period of transition between the time when Nairobi resembled a well-run modern city to the time when the streets were filled with beggars, some in filthy rags and with every kind of deformity. One man crawled on his hands and knees like a giant termite, stopping traffic and dragging his atrophied limbs behind him. Another man sat in a small child's push-cart. He had a fine-looking head, but he had only half a body. He appeared to have no lower limbs at all. Whether he had been born this way or not I do not know. I naturally couldn't ask him. Then there was an old leper and an old blind woman who sat for hours in the entrance to an alleyway which led between two main roads. And there were even the engaging rogues who would stop you with a beautifully bandaged arm and a document which purported to be from the hospital.

'I am supposed to go to the hospital again tomorrow and I have no money.'

This was a favourite technique, especially with warm-hearted American tourists. One man who stopped me in the street with a bandaged leg had stopped me only a week before with a bandaged arm in a sling. I shook my head and said, 'No, I'm sorry,' to his request for money for hospital fees.

'Your arm got better quickly, didn't it?' I said to him.

One felt the greatest pity for the truly unfortunate among them—but there were so many of them that it was impossible to help them all.

Many people said that the beggars were organised into a combine, and that the organisers kept them all in a large godown or shed. All their money was pooled every night and they were then fed and transported back the next morning to places around the city.

These poor people must have been looked after by their family or tribe before the urbanisation of Africa. Whatever had happened to them before, it was after the Lancaster House conference that they descended like a plague upon the city. Besides the innumerable beggars, numbers of hawkers swarmed in the street, selling vegetables and flowers. They importuned their would-be customers. It became disagreeable to go to the bazaar or the post office. Many of the men were well spoken. One felt sorry for them too. They were desperately trying to make a living. The shopkeepers complained loudly because the street hawkers carried on trade outside the shops, selling the same merchandise as in the shops but at cut-rate prices. These itinerant traders inevitably left debris of the widest variety in the streets where they peddled their goods. As they sold foodstuffs, flies and filth were in abundance. There was grave danger that the city might be engulfed by an epidemic.

10 This side leads down to the river. I once saw a leopard here when feeding the cats

11 ‘Who would like to go for a walk?’

(opposite) 12 The incense burner once stood in a Chinese temple. The painting is very ancient and the couch is Ning-Po

(opposite) 13 Chinese room in Africa. The priceless antiques are collected from all over the world and some formed part of the magnificent Bishop collection

14 From the lounge we look into the dining-room. Our house is filled with antiques and works of art from Europe, Asia and Africa

15 The thirty-foot-long lounge has windows on all sides; garden and house blend happily. Suska thinks she is a lap dog

16 Boys from the Stahere Home spend a happy afternoon in my garden. The boys are fascinated by the goldfish

(*opposite*) 17 'Look, Nguku, there's a heron over there.'

18 'I want to show you the garage, Armand.' 'What have you done now, Michaela?'

The political temper of the country at this time was such that no one dared to suggest that the hawkers should be forcibly removed. They were human beings, anyway, and the problem was to where could they be removed? More and more people from the country poured into Nairobi. The pestering of the hawkers became more competitive, more aggressive.

It was my shopping day in Nairobi. I tried not to go more than once a week to the city. My last purchase before my return to Langata was some material in Bazaar Street. The whole of Bazaar Street was exclusively an Asian trading centre. Most of the shops sold materials which were cheaper than elsewhere. A few sold Asian groceries and foodstuffs. From these open-front shops came the most delectable smells. Bazaar Street was, as usual, crowded with busy people. Service wives and their families, looking into the various windows, for all the world appearing as though they lived in Kenya, yet retaining the wide-eyed wonder of the newly arrived tourist. Up-country settlers, although very much in the minority, could be seen on one of their rare shopping expeditions in the city. They usually carried off their purchases to well-worn, dusty Land Rovers. Africans, their women wearing gaily coloured head-scarves and carrying fat velvet-skinned babies on their backs, were also on shopping expeditions with their husbands. Some of the women wore shukas over their dresses, tied across one shoulder. The shuka is a rectangular cloth and can be worn with or without the dress. Many shukas have mottoes printed on them in Kiswahili. A friend of mine, Pat Chilton, told me she had seen one which read, 'You had better hurry up or the baby won't be yours.' There were equally amusing mottoes and a variety of gay patterns. Favourite colours were red, yellow and green. These were 'KANU' colours.

One or two Arabs could be seen, their women completely in purdah (veiled from head to toe). Occasionally a tall, lean Masai, magnificently god-like, walked on these pavements. He might have walked from Kajiado, some fifty miles away, or even further. Their tireless lope gave no indication as to how far they had come. Asians were everywhere, dark-eyed, intense both in their shopping and their trading.

Many shops carried 'Closing down' notices. Another sign of the times. Every other shop had sale notices whether they were closing down or not. Everything was cheap, but as a shopper it gave me no joy. Many of the goods were being sold at such wickedly low prices only desperation could have lead to such a mark-down. These prices could realise the lowest profit and some things were being sold at a loss. I got into my car, thankful to be going home. The city always wearies me.

Three hawkers surrounded my car. 'Strawberries, buy strawberries,' one said.

'Very good peas. I will give you two bags for the price of one.'

The other man was selling oranges.

'Why do you never buy anything from us?' he demanded.

'Because I have a Kikuyu farmer who calls at my house once a week and from whom I buy all my vegetables. It helps him, and if I buy from you people I will have to buy less from him. I am a loyal customer and he is my friend.' This was quite true. The farmer operated with a small van and collected vegetables from his neighbours. He was running what was really a small co-operative venture. Much as I would have liked to help the hawkers, I thought the farmer's enterprise should be encouraged.

The next morning, glancing through the newspaper, I was stunned by what I read. When disaster strikes it is always more horrible when its setting is familiar. Armand was looking over my shoulder. 'Weren't you there yesterday?' he asked me.

'I was there half an hour before it happened.'

'It could have been you, Michaela.'

Indeed it could have been, because I can never resist coming to people's help, whatever the odds.

The story which shocked us had the same impact on the whole of Kenya. Yesterday, so it was reported, an Asian shopkeeper, Shah Kantilal Deuraj, was slain. He was shot in Bazaar Street by Africans making their getaway from a raid on one of those little grocers' shops which sold the exotic spices and foodstuffs I so often sniffed with delight. The raided shop was kept by Wallibhai Karim.

Wallibhai Karim was in his shop. It was just after six-thirty. A Peugeot saloon drew up to the kerb. In it were five Africans. Four got out. Two remained outside the shop and both were armed with pangas. The other two entered the shop. They asked Wallibhai Karim for a bag of rice. The shopkeeper asked what kind they wanted. Each African drew a gun and told him to be quiet, as they would take it anyway. Wallibhai Karim bravely struggled with them. They held on to him, but he managed to break free and run through the shop door to the street, shouting for help. The men with the revolvers rushed outside and one of them fired two shots at Karim. Both shots missed, and struck the windscreen of a car which was parked outside. People in the street were too horrified to know what was going on.

A forty-three-year-old business man, Shah Kantilal Devraj, was passing. He knew Wallibhai Karim as a neighbour and came to his assistance. Two more shots were fired. Shah Kantilal Devraj fell dying to the pavement. The gang jumped into the waiting car. In spite of all their carefully laid precautions to escape, the crowd was still too stunned to move away. They fired two more shots into the air and the people scattered.

A most thorough man-hunt was immediately started. The C.I.D. worked continuously round the clock on the case. On the 17th of August every shop in Bazaar Street was closed, and Asian shop-keepers in Nairobi closed as a mark of protest and sympathy for the brutal murder of Shah Kantilal Devraj. It was estimated that £100,000 worth of business was lost in one day, an especially touching tribute when trade was so bad. Nearly 11,000 people of all communities attended the funeral. At one o'clock people started gathering in front of the house of the bereaved widow. The funeral procession started to move at half past two. It travelled slowly through the streets until it reached the Hindu cemetery in Digo Road. All traffic was paralysed as the procession went by. It was an awe-inspiring spectacle to see the halted traffic in the mourning city. Outside the cemetery were another 1,500 cars. Many Africans arrived to pay their respects to the murdered man.

The prayers were ended. The pyre prepared. Relatives of the murdered man reverently carried the body and placed it on the pyre in the cremation hall. The crowd of 1,100 chanted, 'Ram, Ram, Ram.' The flames caressed the body. The huge crowd inside the cremation hall moved off to the garden and joined the several thousands who were already waiting outside.

That night Asian-owned cinemas remained closed. There were meetings of angry Asians and others who demanded prompt action to enforce law and order.

In the meantime the police were busy. The escape car was found abandoned in Pumwani Location. The radiator was still warm. After a careful examination was made of the stolen car three sets of fingerprints were found on it. A search of the area was made. A man, Muragi Kamonje, was discovered concealed under a bed in a nearby house. A loaded .38 Webley revolver was found under a pillow with two rounds of ammunition. It was not the murder weapon, but it would be produced later in court. A second man, Mundia Kanini, was arrested. The accused said his name was Joseph Ndegwa, then admitted that he was lying. A third man, Karia Wahomo, was picked up. He was found lying on a bed in another Pumwani house. Beneath the bed were four simis, one was blood-stained. The fingerprints of the arrested men matched those in the car. To everybody's astonishment three African assessors found Muragi Kamonje guilty, the other two not guilty. On the 24th of November Mr. Justice MacDuff acquitted all three men.

On the 25th of November fresh charges were brought against the criminals. Mundia Kanini admitted his escaping lawful custody, in April 1960, when he was serving a three-year sentence, and there were still other charges against him. Muragi Kamonje pleaded not guilty to being in possession of a firearm without a certificate, and receiving and retaining a stolen .38 Webley revolver. One would have thought that the police had an open-and-shut case, but the bystanders could not identify the accused. The reaction of the three races and prominent people among them was severe.

At his home in Gatunda, Jomo Kenyatta described the murder as 'a terrible thing'. He went on to say that suspects like those who shot the shopkeeper had to be eliminated. Criminals have no friends. They are the type of people who would kill their own fathers and mothers. All decent people agreed with him.

One would have thought that with so much misery and unemployment those who had jobs would have considered themselves fortunate. It was not so. There were many strikes for obscure reasons. Mostly the strikes were for more money, but because of the heavy recession many firms were running at an actual loss. The bankruptcy courts were overflowing. Many firms closed down sooner than sustain heavy losses. One of these was Whiteway Laidlaw. This firm had branches all over the Far East. Our Whiteway Laidlaw was a large old-fashioned building which had the distinction of having European ladies serving in it. The ladies were genteel and softly spoken. They had the dignity which one often finds in old-established shops, as though they took a personal pride in the firm which employed them.

It was not long before the shop had its closing-down sale. I spoke to one of the departmental managers who had been with the firm since he was a boy. His eyes were suspiciously damp.

'It's no good,' he said. 'We just can't go on. The firm has lost too much money in the Far East.'

I wondered if the manager would get another job easily.

'It is not easy to get employment when the better part of your life has been in one job which becomes redundant,' he said wistfully. It was almost as though he read my thoughts. I blushed idiotically, afraid of hurting him and ashamed that my thoughts had been read so accurately. It was as bad as if I had blurted them out.

After the sale the shop fittings were sold. I went in to see if there might be anything I could adopt for our beloved home. The empty shell of the building resembled a carcass which the vultures were picking over. The whole building had a smell akin to death.

The strikers seemed even more unreasonable because they were sabotaging the politicians' efforts in interesting foreign capital. Who would be mad enough to invest in a country where strikes were of daily occurrence? Many people were keeping on employees at great personal sacrifice. The wages were low compared with other countries, but the alternative was to give notice to staff. Unemployment was a still greater evil.

Our own house servants had larger salaries and more allowances than the average. They had free electric light, and paid holidays. They were perfectly happy.

One day Tom came into the dining-room where I was perched on a step-ladder dusting the electric-light wall brackets. He entered the room stealthily. I could see that I was going to be consulted about some impending crisis.

'There is a man outside who wants to take money from us.'

'Why?'

'He says we must belong to a union.'

'Do you want to belong?'

'No, but he says we must, and then we must all stop work.'

'What on earth for?'

'I don't know.'

'Why does he want money?'

'It is for the union. We don't want to give it to him.'

'He may be a crook who has nothing to do with any union. He has no right to demand it from you.'

'We are afraid. He says we shall get into trouble unless we give it to him. Will you speak to him?'

I didn't much relish the job, but it made my blood boil to have my servants intimidated. Even if I might be put on a black list I would protect my people if they needed help.

'You go across to your house. Don't mention you have told me anything. I will join you and the others in a minute.'

Armand met me at the door.

'What's happening, Michaela?'

I told him quickly the problem.

'Want any help?'

'I think I can manage. But you might come out in five minutes to see how I'm getting along.'

I collected my secateurs before I left the house. I wanted to have some excuse for being in the garden. I didn't want it to look as though Tom had told me anything, in case of retaliation by our visitor. I sauntered out and clipped a fading bloom here and there until I reached the servants' house. A city spiv in a natty suit, brief-case under arm, was haranguing our two men. The gardeners were out of sight in the sunken garden well away from the road.

I pretended surprise at our visitor.

'Hello, may I help you?'

'Hello. Why do you not allow your boys to join the union?'

'Our employees can do what they wish. Neither you nor I are going to tell them what or what they may not do about joining a union.'

'So you will not let them join?'

'I said nothing of the sort.'

The spiv and I gave each other a long searching look. He lowered his eyes.

'How is it that you are not at work?'

'I am a worker for the trade union.'

'Show me your credentials.'

His face clouded. He searched in his brief-case. He handed me a dirty slip of paper. It was the receipt for a bicycle repair.

'These are not credentials.'

He had a book in his hand. I took it from him. In it were names with amounts written at the side. I presumed the numbers indicated salaries.

'So you call yourself a worker. Show me your hands.' (I had read somewhere as a child that during the French Revolution fugitive aristocrats were often recognised because of their hands, which had never done a stroke of work.) Taken off his guard, he sulkily opened his hands for my inspection. I snorted.

'*Those* worker's hands? They are as soft as a three-month-old baby.'

I opened my own palms for his inspection. Carrying boulders for my newest goldfish pond had made my hands as hard and calloused as a road worker's. My servants were convulsed with mirth. The 'union' man looked embarrassed.

'*These* are worker's hands.'

I saw Armand emerge from the house. He walked in my direction. As he reached me, another man, the friend of the 'union' man, joined us. Armand heard him mutter something about Europeans having 'to get out'.

The conversation had taken another course.

'Tell me more about your union.'

'We haven't started it yet.'

'But you are collecting money already before it is registered?'

'Madam, I want to ask you a question. Are you English?'

'I am a human being. I have an American passport.'

The men's attitude changed, they were all smiles.

'Americans are very good people. The English are very bad. Very bad.'

'Why are Americans better than the English?'

'The Americans have a lot of money. They are very good.'

'Yes, they are good. But so are the English.'

'No. The English are very bad to the Africans.'

'Yes, perhaps they are. I remember the last time I went to Nairobi the bodies of the poor Africans were lying two deep—thousands and thousands of them. The roads were slippery with blood.'

The men started to laugh. We all started to laugh. We waved good-bye to them as they trundled, two on one bicycle, round the corner of our lane. They were laughing so hard that they fell off their bicycle and had to remount. We never saw them again.

In the minds of the Kenyan people there was no clear-cut definition of what was meant by the word 'uhuru'. 'Uhuru', or 'freedom' in English, is a dangerous word anywhere in the world. Millions of men will go into battle whipped into a frenzy by this word 'freedom'. Each man has his own conception of what he is fighting for, and will maim and kill himself and others for it. It was the same with our people. You asked them what they thought 'uhuru' meant and you would get answers such as: 'We will no longer pay taxes. Everybody will have free schooling for their children. We shall live in the house of the Europeans and the Asians rent free. We shall get money without work.'

Unscrupulous people were not backward in exploiting the backward peasants. A well-dressed African from Nairobi would see a man from the country with his wife and children, quite obviously from the country because of the awesome gazing at the shops and the bustling traffic.

The 'business man' would approach the family and the conversation would go something like this:

'Good morning, sir.'

'Good morning.'

'I see you have just been examining the car which is parked here. Are you interested in it?'

'Yes. It's a beautiful car.'

The 'business man' would open his brief-case, bring out a book and look inside. 'What's the number?' The countryman couldn't read, but his son could. The son, proud to be treated as a grown-up, would read out the licence number. The stranger would look in his book, run his finger down numbers and with a wide smile turn and look at the peasant.

'You're in luck. This car has not been reserved. There is no deposit on it. Do you want to buy it?'

'Is it for sale?' asked the peasant.

'Yes, it is for sale. Do you want it?'

The peasant laughed.

'I can't afford a bicycle, let alone a car.'

'Ah, but you can. After "uhuru" everyone will have cars like this.'

The peasant showed interest.

'But how do I know that I can get this particular car if I want it?'

The 'business man' eyed the peasant, weighing up how much money he might have on him.

'If you give me a deposit of one hundred shillings it is yours. The delivery will be on the date of "independence". Think how splendid it will be to take your son in to school.'

The peasant's cupidity was aroused. He looked in his pocket to count his money. He had eighty-seven shillings. He asked his wife if she had anything. She had another two shillings. The old woman, her mother, produced three shillings and ten cents. After a brief argument the husband collected all the money.

'This is all I have. I can give you some more next month.'

The 'business man' scratched his head, deep in thought.

'You really want the car, don't you?'

'Yes.'

'I am going to make an exception about the price. I shall have to make up the money from my own pocket. Meet me next month and pay the balance. Oh, all right. I'll put you down for it.'

The peasant was delighted. What a good man to help a stranger from out of town! What lies people told about being careful of the city men! He gave his money to the well-dressed gentleman, who proceeded to write down the number of the car.

'One second, I've got the wrong number.' He beckoned the small son.

'Would you read me out the number?'

The son went to the front of the car and read it out. The 'business man' meanwhile crossed out one of the numbers he had already written down.

'You have to be careful about getting the right numbers. There are so many people buying these cars. Now what's your name?' he asked the peasant. He wrote down the man's name and whose son he was. The peasant walked off with his wife and family, delighted with his new possession. He had arranged to meet the city gentleman in three weeks' time to pay him the rest of the deposit, which only amounted to a few shillings.

Albert, his brother, could drive.

'We will start a taxi service,' said the peasant to his wife. They couldn't enjoy themselves much on their visit to the city, but the glow of having bought such a bargain was too much for them. The old woman said, 'How are you going to afford the five shillings a month to pay for the rest of the car?'

'The kind gentleman said that we only have to pay another twenty-five pounds, and that if we couldn't afford to pay by the month the payments could be adjusted.'

After three weeks the peasant came back again. He had managed, somehow, to scrape up the money in spite of innumerable children he had to feed. After all, was it not for their future as it was for his own that they wanted the beautiful shiny car?

He waited on the street corner for the business gentleman. He waited three hours. After that he began to get restive. What could have happened to him? A steel-helmeted policeman, tall and dusky, was passing by. The peasant stopped him.

'Have you seen the man who sells cars waiting here?'

'Which man who sells cars?' asked the policeman.

The peasant recounted the story. The policeman took out his little book and wrote down all the details. As the peasant told his story the policeman's handsome Luo face registered anger.

'Could you identify this man?' he asked the now thoroughly worried peasant.

'Yes, I could. What has happened to the bwana? Has he met with an accident?'

'He will meet with an accident if I meet him,' the policeman said.

The 'business man' had been very active. He had 'sold' a sizeable number of cars. The peasant went back to his family a very sad man. That term he would be hard put to it to find the fees for his sons' school, let alone to plan for his taxi service.

8

Nature and Human Nature

COULD it be two years ago that Bwana Kenyatta was released from restriction? I thought back to the time before his release. The country had been a pulsating cauldron of hot-headed words and hot-tempered deeds, burning hates, anxiety and frustration. The pessimists said that if Jomo Kenyatta was released the country would be plunged into instant civil war. Sir Patrick Renison, a good and honest man, had described the Prime Minister as a 'man of darkness and death'. He said it in all sincerity. It was obvious even to those not in the know that there were sharp disagreements at a higher level. To release or not to release Jomo Kenyatta was in everybody's thoughts. Right was certainly on the side of Mr. Kenyatta. He had served his sentence and he had been confined to Lokitaung and Lodwar. Ten years of a man's life had been taken away for a cause which he had sponsored without counting the costs. Jomo Kenyatta had been in reasonably comfortable circumstances. He was a respected man and a hero, for he had endeavoured to bring mass education to the African.

If he had kept himself strictly out of the struggle he could have saved himself years of exile, but he did not. He was, as far as I know, never tied in conclusively with the bestialities of Mau-Mau. How could he be? He was an educated man. The childish filth indulged in by the terrorists would not have appealed to such an intellectual.

It was all very well to say that there would be rioting if he came home, but it was not just to hold him when his sentence was completed. These were days of agonised uncertainty, of heart-searching. Our friends from all over the world wrote us letters pleading with us to flee the country. I could not contemplate such a move. To me Kenya is a person. If a person is sick you do not leave the sick-bed until the patient has recovered. There were crimes of violence every day. Whenever I went to Nairobi, Africans whom I knew there dropped their voices when they spoke to me.

'You're not going, Michaela?' they asked. 'Whatever happens you will be safe either way.'

'I am not honestly afraid and I don't want to go,' I said. I wasn't afraid for my personal safety but I was afraid for the house. My greatest fear was for our 200 pets. We had heard tales of how the animals had suffered in the Congo. I couldn't bear the thought of any of these dreadful things happening to our animals.

Armand and I decided that we must immediately search for homes for our animals. We had to find a place of safety for them as fast as possible. At this time we heard that a new zoo was to be created in New Delhi. We were told the animals would be allowed the maximum of freedom, in ideal conditions, on small islands. They would be fed on the island but could not be annoyed in any way by visitors to the zoo. This was perfect for the animals who were not very domesticated. We found another place of safety for those animals who could be handled and were pets. A woman in South Africa had an establishment rather similar to our own. She had so many pets that she really had a private zoo. All her animals were well loved and looked after. We prepared to send our animals away months in advance. The animals had to be crated. Those which were going to South Africa were going by ship. Those for India would be flown there. This was an added complication because no one could really agree what type of crate was the best for an animal on a not too complicated plane journey.

We had one chimpanzee called Emily. She had been sent to us from London. Emily came out of her travelling box. She looked at me and Armand waiting to receive her. She held out her arms in a most endearing manner. We each took a hand, Emily between us, and we walked around a friend's garden. Armand and I were going safari the next morning. The kind lady who was looking after Emily begged us to consider selling her Emily, for she always wanted a chimpanzee.

When we returned after our three weeks' safari it was a very different story. Emily had the temper of a virago, and the strength of an All-American full-back. She was completely unmanageable and the household who had given her shelter was in a state of terror. She had even managed to besiege the household for two days when she had escaped from the garden into the house. The unhappy family locked her in their living-room, which was promptly wrecked. They finally managed to get her into a very strong cage, well baited with strawberries. Yes, she had expensive tastes too. They were very glad to see the back of Emily.

Armand has great experience of transporting primates. He made a box for Emily which was just big enough to prevent her from trying to break it by levering her body against the roof. The case was inspected, and pronounced too small by the vet, who had never transported a large aggressive chimpanzee.

'We shall have to construct it so that she cannot touch opposite sides at the same time,' said Armand.

'It will cost a fortune just to send Emily to a place of safety. And will she be grateful? No!'

There was no alternative. The thought of Emily running amok on the plane was not to be contemplated. We couldn't order Emily's execution; we couldn't leave her to face the cruel death which might be hers if there were to be large-scale riots. Eventually the vet pronounced the travelling box to be satisfactory. We said good-bye to Emily with relief. Her inscrutable gaze was the last we saw of her, peering out of the wire mesh of her titanic cage. It took eight men to load it aboard the plane.

Emily's adventures were not over. She was off-loaded in Bombay to continue her journey to New Delhi. As she was waiting to be reloaded a rich and eccentric Indian lady saw her. It was love at first sight.

The Indian lady found out where Emily was going to be shipped. She sent a telegram to New Delhi, and managed to persuade the dealer in charge of transporting the chimpanzee to the zoo to allow her to adopt Emily. We were consulted, as we had stipulated that Emily should not be sold to anyone else. We gave our consent, happy to think that Emily would have a devoted foster-mother to look after her. It was amazing that the Indian lady should have been able to make contact with our irascible pet, which proves once again how very similar animals are to human beings with their likes and dislikes.

The Asian bears were also a heavy item in every sense of the word to send away. Our bears were at that time the only ones in East

Africa. Added to all the complications of sending the animals away, the drought was abruptly terminated by the most devastating flood the country had seen for a decade. Where we often walked with the dogs there was now a waterfall.

To get to Nairobi was quite an adventure. Our own road is a murram one which branches to the left where the tarmac begins. It was at this point that an underground stream burst forth from the earth, undermining the tarmac. The tarmac disappeared completely, literally collapsing into mud which resembled cocoa. One day I had to abandon my car behind a line of others because the road was impassable at that point.

The animals which had to be sent to South Africa were to be shipped at Mombasa. We had intended to put them on the train and one of us was going to travel with them to see that they got safely to the ship. The rain was so torrential that railway lines were washed away in places. There was no alternative but to have the animals sent by road.

Armand had promised to let me keep Bamboo, my pet gibbon. As though we didn't have enough troubles already, Bamboo died. The autopsy proved that he had an intestinal complaint. I was heartbroken and took several days to get over his death. Bamboo was very attached to me. I often took him for walks, too, but he was very demanding. He would not let me go back to the house to get on with my work. He would wait until I had headed in the direction of the large, 100-foot aviary where he spent his time with other animals. He would watch his opportunity when my grip slackened from his slim delicate hand, then race off, straight up the telephone pole and hang from the telephone wires. What effect it had on the telephone service I hate to think. He would then proceed to pretend to come down, and when within grasping distance he would clamber up again, and swing with his long thin legs and toes hanging gracefully below him. There was only one sure way of getting him down. It was very mean to do it to him, but I was always afraid that he might come down from the telephone wires, and go up on the power lines and electrocute himself. At such times I called Armand and we made the most outrageous noises, kissing one another in the middle of the road to the astonishment of all who passed by. Bamboo, the gibbon, couldn't stand it. He was consumed with jealousy. He clambered up Armand's legs and inserted his face between mine and Armand's. Taking Armand's nose in his hand he would push him away, making little crooning noises to me, and showing his teeth to Armand. Then I would be able to carry him back to his place of safety, which contained trees for him to clamber on with the other primates.

One day Armand was visiting Nairobi when Bamboo played his trick of running away from me. He refused to come down for any reason, whether it was for bananas or biscuits which he normally enjoyed as a special treat. After half an hour, during which the whole household was occupied exclusively in trying to recapture Bamboo, I had an inspiration.

I fell face downwards into the dust, hoping I would not be covered from head to foot with the chiggers, small parasites which burrow under the skin. Then I howled and cried, as though my end had come. I felt gentle hands upon my cheek and furry arms encircling my neck. A gibbon voice whispered into my ear, soothingly. If I had not been capturing him for his own good I would have felt a monster of deceit.

That I would see Bamboo, the golden gibbon, no more was tragic.

At last all the animals were sent away, many in our absence, because we went on an expedition to South America.

When we returned our land seemed denuded and bare. It was like a house where childhood has been spent and the parents have insisted on moving to another home. The last look around a house which has contained a child's dreams, and is then stripped bare of everything, leaving the shell of what was once a home, this was exactly how I felt. Everything was familiar, but the heart and soul had gone out of it. People still stopped us in the street to ask whether they could come and see our animals, and there were no animals to show them. Our only consolation was that we had done what was morally right, considering the safety of the animals before our own feelings.

The floods were part of the overall illness from which the country suffered. The heavy deforestation in Kenya resulted in baked earth, left raw, without the protective covering of the shade trees. Large areas of Kenya began to resemble gigantic paddy fields. Many of the people were completely cut off and were in danger of starvation. Again the Army helped in distributing supplies sent by generous people from all over the world. The Air Force helped too. Volunteers flew tirelessly to distribute foodstuffs to isolated regions.

I was told a story by an army sergeant. He and his men were told that an aircraft had spotted some Masai Moran (young warrior class) on a small peninsula of ground. They were obviously stranded without food. The sergeant and his soldiers reached the young men after a terrible ride in a four-wheel drive lorry. Filled with love for their fellow men, they pointed to the sacks of food, and in sign language indicated the Masai should unload the food. The Morani pointed to the soldiers and indicated they should unload the sacks of food. The soldiers pointed to the Masai again who refused to unload. There was deadlock, only ended when the sergeant jumped back into the lorry and drove off. The Masai chased after the lorry, shouting for him to stop.

He said: 'I only wish you had been there with your movie cameras. It made quite a scene.'

I could imagine it. The young men running in their shukas, the wind blowing the cloth, exposing their long lean bodies, their elaborately coiffed red painted hair flying out behind them. The sergeant stopped the truck and the now breathless Masai unloaded the sacks without being urged.

An American I met at the New Stanley Hotel told me that he had delivered corn to another region. The people had refused to eat it because it wasn't the same colour as that to which they were used. Another group had said, 'Where's the salt?' Most of the stranded Africans, however, were deeply grateful for the efforts being made on their behalf.

Although we were not short of food, we were experiencing other difficulties. Because there had been such an exodus of Europeans from Langata we were in trouble about the maintenance of our roads.

The tenants of the Hardy Estate used to give Shs. 200/– per household a year towards the maintenance of the roads. Now there were not enough people to collect the sum. The roads got steadily worse. The falling in of the tarmac was an emergency. No one could afford to be isolated from his or her place of business. There was a tenants' meeting, and all of us set to to repair the damage. In one part of the road there was a three-foot-deep hole. Africans and Europeans worked together on the road.

Armand and I supplied stone. We had recently ordered several loads from a quarry to do a building job. The road emergency was more urgent than our plans for building, so we decided to give this stone for road repairs.

I changed into my oldest safari clothes, khaki slacks and shirt. We took several Land Rover loads of large stones to the twenty-five-foot-wide breach in the tarmac. It was at this point that an underground stream had emerged from its hiding place under the earth. The three-foot hole seemed to be bottomless. I began to wonder who had first described it as a three-foot hole in the first place. It was an understatement. There was no culvert at this point to take the wayward water away. It was the first task of the men to dig a ditch on one side. My experience in building goldfish pools had developed my muscles to the point where I could carry boulders. That day I used brawn instead of brain. The technical know-how of building roads was not my strong point, I merely tried to do what the others who knew told me.

Only one car passed through that morning. The road workers left off work and pointed the way through the morass. At the really bad places we had put upright sticks. We kept well off the road as the brave driver gritted his teeth and took the plunge.

'Don't stop for even a second,' I shouted advice, and then leapt out of the way of the moving car—straight into the three-foot-deep hole. I struggled to keep my balance, illogically afraid that if I disappeared under the surface of mud I would be lost for ever. I floundered out of the sticky goo. My clothes were plastered on me, one shoe had disappeared. I pushed the hair out of my eyes with a muddy paw.

An African tried with a stick to fish out the missing shoe. There was a million to one chance of finding it. It was extraordinarily lucky that it came out at the first attempt. I stuffed my foot into the caked shoe and continued working. There were about fifteen of us, Africans and Europeans, men and women. Although it was back-breaking work, there was a nobility about it because it was a community effort for the common good.

At that time in Kenya there was a slogan '*Uhuru na Kazi*', which roughly translated means 'Freedom through work'. When it began to pour I started to sing '*Uhuru na Kazi*' to the tune of a popular song. It was good to hear the laughter, for all appreciated the joke.

We worked for several hours until the office workers started to return. A couple paused to talk to us. The wife said:

'Michaela, if only your fans could see you.'

'Why?' I said innocently.

She held up her handbag mirror for me to see and the sight was really funny. There was a broad diagonal stripe of mud across my face, and even my hair was caked with lumps of mud. I looked down at my shirt and trousers, which were stiff with mud.

Two days later the weather improved a little. We owed some friends who were visiting Nairobi an invitation.

'We had better invite them to the New Stanley or the Grosvenor Grill,' suggested Armand. I agreed.

'If it rains again tonight they could easily get stranded.'

Our friends, who had come from Europe, wouldn't hear of it. They wanted to see our house. The house had been featured in our television programmes and we had both written about it at various times. Other people had fallen in love with it besides ourselves. People often wrote to us requesting permission to see it. There are often letters addressed to 'The Secretary' of Armand and Michaela Denis, requesting an invitation to see our home, adding that the writers would not invade our privacy.

We didn't argue about our friends visiting us. We merely pointed out that it was the rainy season. There might be a little inconvenience, but of course they were welcome.

'What are we having for dinner, Michaela?' asked Armand.

'Chicken stewed in a sauce of dried mushrooms and onion, and a cabbage soup, and stewed fruit.'

'Why all stewed?'

'Because I'm a pessimist.'

Late that afternoon the sky became a dramatic indigo, pregnant with unshed rain. Everything was hushed, still.

Armand looked at the sky and shook his head.

'Do you think they will be able to find their way safely here?'

'I recommended them to call United Touring or Archers. The taxi drivers, to a man, know our house.'

A large drop fell at our feet. Too late I remembered the best cloth on the line in the laundry. I ran across the garden. I nearly bumped into Tshikadi, unrecognisable with a red plastic hand basin on his head. We hurried into the special garden around which I have grown a tall hedge of yellow-flowering vines to hide the laundry. There on the line hung limply the best cloth. I have no spin-dryer.

'Oh, Tshikadi, what shall we do? The visitors are coming tonight.'

'We will put on table mats instead. I will arrange a special bowl of flowers. It will look like the home of Queenie.'

I and my servants have a private joke. They often refer to me as 'Queenie of Langata'. This name originated when I used to praise them on a particularly energetic polishing of the house.

'You have cleaned this piece of furniture good enough for Queenie' (Kiswahili for queen).

Later they would say, 'Today you are dressed well enough for Queenie.' Soon by an association of ideas I became 'Queenie' myself.

The rain pelted down. In one place it covered the ankles. I waited under the shelter of the garage roof. I thought it might abate, but the rain continued to fall in streams, as though it wished to annihilate anything which stood between it and the earth. It softened and I ran back to the house.

It was useless to delay, any more, the preparations for our visitors; it was already dusk. We turned on the electric light to find that it was at half-strength, possibly even less.

Tom was in the kitchen with a glum face.

'The food will not even be heated in time, let alone cooked.'

At that minute the lights went out altogether.

'What are we going to do?' asked Armand, who had just come into the kitchen from downstairs. I groped my way to the store and produced candles and matches. I returned with the small gas cylinder which had a cooking-ring attachment on top.

'Now you see why I wanted all stewed food tonight Armand. I had a strong feeling that something like this was going to happen. It always does when you have guests during the rainy season.'

The dinner was cooked in time, but the rain was pouring through the house. It was like being on the receiving end of a gigantic sieve. Hand basins and saucepans marred the elegance of the house.

Our guests arrived late, not having been able to locate the house, after all. Ted had insisted on driving himself instead of taking a taxi driver. When Ena, his wife, had called me that morning I had said: 'You can't miss it. It is the only two-storey house in the road on the left.' It was at that time. As the lights had failed they couldn't see the dim candle in the kitchen. Our house lost its two-storey feature in the anonymity of darkness. They had passed the house twice before the lights came back again. Their lateness had helped instead of hindered us. The dinner was perfect. We settled down to coffee in our big lounge.

'How are you getting on with your safari?' Armand asked them.

'We are having a wonderful time in spite of the rain.'

'Well, not all the time,' interjected Ena. 'What about the Africans you wanted to photograph?'

'Yes, that wasn't a very pleasant incident.'

'What happened?' I asked.

'We were travelling along that escarpment.'

'The Rift?'

'Yes, that's right. We wanted to go to the Brown Trout. We heard it was a good place to have lunch. On the way we passed a group of colourfully dressed women. I stopped the car to take a photograph. Before I did so I offered them each a shilling. They were well pleased. I was just focussing on them when two men came out of the thick undergrowth at the side of the road and spoke to the women. They then refused to have their picture taken. One of the men, who looked a real ruffian in a long army overcoat and a panga in his hand, said they wanted ten shillings each for one photograph, for himself and the other man to act as interpreter.

' "Certainly not," I said. "I am only taking one photograph of all of them."

' "Why do you want to take their pictures? You think these people are savages?"

' "Of course not," I said.

' "Then why do you want to take the pictures?"

' "Because they look beautiful and I want to show them back home your national costume."

' "I don't believe you," said the man.

'His friend said something to him in Kiswahili. "He says you have taken pictures already."

'The man started to jostle me. He tried to snatch my camera from me.'

'I was really frightened,' said Ena. 'Within minutes there were several people round us and two or three of them started to throw stones. We managed to get into the car, but only just in time.'

'If that's what you call making tourists welcome,' said Ted, 'I think it's about time someone told these people how to win friends and influence people.'

'Did you tell the police?' I asked.

'We didn't bother. I guess the police would have enough on their plate without our complaints, and neither of us were injured, although it was sheer luck that we weren't.'

The loss was far greater than the shilling each the women would have earned happily. It was the loss of prestige for the country.

Ted and Ena were not millionaires, but they were quite well off. They had a circle of friends to whom they would undoubtedly tell about the highlights of their tour. They certainly wouldn't recommend photographing the local inhabitants.

'Are you going to Japan?' I asked.

'Yes, we thought we would on the way back.'

'Japan is as different as can be,' I continued. 'I well remember when I was there everybody of over the age of six seemed to be carrying a camera. Wherever I went I found that while I was discreetly photographing the Japanese they were discreetly photographing me. Often we bowed and smiled at one another during our photographing. When I visited one of the "famous beauty spots of Japan", as the Japanese describe it, a whole school party asked me if I would pose in the middle of them, which, of course, I did. I was highly flattered to think that the Japanese schoolgirls would want to have my picture taken with them. That is the difference between these people. We look upon photographing someone as a compliment to the person chosen as the subject. Our people just don't realise that you usually only photograph the good-looking girls and men. Besides, the Japanese are proud of their national costume, proud of their national character. Our people are often too fond of trying to copy the European dress and costume. They *want* to forget that they have something different, almost as though they are ashamed of their indigenous culture. I blame the early missionaries and settlers, to whom anything not conforming to Victorian England smacked of the Devil. They were not, unfortunately, anthropologists. Many of them were not very cultured themselves. Their viewpoint was appallingly narrow. Almost as narrow as your stone throwers.

'We have heard so much talk of the big enemy being poverty, ignorance and disease. I think our only enemy is ignorance. When that is conquered poverty and diseases are well on the way to being eradicated.'

The dinner party was a success in spite of the rain. Our friends waved us good-bye. They were on their way to India in the morning.

I praised our two house servants for coping with the unusual problem of serving dinner by candlelight, and in managing to cook a three-course meal on one small ring.

Tom has not been with us very long. Originally Tshikadi's friend John had worked for us for many years. He was a good-looking man, well built and always cheerful. One day I noticed that Tshikadi was doing all the work by himself.

'Where is John?' I asked.

'He is over at the house,' said Tshikadi. 'He doesn't feel very well.' Tshikadi is always loyal, whether it is to us or to his friends. Something in his manner made me sure that he was covering up for John. I went across the garden to the servants' quarters and nearly fell over John's prostrate body. He was lying on the ground outside his house. I didn't need to have a very keen sense of smell to know the nature of his illness.

'Get up at once,' I ordered.

He staggered to his feet and would have fallen if I hadn't gripped him by the elbow.

'You've been drinking,' I said, rather unnecessarily.

'No, I am ill.'

'I don't wonder. You will be worse in the morning.' I guided him to his house and made him lie down on the bed. I went back to the house and helped Tshikadi in the kitchen.

The next day John was apologetic and swore he would never get drunk again on a day when he was supposed to be working.

'Don't drink as much as that, even on your day off. As you see, Bwana and I drink a little in the evening, but only one glassful. That is why it is a pleasure.'

'Yes, that is very intelligent,' John said. He touched his head gingerly with his forefinger. I suppose he had an outsize hangover.

All went well for several months. Occasionally his breath smelled like the fluid we put into our lamps when on safari. I had warned him, I couldn't very well interfere. He was, after all, a grown man.

All went well until Christmas. Each one of the household had a day off during the festivities. John went off cheerfully in the morning on his bicycle. I went up to our local duka, or store, to buy some dog biscuits. There was John. He looked wild-eyed. Obviously he had fortified himself for the journey before leaving the house.

'Give me a shilling, please,' he demanded, without an explanation. Taken off guard, I gave it to him. He mounted his bicycle and rode off looking neat and prosperous. He was clad in the clothes we had given him for Christmas. Clothes were something they appreciated more than anything else. It was quite a ceremony for me each year to measure them all. Each gets a new shirt and a pair of well-cut trousers, which I buy from one shop in town.

The next day I asked Tshikadi where John was, because he had not prepared the breakfast in the morning.

'He hasn't arrived back yet,' said Tshikadi. 'Perhaps he is staying in town with friends because it is Christmas. He may have had something to drink and been afraid to come home on his bicycle late at night.'

Another thought had occurred to me. John would not have been alone in indulging himself. The roads would have been full of drunken drivers at Christmas. I telephoned all the hospitals in Nairobi, and the police were informed that we had a missing servant. I didn't want to become too alarmist in case John returned during the day. Another day passed, and then another.

This time I personally went round to traffic control. I asked about the various accidents which had occurred over the holidays. There seemed to be no accident which would apply to John. I went back home completely mystified.

Later that afternoon a taxi drove up.

In it were some people with glistening eyes.

'I am John's friend,' said one. 'We have just come from the hospital. We went to see him. They were discharging him today. Has he come back yet?'

'No, indeed he hasn't. What was wrong with him?'

'He had an accident. He was knocked off his bicycle.'

'But I asked everywhere for him.'

'He couldn't think of his name.'

I called the hospital. Yes, they had had such a patient.

'We let him go this morning,' they said.

At six o'clock poor John arrived home on foot. He was very subdued. His eyes had a vacant stare.

'Where is your bicycle?' I asked.

'It is smashed up completely.'

He gave me a card which had been issued to him from hospital.

'I have to go back for treatment every day,' he said.

Vitamin B2? What a strange treatment for such an accident case, I thought to myself. John spent the next day in bed, just getting up to come with me to the dispensary to have his injection. I didn't take him to the hospital, as the dispensary was nearer and he told me that he did not have to go back to the hospital again. He had been discharged.

The second day was spent in convalescing. I again took him to the dispensary. He didn't seem to be improving. On the third day he said to me:

'When I look at you I see two of you. When I look at Tshikadi I see two of him. When I look at the Bwana I see two of him. When I turn over in bed from left to right all the things inside my head go *shonk*. When I turn over from right to left all my things in my head go *shonk*.'

'Poor John,' I said to Armand, 'must be suffering from concussion. I am going to take him back to the hospital to see if they can do anything further for him.'

I telephoned the hospital and made an appointment to see the matron. At the appointed time I arrived. The matron was a motherly Scotswoman.

'Yes, indeed I remember John. We did all we could, I don't think any more can be done for him.'

'But surely he has concussion, hasn't he? Was he X-rayed?'

The matron's blue eyes registered surprise.

'Why, don't you know what is wrong with him?' she asked me.

'He had a road accident, so I understand. His bicycle was smashed to pieces.'

'So that's what he told you. It's true in a way. His bicycle had the accident but he didn't. He had been drinking methylated spirit. He left his bicycle in the road and it was run over. John wasn't on it. The car owner who demolished the bicycle tried to arouse him, also thinking that he might have swerved and been thrown off his bicycle to the side of the road. They called the police, who brought him in here. It didn't take us long to diagnose what he was suffering from, even before he opened his eyes. He was reeking of the stench of methlyated spirit. No wonder he had double vision. He is lucky to be alive.'

I took John home and talked to Armand. We decided that the best thing for him was to send him home to his family. Obviously we could not watch him night and day.

'As soon as the injections are finished we had better send him back to his family,' I suggested, and Armand agreed.

He stayed with us another two days. When the injections were completed I told John that he must go back to his wife Mary and tribe. He still seemed bemused, but cheered up at the thought of seeing Mary. She had often stayed with us and she seemed to be a nice, sensible sort of woman. We gave him a month's wages with instructions that it should be paid over to Mary.

Three weeks later we heard that John had died soon after his return home. I felt very sad about it. I remembered how he had looked when he first came to work for us. Keen, alert and smiling. Now he was dead, leaving a wife and children. I was angry at the people who had sold him the lethal methylated spirit. They had been responsible for his murder as much as if they had taken a gun and shot him. I gave all our men a little lecture on the evils of drink, especially strong drink.

A few weeks later Tshikadi came to see me.

'Would you please write a letter to Sub-Chief Stephen?'

'What about, Tshikadi?'

'Would you please tell him that it was not my fault that John died?'

'Of course it wasn't your fault. Why, what is happening at your home?'

'Mary has called in the witch-doctor and cursed my whole family. Every one of them. She has also gone to my house and beaten my wife.'

I wrote to the Chief and told him the circumstances in which John had died. I sounded like a temperance worker. It had the desired effect and presumably the curse was taken off Tshikadi's wife, because she paid her usual visit to our house after her planting, and she and her children looked in perfect health.

9

One Damn' Thing after Another

WE DECIDED to go to Kariba to visit our good friends Ronnie and Erika Critchley, who had been instrumental in saving the wild life threatened by the rising waters.

Erika is a tireless champion of wild life and will go to any lengths to ensure its preservation. One of the vessels used in operation 'Noah' was named after her. People often say we feel so helpless, so impotent, to do any good. I remind them, always, that all causes have started in the minds of two or three individuals, and that nothing has ever started unless it has been in the mind of one person only. If we remember that even General Motors started off as one man's private dream then we shall not lose courage. All progress is achieved by persistence. In fact, all achievement is mostly a matter of stubbornly not giving up. Erika Critchley had that kind of courage and persistence.

We had to visit Kariba. I had the same kind of sadness in my heart when I saw the great dam 400 feet high and 2,000 feet in length as I did when I heard Everest had been conquered. Instead of marvelling at man's conquering of nature I could only marvel at his impudence. The Africans had said that the gods would be angry that the river had been tamed. I could imagine the chained god, a giant harbouring his strength until he could strike back at puny man, and I shuddered.

As the waters rose many animals made for the shoreline, but some went to the high ground, which often was cut off, as the waters continued to rise and form islands. It was these animals which a handful of dedicated people determined to rescue. Nature lovers all over the world rallied to the help of the gallant handful. We did a programme of the rescues at Kariba which showed how old nylon stockings were plaited and used as ropes for binding the animals when they were transported in the boats. Kind-hearted people still write to ask us where they can send their old stockings to help the animals!

The leader of the rescue team was Rupert Fothergill. He and his men worked tirelessly, day in and day out, capturing an amazing assortment of wild animals and bringing them to safety. Sometimes it was dangerous work, for the animals could not know that the capture was being done for their own good. Wart-hogs were difficult to capture and sable were not easy either. Everything from snakes to rhinos was rescued.

Kariba Lake was a thing of beauty. But it depressed me because it was a thing of death. Trees were being drowned, doomed, their heads forlorn as the waters slowly mounted up their trunks. Nor were the trees the only casualties of this interference with nature.

One species of small bird which used to live at the water's edge disappeared completely. Perhaps it was a highly specialised feeder which couldn't adapt its diet, and move back to other vegetation as the water crept up and destroyed its normal habitat.

The Ba-Tonga tribe were affected when they were moved to another area. For centuries they had kept their individuality and their culture. When they came in contact with other tribes their wives complained. The other women laughed at their tribal dress, which was distinctive, and infinitely more becoming than that of those who mocked them. So the Ba-Tonga were already dressing like their neighbours, who had long ago discarded the precious birthright of individuality. The move had been carried out most sympathetically by Ivor Cockcroft.

His wife May had created a fascinating garden at their headquarters at Binga filled with exotic-looking plants, some of which were quite new to me. I recognised one old friend from the Congo, the elephant-ear plant. May presented me with an elephant-ear plant which flourishes to this day in our garden.

After Binga we were going on to Wankie National Park.

Les Stuart, the Director of National Parks, had seen during his administration many great strides forward in parks management, one of which was the restocking and moving of certain species to places of safety. There were many other important innovations which had been instigated by Les, and the Rhodesian Parks had very generously given the benefit of their experiences to other National Parks.

We were lucky to have Ted Davidson, Assistant Director of National Parks, with us for our journey to Kariba. Ted was going to take us to see the Wankie National Park.

The country through which we travelled was beautiful, with many valleys, gorges and escarpments. It was there I first saw bauhinia trees, whose flowers resemble orchids. I planted several in our garden the moment I got back to Kenya. A garden is often a history of happy memories stored up in a lifetime, even more intimate than the contents of the interior of the house. Only local byelaws have stopped me from importing some of the lovely things we have seen in our lifetime of travel. To this day I regret not having the hibiscus I saw in Surinam, with its variegated leaves white and pale green and its pink flowers. The leaves alone were as ornamental as the flowers themselves. Unhappily I had neglected to get permission to import them from Surinam to Kenya.

The roads of Rhodesia were admirable. I had been told by a Rhodesian friend, Clive Poulton, that Rhodesia had a unique method of constructing roads. He assured me that a very simple method was employed and that it was exceptionally economical. Mile upon mile of tarmac criss-crossed Rhodesia. Parts of the road are closed and when the first surface of tar is laid on, the road is opened. When the tar has been well worked into the soil that section of the road is closed again to have another layer of tar put on it, then again it is opened. The traffic itself helps to lay the surface.

Rhodesia was in a state of near jitters. No one knew what changes might take place and how rapidly. As in Kenya, there were many Rhodesian-born Europeans. What was in store for them? they wondered. Changes had taken place already, which I applauded. One was the opening of restaurants and hotels to people of all races. I spoke to an African woman I met in Salisbury about these changes.

'How has it worked out?' I asked her.

'There are objections, of course. There are bound to be objections,' said my newly found friend. She was a schoolteacher. A bright-eyed, dusky, sturdy daughter of Africa.

'Tell me about it,' I asked her.

'First of all,' she said, 'I went to a hotel with one of my friends.

No one came to serve us. I finally got impatient and went to see the manager. "My friend and I have been here three-quarters of an hour. People who came here after we did have already been served. I thought hotels were not supposed to practise discrimination." He was a very nice European. He said certainly they were not to practise discrimination. "They have strict orders in the restaurant to attend to everyone. I cannot understand why you have not been served, but come with me, madam, and we will find out." I sat down at the table with my friend and the manager stood beside our table. He beckoned to one of the waiters who had avoided our eyes all the time.

' "Why haven't you served these ladies?" he asked the African waiter who grudgingly at last came up to the table. "Because they're women," said the waiter. "Men won't wait on women."

' "But you're waiting on European women," said the manager sharply.

' "That's different," replied the waiter. "Not one of us will wait on African women. We'd sooner lose our job."

'The manager muttered something under his breath.

' "What would you like, madam?" he asked me and my friend.

'We ordered tea and cakes. The European manager himself brought us our order. Our men can certainly learn from the Europeans how to treat their wives.

'There was yet another incident,' my friend said when I had commiserated with her.

'The swimming pools are now open to people of every race. Three days ago there was a terrible scene at one of the public swimming pools.'

'Why?' I asked, fearing that she would tell me that Europeans had refused to bathe with Africans.

'Because some African women attempted to bathe in the same swimming pool as some African men.'

'Don't despair,' I said to her. 'Africa will never be free until the women are respected and honoured and take their rightful place beside the men. In Europe only sixty years ago a woman could not keep her own pay packet if she worked. She had to give it to her husband, and he could, if he wished, go and drink away the entire salary in one night's binge. The woman had no legal redress.'

'How are things in Kenya?' asked my friend.

'The women are gradually coming upward, but the men will have to help them. We still have a system of bride prices, and even some of my most educated friends have been married in the traditional way with the paying of a bride price. But this bride price in reverse is practised in many countries in Europe. Every French girl, I am told, has to have a dowry. In Belgium it is the custom to have a dowry and often the ugliest and most stupid girls are the most sought after solely because of the size of the dowry. No wonder a Frenchman or a Belgian thinks he has done you a favour when he marries you without one.' The African girl and I laughed, drawn together by the need for unity amongst women of every nation.

'My friends in Kenya,' I continued, 'tell me that their husbands sometimes go out to buy a newspaper in the evenings just before dinner, and then arrive home hours later, which makes them worried and unhappy. When they ask their husbands to let them know when they are going out for any length of time there are bitter quarrels. Traditionally Kikuyu women should have a very important role in the nation. Have you read the Prime Minister's excellent book?' I asked her.

She shook her head.

'According to Mr. Kenyatta, the first Kikuyu, Gikuyu, the founder of the tribe, and his wife Moombi had nine daughters and no sons. He called upon Mognai, or Ngai, Lord of Nature, to help him to find sons for his daughters to wed. He told Gikuyu to sacrifice a lamb and a kid under a big fig tree (*Mokoyo*) and to pour the blood and the fat of the two animals on the trunk of the tree. He then told him that he and his family should make a fire under the tree and sacrifice the meat to Ngai in the flames. "Then go home, come back later to the sacred tree and you will find nine handsome young men." Gikuyu did as he was told and Ngai or Mogai had kept his word. The young men married the daughters of Gikuyu and Moombi. When Gikuyu and Moombi died the daughters inherited everything, which they shared equally amongst themselves.

'Women continued to be the heads of the family groups for many generations. It was said that whilst holding this position the women became tyrannical. They had many husbands and men were often put to death when they became jealous. The men were treated as inferiors. The men decided to revolt. At that time the women were much stronger in physique than the men and were skilled fighters. The men formulated a plan. They systematically seduced the women leaders with flattery, and managed to make all the women pregnant at the same time. When the women were in a state of late pregnancy the men overthrew their leadership. Polygamy instead of polyandry became the order of the day.

'Kikuyu women still have great intelligence and when they are encouraged to come out of the shell into which they have been pushed they become great leaders and public figures, of whom Miss Margaret Kenyatta is a shining example. If the men will help the women to have the same opportunities as the young men the whole country will progress at a faster rate. It is the women, after all, who have to look after the young children. With educated women, the children have a better background and start in life. Besides, from the humanitarian point of view, women should be educated. . . .' My voice trailed off. I didn't want to be too personal or to hurt her feelings.

My friend sighed and nodded. 'I know what you are going to say because I have seen it with my own mother. My brothers are all well educated. My father is educated too. My brother's children are already able to read and write. My mother is completely illiterate. She is imprisoned in her own ignorance.'

'And yet I am sure she is highly intelligent,' I said, 'because she has obviously helped in pushing you ahead and encouraging you to be an educated woman.'

'You are right,' said my friend. 'It was she who begged my father to let me go to school. When I have children I will see that my daughters have as good a chance as I had.'

'Your family then will go from strength to strength.'

I said good-bye to my friend, telling her that if she came to Kenya she should come and stay at our house.

That women of Africa can obtain high positions is absolutely true. One of my friends is a lady doctor: Dr. Carroline Nompozolo is brilliant. She has been practising in Britain for some time now. Everyone thinks highly of her and her capabilities.

A cause of great unhappiness and many difficulties in Kenyan marriages is when the wife is educated and the husband practises polygamy. It is a most difficult and delicate situation for many of the girls. Those who are Westernised cannot tolerate the practice. An educated friend of mine was shocked when one of her ablest politicians invited her and her husband to his house and introduced them to his pretty new wife. He had two others besides the new one, and all four people were living happily ever after in the same house.

'Don't you think it is shocking, Michaela?' asked my friend.

'It's not so shocking if the three wives don't mind about each other.'

'But wouldn't you object to it?'

'Yes, I would, because it is our custom to have one wife and one husband. That is how I have been brought up since a child. I must admit I would be very jealous and unhappy about it.'

'And so would I, Michaela,' said my friend.

Luckily her husband sees her point of view, and she is the only lady in the household. My friend is, of course, a Christian convert, but even with non-believers I think the time will come when polygamy will vanish.

An educated wife is so much more interesting and satisfying for a man, so that he can well do without several wives. There is the economic factor, too, which will make the custom of polygamy disappear.

In Muslim countries, although a Muslim is allowed to have four wives, very few men do so. A good Muslim husband has to treat all his wives equally. If he gives one a diamond bracelet he must give all four diamond bracelets!

We hastened back to Kenya after our stay in Rhodesia. We were off almost at once on another safari, this time to Lake Baringo in Kenya. We were going to film the fishing industry which David Roberts had set up. We drove to Baringo in our Land Rovers. We would be camping beside the lake. The whole area of Baringo was incredibly desiccated. It was hard to believe that a century ago the area round Lake Baringo had been the centre of a thriving agricultural community. Now the country was semi-desert. The furrows were broken and were not repaired. The area directly round where the people lived, with their cattle and goats in enclosures, resembled a battlefield. Tree stumps, blackened and ugly from fire, thrust accusing fingers upwards. The wanton destruction of the trees had been accelerated by goats climbing up on the branches and devouring everything within reach.

The whole country was overstocked. Wild animals feeding, as they do at different levels, could never have encompassed such destruction.

It was said that the Arab slave traders used to halt here to buy fresh vegetables from these long-vanished farmers. There were great movements of peoples in Africa before recorded history, but one can still trace a little of the movement of peoples from the old men and women who have heard the tales from their mothers and fathers. Artefacts are sometimes found on several sites of long-forgotten peoples. At Langata we had to make a new enclosure for a small antelope until it was used to staying with us. We thought it should have the protection of a pen. Our men dug some holes for fence posts. After they had dug the first one they started on the second and unearthed an axe-shaped piece of stone. They dug further and found beads and pieces of pottery. The find was between our two houses. Des Bartlett took the objects to the Leakeys who said they were several hundred years old. It was the Leakeys' theory that the site had been used as a slave camp.

David Roberts and his wife Betty lived amongst some of the most interesting-looking people still to be found in East Africa. It was true that the Njemps, Sukh and Turgen were unsophisticated, but they were romantic-looking, with a fine physique and an independent bearing. They knew nothing about politics.

David loved his work-people. They had respect and liking for him. David and his parents had lived in Egypt but had moved to Kenya to make a new life there.

Somehow or other he had installed a modern refrigeration plant at the lakeside. It was a miraculous achievement to have transported such complicated and bulky machinery to this isolated place. The machinery was not only installed but was in perfect working order, thanks to David's technical skill.

David had been a crocodile hunter at one time of his life, but as nearly always happens with intelligent people he had changed his attitude towards animals and become a conservationist. Even his former foes became his friends.

The waste from the fish industry was used to feed the crocodiles, who lay all day in the water in close proximity to the fisheries and David's house beside the lakeshore. The golden-eyed monsters became so tame that it was easy to forget their presence. David and Betty had several children and the crocodiles ignored them completely.

David's workers worked in an open-air yard which had good shade from the large thorn trees. The men were resplendent in their tribal dress. The Sukhs costume resembled Turkhana costume. The head-dress was especially interesting. It had the same concoction of ostrich egg-yolk and deep blue powder which elongated the head at the back, as the male Turkhana coiffure, and had also the curved-shaped spring with a pompon, which bobbed over the face at every movement. The men wore many colourful beads and ornaments.

The men cleaned the fish first, and then packed it into rectangular tins to be taken to the freezing plant.

David provided the men with the fishing tackle. He also told the men not to take the very small fish.

Fishing regulations are not always understood by the very people the regulations are designed to help. On a visit to Lake Victoria, Armand and I heard that soon after self-government the fishing regulations had been lifted. In three years there was not a fish in the lake. The local inhabitants begged the Fisheries Department to help them. Regulations were once again introduced about the size of mesh in fishing nets. The lake would have to be restocked with fish, and it would take many years to repair the damage caused by ignorance of the laws of conservation. Meanwhile not only were people short of food, but they could no longer export it, or even keep the Lake Victoria Hotel supplied in fish. Fish had to be imported from Kenya.

The Njemps and Turgen are closely related to the Masai, whom they resemble in culture and costume. The two tribes have the Moran system. At a certain age the young boys are initiated into manhood. They are circumcised, grow their hair long and go to live by themselves with the other boys in a maniatta (Masai hut or group of huts). The youths are then known as Moran or warriors. The young unmarried girls visit the Moran at their maniatta but do not have babies. The girls are immature.

The Moran are greatly honoured by the rest of the tribe. In the old days they were responsible for the safety of the tribe or clan. The men will stay Moran until the next period of their life, when they become elders. The elders are not necessarily old, but the Moran system is comparable to military service. When the service has been completed a Moran automatically becomes an elder.

The Moran are highly photogenic, chiefly because of the distinctive style in which their hair is dressed. It is braided into long pigtails and coloured with red powder and fat. Another Moran undertakes the task of hairdresser for his companion. We photographed the dressing of the hair of a Moran. The finished product is handsome, its smell mercifully worn off. I am a vegetarian and meat fat and its smell makes me faint with repulsion. With great self-control I was photographed with the young men, watching the work as it progressed. The air seemed to take the smell away after a few hours.

The following day we were invited to a big dance or ngoma. We took some of the Moran with us in our truck, the open Land Rover. They piled in until we had to beg them to stop, as we feared for our springs.

We set off with the young men crowded in with their seven-foot-tall spears sticking out in all directions. It was quite bumpy on the way, and the thought occurred to me that it would be extremely easy to become impaled on one of the spears if we went into a hole. Armand must have thought of the same thing, because he suddenly said:

'Hang on, Michaela, and watch the spears.'

We drove into a steep donga immediately after his words. (A donga is a dried-up river bed.) This was an extremely steep one and as we went down and up the other side our young Moran screamed with delight and surprise at the weird sensation.

They seemed to enjoy it so much that Armand retraced the steps and did it two or three times. When the other Land Rover drove up with the Bartletts and the cameras Armand suggested we should film it.

'Let's hope they haven't become blasé about it,' said Armand. There is always a danger when repeating some new experience that the pleasure will pall and when the same scene is photographed it lacks the original spontaneity. Fortunately this had not happened with our Moran. They screamed and laughed with as much gusto as they did first time across.

We arrived at the appointed place for dancing. Many of them must have walked many miles, as the country of necessity was sparsely populated and there was a considerable crowd of men, women and children.

The women were as tall as I. One or two of them were even a little taller. They had a similar beauty to that of the Masai, rather masculine, slim-faced, straight narrow-nosed, well-formed lips, oblique eyes and high cheek-bones.

The women wore skin skirts, sarong style, around their hips, and toga-like garments fastened on one shoulder. The skins were soft and supple, almost like chamois. The garments were ornamented with bead embroideries. The girls wore several necklaces one on top of the other. The necklaces were circles of beadwork, three or four inches in depth and stiff. The women's ears were loaded with ear-rings, which were large circles of brass. These were so heavy that the ear-lobes had been stretched to breast level. Some of the women wore a little chain which connected between the two circles. I wondered about this ornament, and the woman, guessing what was in my mind, showed me its use. She lifted up the chain and rested it on her head. In this way she took the weight off her ear-lobes.

All the women and young girls had shaved heads, Masai fashion. Many wore an ornamental band round the head. On it was fastened an ornament which dangled on to the forehead, usually in the shape of a silver crescent. Most of the women's garments were reddish in colour. The Njemps and Turgen men were very tall on an average. Many were as tall as Armand, who is six foot three and a half inches.

The dancers induced me to dance with them. They were greatly pleased that I knew the dance steps, which was not surprising as they were identical to those of the Masai. In no time at all I was completely identified with part of them. Arms were put round my waist and we moved forward in the dance in great circles or in lines. The dust rose up in clouds above us with the stamping of our feet. The singing and dancing had a completely intoxicating effect on me, as it did on the other dancers. I could have danced for several days and several nights with them if I had not been recalled to reality by Armand, every now and then, when he took me off to be photographed with another group dancing at the same time.

It was nearly dusk, but the dance was in full swing. Armand gripped my arms and pulled me bodily out of the dancers. He pushed me into the Land Rover, holding me tightly, as though I would escape and run back to the ngoma. He looked at me and said:

'It was quite hard to find you, Michaela. Just look at yourself. You look like a Njemps.'

I looked at my trousers and shirt. I was covered with red powder mixed with grease like my fellow dancers. I looked in the mirror which I carried in my handbag, and which I had left in the Land Rover during the ngoma—even my hair was red. Armand laughed at my expression as I looked into the glass.

'I was in two minds whether to take you home or to leave you there for two or three days' dancing. I don't think you would have noticed if the trucks left. It was only the thought of leaving my herbivore without food which made me decide to disturb you. After all, you wouldn't take kindly to blood and milk as food.'

I came back to the camp tired and happy.

Betty Roberts kindly suggested that I should take a bath at their house.

'Cold water will not remove the "paint",' she said, which was true. I slept like a log.

The next morning we were up bright and early. Armand and I took a long walk along the lakeshore. There were several marabou storks congregated around the jetty, where David fed the crocodiles every day. The tall birds, with the pink sack-like appendages which hang from their necks, were picking their way warily between the crocodiles. The birds seemed to know that the crocodiles were not a serious menace, and as they scavenged went insolently close to them.

'Look, Michaela. What's the matter with that one?'

Armand pointed: 'No, not there. Over there.'

He took my shoulders and twisted me in the other direction.

'Now.' He pointed again.

'How dreadful. It has something sticking out of its side. Is it an arrow or a spear?'

'It's an arrow,' said Armand, after further scrutiny.

'The poor thing, Armand. We must try to save it.'

'Let's go back to camp,' Armand said. 'On our way we'll call on David and see if he has any suggestions to make.'

David had just finished breakfast. He listened as we told him what we had seen.

'Yes, I saw the bird yesterday. I was coming down to your camp to ask if we could combine forces to try and capture it. It might stand a chance if we can remove the arrow and give it some medical treatment.'

We left everything we were doing back at the camp and set off for the jetty.

David, the Bartletts and ourselves surrounded the bird. We were going to try and throw a net over it before it could take off. In spite of every precaution not to alarm it, the bird flew away painfully, slowly, the arrow quivering in its side. It flew out of sight.

'I am afraid this will happen each time we try to come near it. The best thing is to wait until nightfall,' David advised.

'It will then have to roost, and we will have a better chance of finding the tree on which it is perched, and to grab it before it can fly away.'

'It's a good job we brought our lighting equipment with us this time,' Armand said. 'It will be useful for illuminating its roosting place if we locate it.'

That evening we set off with a pole with a loop attached and the lighting equipment. We took two vehicles and cruised around in search of the wounded bird. We went first to one tree, and then to another, peering into the branches. There were several hundred birds roosting in the large thorn trees, but not the one we sought. We kept up with our search but were beginning to lose hope.

At last we came to the tree in which the poor bird had taken refuge. We shone the light upwards. It was dazzled by the light and stayed perfectly motionless. David reached on tiptoe, holding the pole upwards.

'It's too short,' he said. 'What on earth can we do?'

He looked around him.

'I know, I will stand on the roof of the other Land Rover—that will give me extra height.'

We drove away from the tree to the covered Land Rover. We transferred to the other truck, David mounted on to the roof and we passed him up the stick with the loop in it. Carefully he reached up, and was about to slip the noose over the bird's body. The bird flapped off before he could quite manage to slip the loop over its head. David swore under his breath. He still wouldn't give up. We searched again and once more located the bird. Unhappily, it had gone into a taller tree this time. Even on tiptoe, and with arm outstretched, David was unable to reach it. While we were debating amongst ourselves how we could best reach it, by placing something else on the roof of the Land Rover to give some extra height, the bird flopped out of the tree and flew off. We could not follow its flight this time. We drove round in circles again to try to find it. There was no sign of the bird and after half an hour we gave it up.

It was depressing to think that we had nearly but not quite rescued the now doomed bird. It was certain to die wihout medical attention.

We drove back to camp feeling terribly disappointed after all the efforts we had made to try to rescue the bird.

'If only one could communicate with animals and tell them that we are trying to help them everything would be all right.'

'They have no reason to think that we are going to help them,' said Armand. 'Too often animals have been betrayed by human beings. Why should an animal have trust in man?'

10

Serious Matters

THE GARDEN was beginning to look like an old-established one. If one concentrated on plants which enjoyed growing in the tropics, and didn't attempt to grow Alpine plants in the lowlands, one established a garden very quickly in Kenya. I always pitied the D.P.s of the plant world, who were compelled to eke out an existence in an environment so hostile to them that they would always be sickly and stunted. My plants without exception were exuberant growers. Some were rather touchy about where they were planted. They might have to be moved around until they found the spot they liked. When I had first employed a gardener I thought I should try a girl, which is quite usual in Kenya. I hadn't been very long in Africa. I foolishly asked one of our employees to find me someone. The little lady duly arrived. She was plump and smooth-skinned, like a ripe plum. Although she was plump, she was very sexy, and moved her hips provocatively. She was attractively dressed in Kikuyu costume, an orange shuka held on one shoulder. I soon discovered that the little gardening girl was not much good at her chosen calling.

'Mary,' I called her. 'Would you please plant these mugumu poles.'

The mugumu, or sacred Kikuyu fig, is a most obliging tree. It will grow from a pole into a fine tree with glossy dark green leaves. It needs a deep hole with soil well broken up to plant it in. Even I knew that, limited as my gardening knowledge was at that time.

I left Mary the expert to do it. Later on that day I needed Tom to help me with another job in the house. He was nowhere to be seen. Neither was anybody else. What had happened to our household? I went into the garden, calling names. I found everybody helping Mary to plant the poles. She was in a state of giggling hysterics. The hole she had made was three inches across and six inches deep. It was just the right size to plant a dandelion.

'It should be just a little bit bigger,' I said to her.

'If it is any wider it will not stand up.'

'It should surely be deeper too.'

'The ground is too hard.'

'Give me the jembe [hoe].' I took it from her and started digging. The others stood open-mouthed. I didn't stop until I had a decent-sized hole three foot across by three foot deep. A really large mound of earth was piled on one side of the hole. I got some water and poured it into the hole and then some earth.

'Hold the pole, please, Mary,' I asked her, and then I pushed the earth all around. The pole stood upright and firm.

By this time it was four o'clock. Elija, the man who had recommended Mary to work for us, was at our gate with transportation. 'Ding, ding' went the bicycle bell.

'Good-bye,' said Mary, 'tomorrow I have to take my baby to the doctor.' It was the first time I had heard anything of a sick baby. I felt ashamed of myself for the suspicion which had come uninvited into my mind. I tried to suppress my doubts on how conscientious Mary was as a mother, even if she wasn't the world's best gardener. I would ask her the day after tomorrow to bring her baby, and I would take a photograph of her, something which our servants always appreciate.

Two days later there was no Mary. Could something dreadful have happened to the baby, and the poor girl was unable to get news to me? Mary didn't appear the next week either. I was thoroughly alarmed. Then I remembered that she had been recommended by Elija. He would certainly have some recent news of her.

'Where is Elija, Tom?'

'He is not here today.'

The next morning I went in search of Elija. I found him mending a fence post.

'Why weren't you in to work yesterday?'

Elija looked down at his feet in sorrow, then he looked up at me.

'My wife and child are covered in boils. I had to take them to the doctor.'

'What has happened to Mary?' I asked.

'She has gone to stay with her mother.'

'But what about the baby?'

'Baby, what baby?'

So my suspicions had been right, after all. At least after her stay with her mother, *if* she had a mother, I would be able to say that there was no more job.

I was busy writing a book at the time. Writing always preoccupied me fully and if the servants wanted to get away with murder there was no better time for it. Luckily, Tshikadi is thoroughly reliable. But in those days he was the only thoroughly trustworthy one. At this time anyone who wanted to keep out of sight could do so, and I would not even know if they had arrived at work that morning.

Exactly a week later and on the same day of the week I again needed some odd job done by Elija. Elija couldn't be found.

The next day I located him.

'Why didn't you come to work yesterday?'

'My child has fallen down the cho,' he said (cho is lavatory in Kiswahili). Many of the lavatories are the rural type which I have used on safari—basically a hole in the ground over which is set a pole.

'What a dreadful thing.'

'Yes, I had to take the child to hospital.'

'Did it break any bones?'

'I don't know, the doctor didn't say.'

It was strange that such bad luck befell Elija on that particular day of the week. Could it be coincidence?

'What is the matter?' said my secretary, as I came into the house. 'You look worried, Michaela.' I explained the coincidence.

'Yes, it is extraordinary.'

'Let's see if fate deals him any more sharp blows next week.'

Sure enough, the next week Elija was missing on the same day. This time I sent Tom off to find him the next day, and to escort him upstairs to my writing-room. I went on for two minutes with my work so as to allow his anxiety to grow a little.

'What happened yesterday?' I asked. 'Did your grandmother fall down the cho?'

Elija smiled sheepishly and looked uncomfortable.

'I had to go to court yesterday.'

'Ah,' I thought to myself, 'that sounds more likely.' My intelligence service in the house had already informed me that the police had arrived one morning when I was out picking up my mail, and that Elija had hidden down by the river. The police had gone away after waiting an hour.

'What have you done?' I asked.

'It is not my fault. You know that I have a store.'

I hadn't known, but I was ready to believe that Elija had, as he always looked prosperous.

'I bought some scales from a man. They are incorrect. A police inspector came to my shop and tested them. I was arrested and I have to pay a fine. I had to go to the court yesterday.'

'You must have some document or other on you. Show us.'

My secretary and I looked at the little form which he produced. On it was written Elija's name and the charge—'Assault and battery.'

'But this is nothing to do with weights and measures, Elija. You are charged with assault and battery.'

Elija looked surprised.

'They have made a mistake on the form. Fancy their doing that.'

'You didn't know what was on the form?' I asked.

'No, I thought it had my name on it '

Somehow neither I nor my secretary was convinced that the efficient clerk at the court could have made a mistake of this nature, but it was obviously unjust to allow poor Elija to walk around with such a damning document.

'Let us call the court,' suggested my secretary. 'We can easily find out about it.' She went into the other room to telephone.

'Michaela, I think it is our friend Elija who has made a mistake in showing us the document, not the clerk in filling it in.'

'What has he done?'

'It was an assault-and-battery charge on a woman named Mary. She is lying in hospital with a knife wound.'

I was cross about the lies, but Elija was a very good worker and we didn't give him notice. Mary fully recovered. As far as I know she and Elija made up their lovers' quarrel, but my garden flourishes without Mary's ministrations.

People still gave sundowners and parties in Kenya. Some had a note of sadness in the gaiety, for many were farewell parties.

Not all the people were going willingly. They had become redundant. The farm or home they had bought to retire to was no longer the sanctuary for which they had longed. It was too isolated in these violent days. Elderly people were unsafe, and many couples with grown-up children who lived alone feared that either one or the other partner might die. It would be decidedly unsafe now for one old person to live alone, and even two together would be under a nervous strain. If people fall upon hard times through their own fault it is not nearly as sad as when it is undeserved.

We went to one such party to say good-bye to our friends. They were going to settle in Canada.

'It is like uprooting an old tree,' I said to Armand as we drove to Nairobi. 'Let's hope they can survive being transplanted.' Many couldn't. A home would be sold. A family would say good-bye to all their friends and in under a year would be back again, unable to keep away, like moths around a candle flame. It would mean having to buy another home and entirely new furniture.

We parked our car on the side of the road behind the long line of cars of the guests who had arrived before us.

The house of Bill and Mary was old for Nairobi. It must have been one of the first houses in the area. Other houses had mushroomed around it, until what had been a piece of African bush had become a fashionable Nairobi suburb. It was spacious, with several good antique pieces of furniture in it. Some huge jacaranda trees stood in the drive and carpeted the ground with mauve blossoms.

A babble of voices greeted us as we walked up the drive under the tall trees. We had difficulty in finding our host and hostess in the crowd. Nearly everyone was standing, and talking, all at once. We found Bill and Mary almost in the centre of the room.

'Let me get you a drink,' said Bill, and left us with Mary.

'We are very sorry that you are leaving us.'

'I would never go,' said Mary, 'but Bill insists on it. He is too afraid of something happening to him and my being left alone.'

'That is understandable.'

Bill came up with our drinks. He took us off to introduce us to some of the other guests, most of whom we knew.

'Do you know Norman's son? He is a white hunter.' Armand and I greeted the young man, who was bronzed, with very white teeth. Neither of us like people who kill animals, but some white hunters are reformed characters, and only take out photographic parties.

'This is my client,' said the young man, introducing a plump swarthy man who spoke with an American accent.

'He has come over here for leopard.'

'To photograph leopard?' I asked.

The client said: 'No, lady. I have a trophy room and I want a leopard for it. Last year I got a polar bear.'

'Don't you hate seeing all those dead animals around you?' I asked.

'No, I don't. I never think of them as animals.'

'What a pity,' said Armand. 'We have so few animals left and it is hard to try and eradicate poaching when rich people kill animals for so-called pleasure.'

'Well, surely you kill animals sometimes in the course of your work?' said the young man, who had obviously not seen our pictures on TV.

'Certainly not. Both I and my wife find the greatest pleasure in photographing living animals. We give pleasure to millions of others all over the world in watching the beauty of wild life.'

'You talk about the poachers,' said the young man huffily. 'People like myself and my client do hardly any damage at all compared to the Africans who are going to take the country over. Just wait until they get uhuru. They will destroy everything.'

'Can you honestly say that the Europeans have preserved wild life? When the Europeans first came to Africa were there less wild animals than there are today?'

'That was different.'

'Why is it different?'

'That was for sport and for farming.'

'Don't call it sport,' I interjected. 'Call it perversion.'

'But it brings money into the country,' said the young white hunter.

'So would public hangings. There is no moral justification for doing something which is morally unjustifiable, just because it brings in cash.'

The client shrugged.

'All I want is that skin for my trophy room.'

The young man looked uncomfortable. His client's callousness seemed to have touched a chord off in him. Armand and I left him and talked to some of the other visitors. The young man was at my elbow fifteen minutes later.

'I know what you meant when you were talking to my client. I must say he is a butcher and if I had my way I would dump him at the airport and tell him to go home. It's not true when he makes all that song and dance about getting his leopard. He would kill anything and everything if I didn't restrain him.'

'Then why do you put up with such people?' I asked.

'I do it because I like the outdoor life. I love to be on safari.'

It seemed rather hard on the animals that they had to be sacrificed just to give this young man an opportunity and the funds to go on safari.

'Besides, I like to go on a bit of shooting even if it's only for the pot. After all, you eat meat, don't you?' Armand heard the last part of the conversation and laughed.

'I am sorry, you are out of luck. Michaela is a vegetarian.'

'Even if people are butchers and they kill the animals humanely,' I said, 'I doubt whether they get any pleasure out of the killing. It is the getting pleasure out of taking life which is, in my opinion, so very wicked. An animal, bird or human being is a beautiful complex piece of machinery. It is vandalism to smash it to pieces.'

The client came up to our group. He hadn't heard all the conversation, but by the way we stopped talking when we saw him he guessed we had been talking about the same subject.

'You just wait till the whites go and then watch the extermination squads take over.'

'You might be surprised,' I said to him. I wasn't too sure myself of what would happen to the animals. The European attitude about wild life was changing rapidly from the days when a pioneer's diary read like a holocaust. Indeed it was such a new outlook that it had not been possible to educate everyone quickly enough. Had we not ourselves seen some of the European schoolboys with guns prowling in the gardens around Nairobi? But there were more camera-minded people in the vanguard who truly despised hunters. I have often said to Armand that photography has done more to save the wild life of the world than any other single factor.

Soon after the party we were once more on our way to attend the International Union for the Conservation of Nature, which was being held that year in Arusha in Tanganyika. Armand and I drove down in my Buick convertible. We were invited to call on the film company which was making the film *Hatari*.

For some reason Armand thought the Buick would be the right

car to have in Arusha, besides our Land Rovers. I was not against taking it with me. If it became necessary to evacuate the country I wanted to test the roadworthiness of the car. I would then be able to drive Armand and our pets in the Buick to safety. My Buick is of 1951 vintage, but so advanced is the design that it looks almost new. It has every possible convenience. Hydromatic gears, push-button windows. A roof which lowers itself or raises itself at the touch of a lever. A radio which works perfectly. It is, besides, tremendously comfortable. I become attached to all the utilitarian objects in my life. Almost as though the inanimate object has a life of its own. Whether it is car, fountain pen or typewriter, or even the chair I usually sit in when I write, or my desk, or cameras, I feel that they are old and trusted friends. I hoped that the Buick would be able to make such a journey. There was one part of the road to Arusha which was very bad indeed.

We set off early in the morning. It was the Kenya part of the road which I feared. After Athi River we had to drive to Kajiado. The road was corrugated. I had never driven the car on such a road before. I tried going slowly. I hung on with all my strength to the steering wheel.

'Michaela, I don't want to be a back-seat driver, but try going faster.'

I took Armand's advice and found I managed much better.

For the first part of the journey the dust was almost white and followed behind us in ghostly clouds. Soon after Kajiado the dust changed in colour to pink and then later to a deep copper red. The road was slightly better, but there were often sudden bends, and a bridge to cross which we suddenly came upon. Anyway, I managed. We drove near the National Park. An antelope sprung straight out from the bushes in front of the car. I missed it by inches, the car instantly obeying my evasive action at the wheel.

'Good work, Michaela,' said Armand. I felt as childishly proud of his praise as a schoolgirl presenting a good school report to her parents! Further along the road we came to a dried-up river bed.

'This is where Abdul and his friends nearly got drowned, isn't it?' I asked.

'Yes, I believe it is,' Armand said.

Abdul Gahfur Sheikh is the son of a Nairobi business man who was one of the earlier settlers in Kenya. The Sheikhs amassed a considerable fortune, which is entirely dedicated to good and charitable works. Abdul administers the foundation. He is a young, good-looking, intelligent, always faultlessly dressed man, whom we first met in the United States. When we heard he was from Nairobi we instantly exchanged addresses and he became one of our best friends. He was interested in everything and everybody. Most of the V.I.P.s who come to Kenya know him. Abdul is also very active in the East African Wild Life Society.

Some important American visitors were in Kenya and Abdul was taking them to see the National Park. The party set off in two cars. When they reached the river near Namanga they got carried away by the floodwater. Abdul and a companion clung to one another and managed to grab the trunk of a tree. The water swirled around them. They were saved only just in time. Abdul nearly drowned. After the rescue his feet were in very poor shape, and he went around for nearly a week in bedroom slippers.

The river was a mere trickle now. We stopped at Namanga for lunch. Armand and I consider that Namanga is one of the best hotels in Kenya. It is exactly right for the tourist. It does not disillusion the visitor's ideas of romantic Africa as do some of the modern hotels. I remember meeting a German husband and wife in the streets of Nairobi, who stopped me outside Woolworth's.

'We enjoy your programmes so much,' said the wife. 'The programmes really persuaded us to go to Africa. It's too bad that we haven't seen any of the exciting things which we saw in your films.'

'How long have you been here?' I asked.

'We arrived yesterday.'

'Go and see all the National Parks, as many as you can, and you will be back in the Africa of your dreams. In fact you will never want to leave this country.'

'We are going to Amboseli tomorrow,' the man said. 'But surely we cannot see very much. We are not millionaires and can't stay here for long.'

'You can see everything a millionaire can see if you are here for three weeks, and I will tell you how to do it. Come and have a coffee with me.'

I took the strangers to the Rendezvous, a café with a continental, boulevard appearance. We sat outside at one of the little tables on the pavement. I wrote down on a piece of paper an itinerary covering most of the National Parks.

19 *From the right* Melville Grosvenor, President of the National Geographic Society, Mervyn Cowie, Director of the Kenya National Parks, I and Armand, fondle three cheetahs in the animal orphanage

20 When photographing hyena we drove into a warthog hole hidden in the long grass. My forehead came into painful contact with the metal frame of the windshield. We were on our way to Olduvai Gorge and Armand acts as 'doctor'

21 and 22 Dr. Louis Leakey indicating to Armand the various levels of geological beds where he and Mary Leakey have been working. *Zinjanthropus boisei* was found in this area

23 A crowd gathers around the car with smashed windscreen (Bazaar Street murder)

24 The Bazaar Street victim's widow and family mourn his passing

25 Thousands of people of every race and sect attend the traditional Hindu cremation of Shah Kantilal Devraj

26 Armand and I survey Kariba, which has tamed the Zambezi

27 An antelope is rescued to be put aboard the boat which will take him to safety

28 Kariba rescue boats are towed to their assignment

'When you come back please telephone us and let us know how you got on.'

In three weeks' time Herr Schmidt and his wife called me.

'We saw everything. We shall certainly tell our friends to come here, and to make the same journey. How did you ever find out that one could see so much?'

'Armand worked it out.'

'I don't think you could find a better itinerary anywhere. You see the maximum amount in the minimum of time and you don't have to spend a fortune doing it.'

I had highly recommended the Namanga Hotel. I thought of the Schmidts as we drove up the pleasant driveway with its flowering trees and indigenous plants. There was a great chattering of birds, whose voices we did not recognise. We looked around the garden, following the noise, and found a very large aviary filled with budgerigars. They were obviously happy and in well-adjusted families.

The hotel itself was made entirely of local material. It had a thatched roof and was spacious and airy.

Peter Gethin greeted us at the door.

'Welcome back. Where have you been all this time?' he asked us.

'We have been in Africa, but terribly busy. Sometimes we even have to fly wherever we are filming, because we are on a deadline with our work.' Armand answered him.

'I long to come here one day and write a book,' I said. 'I would shut myself away in one of your nice cottages, and only appear in public at mealtimes.'

'After you have had your lunch I want to show you something,' Peter said.

We went to the dining-room, and found it filled with two separate groups of tourist parties. One group came from Western Germany, the other from France. Armand and I sat down to have lunch and couldn't help being aware that everyone was looking in our direction. When we moved out to the large verandah for coffee, first one and then the other group came up to speak. We were thrilled to hear that they all watched our films on television, and that we were almost like old friends to them. One of the French girls said:

'Now we know we are in Africa because here are Armand and Michaela.'

After lunch we went in search of Peter Gethin.

'Come with me,' he said. He took us to the back of the hotel to his own house. We went into his garden. There in the middle of the garden, looking at us solemnly, was a giraffe, which was only an inch or two taller than he was. When it saw him the baby giraffe walked up and nuzzled him affectionately. He stroked the silky head with its large eyes and one-and-a-half-inch-long eyelashes.

'Where did you find it?' Armand asked.

'It wandered in the other day. I don't know what happened to its mother, but it has adopted us.'

Armand and I approached the young giraffe and stroked it. It seemed to enjoy being petted.

'I won't be a minute,' said Peter. He disappeared and returned with a bucket filled with milk. She buried her velvety nose in the bucket, only pausing to look up and shake herself. She spattered us with milk, but we were too fascinated by her to move away quickly enough. And, as a Roman empress would have said, 'Milk is good for the complexion.' The little giraffe followed Peter around. He was very attached to it. We said good-bye to him and his giraffe and drove on towards Arusha.

There was a frontier post between the two countries. There was not too much formality in getting over the border. Usually it was only necessary to put down the names of the occupants of the cars and the numbers of the vehicles. The minute we were in Tanganyika the road was remarkably well kept. It was tarmac most of the way. We arrived in Arusha, a place Armand and I have always liked, as it has character and period charm. Tanganyika's first contact with Europeans was through the Germans. Until World War I it was a German colony. There is a Germanic atmosphere about Arusha, even to the old fort which is now a government building.

The next day we went to the opening of the conference. Many of the delegates we already knew. Sir Julian Huxley was one of Armand's first friends in England. They were both Oxford men, but at different colleges. We are very fond of both Julian and Juliette (Lady Huxley). Besides the common interest in the conservation of wild life we could not have endorsed Sir Julian's views on overpopulation more strongly. But perhaps it is because one is a conservationist that one has such decided views on overpopulation. A true conservationist is even more acutely aware of the terrible crisis which faces the world, and whose problems are just beginning to show themselves. Quite apart from the overwhelming destruction of natural resources, and the impossibility of managing to educate everybody, it is the disappearance of the dignity of man through loss of the countryside which worries me most.

We had made a film especially to show the delegates on the problems of conservation in Africa. Both of us were most pleasantly surprised to find a large number of the delegates were African.

'Remember that conversation we had at the Nairobi sundowner just before we left for Arusha?' I asked Armand. He nodded.

The Governor, Sir Richard Turnbull, gave a scholarly opening address to the assembled delegates. It was an appeal to the Africans to face the challenge of saving the painfully small remnant of their wild life. I saw two or three of the delegates square their shoulders at the Governor's words. The Governor received an ovation. The speech had left little doubt in my mind, as the conference progressed, that there were many Africans who would fight for the cause as devotedly as, and even more devotedly than, the most ardent conservationists we knew.

'If only that Texan could hear some of these speeches. Or that selfish young man,' Armand whispered.

There were delegates from all over Africa. Some spoke French and some English. The speeches were translated in either one or the other of those languages. At one of the sessions a politician from Dahomey gave an impassioned speech on the need for the preservation of wild life. Neither Armand nor I spoke at this conference, but I was enthralled by all that I heard and, consequently, applauded most enthusiastically. The delegates were greatly amused because they knew exactly when I enthusiastically believed in something and when I didn't, for I would not applaud. Armand and I were on the platform most of the time. One could sense the undercurrents at the conference.

'I shouldn't be surprised,' I said to Armand, 'that when the Africans have full power they will be able to ratify the various proposals far better than any colonial government will be able to do. After all, the prosperity of their country will be in their hands. Every educated African has a far greater burden of responsibility than his equivalent in other countries. He is still in a minority, as most of his people are illiterate. He has to be the eyes, the ears and the conscience of the masses, who live a twenty-four-hour day with no thought to the lessons of the past and with little regard for the future.'

'Do you think they will be able to do it?' asked Armand.

A delegate from another continent overheard our conversation. '*You* think they will exert themselves to the full?'

'I am sure they will. The African politicians I know, and men in public life, work a sixteen-hour day, if not more. When they are not doing their usual work you will find them on committees. Even when they are at parties they can't forget their country's problems.'

A tall man sat on the platform next to us. He was an observer. He smoked a pipe and had a strong, clever, bearded face. I wondered what his field was, for it was obvious he was deeply interested in every phase of the discussions. We introduced ourselves. He told Armand and me that he was Ian MacPhail, a journalist. He had become more and more worried by the rapidly diminishing animal population, not only in Africa, but throughout the whole world. Being a practical man, as well as having enough insight to see the urgency of the problem, he was formulating a plan. He told us what he intended to do. He was going to organise a world wild-life fund. He was going to campaign on a scale which had never been contemplated before.

His plan was so brave, so bold, it didn't seem possible that such an organisation could be built up fast enough to meet, what we who attended the conference knew was an emergency. We should never underestimate the power of a single dedicated human being.

When a mission is Herculean, strength beyond the human seems to come to us. So it was with Ian. He launched the World Wild Life Fund. Help came from all over the world to make the fund one of the most influential bodies ever devised. It is entirely due to the vision of this one man.

11

People and Animals

IN BETWEEN the sessions at the conference we called on the *Hatari* film company. A whole camp had been built to look like an animal-capturer's farm. The camp and personnel were very different from an 'On Safari' camp. Even when we make films for the cinema our expedition rarely numbers more than six people. We sometimes take a married couple with us, either the Bartletts or the Halbertsmas, on our TV expeditions. Often Armand and I work with only one assistant with us. The reason why our party is so small is because more work gets done. The more personnel, the more the whole operation tends to be unwieldy and slow.

There were three delightful baby elephants in the cast, besides the humans. The cast was international. Elsa Martinelli, John Wayne and Red Buttons, Hardy Kruger, and there were also some French actors in the cast.

The technicians and their wives and the directors were all extremely pleasant people and seemed a happy group. I heard news of a friend and neighbour of ours from one of the wives. Diana Hartley lived not far from us. We had known her for many years. The first time I had ever met her she had a caracal with her. It was extremely tame and followed her everywhere. At night it slept beside her bed. She was a tall blonde who wore glasses. She had one of those faces to which glasses add something. Years ago, Diana and Lionel, her husband, ran Mac's Inn, in the Tsavo National Park, which is almost halfway to the coast, 149 miles from Nairobi and 152 miles from Mombasa.

Visitors coming by ship to Kenya usually see Tsavo Park first, as it is on the main road to Nairobi and Mombasa. It is one of the best places to see rhino and elephant. The impact is tremendous. Much of the year it is very dry. Scenically it is different from the Nairobi National Park. It is more rugged-looking country, with different vegetation. The baobab tree is a prominent feature there. The baobab has a grey bark which is almost the colour of a rhino skin, and fibre can be obtained from it. Its shape is like an enormous bulbous bottle. Its branches spread wide, and its flowers are large and white. The width of the trunk is so enormous that neither Armand nor I could encircle it even with our arms outstretched. It was said that there was a sentry post made in the trunk of a baobab tree by the Germans many years ago. The fruit and seed pulp are edible and its leaves are an African vegetable.

Mackinnon Road, an army base, is near Mac's Inn. Mackinnon Road was originally a naval air base. There were two blister hangars, a grass landing strip and ten miles of tarmac. A very large army camp replaced the naval air base. The Government developed the camp and then for some mysterious reason they vacated it the minute it was completed. During all this time Lionel and Diana helped to make life enjoyable for the Army. There was no other place of amusement, or hotel, for many miles, although the soldiers did much to amuse themselves by forming a flying club. Lionel and Diana were the perfect people for the job of living so close to nature. Both were passionately fond of animals and never grew tired of watching them. They also enjoyed making the lonely servicemen feel at home. They greatly appreciated the hospitality of the Hartleys and often tried to show their gratitude. There was one serviceman who owned a Tiger Moth. He offered to give Lionel a joy-ride. They set off in a carefree spirit. Unfortunately, the aircraft crashed. The pilot was unhurt. He looked at Lionel, to find that he was dead. There appeared to be no injury, and it was assumed he had died of shock. Diana was left with two small children to support. She became an animal dealer and started a thriving business. Her partner was Heini Demmer, a blond German giant whom Hitler would have given half his misbegotten life to have been like. He was a perfect Teutonic type. The partners soon built up one of the largest animal-export businesses in Africa.

Heini Demmer had procured a giant panda for the London Zoo and also brought to the West one of the famous snow leopards of China.

Life seemed to be going smoothly for Diana. . . .

During Mau-Mau she visited her father and mother. They were having dinner. Suddenly there was a rain of blows on the door; terrorists streamed into the room. Her father blocked the way and kept the terrorists talking whilst she and her mother and children fled to another room. This room had a trapdoor in the ceiling. Diana managed to scramble inside the hiding place. She pulled up the two children after her and then tried to pull up her mother. She was too heavy. The door burst open. Diana had no alternative but to hide. Her mother was hacked to death beneath them as she and her children crouched above. Her father was dragged from the house and was missing for six days. The whole of Kenya searched for the missing man. It must have been one of the most nerve-racking experiences that a woman could have endured. The very uncertainty of it, besides the horror of having her mother killed and hearing all the terrible sounds of the murder, would have been enough to have made most women give up in despair, but Diana was tough and brave, and she had her children to look after.

At last her father's body was found. He had been buried alive.

Diana carried on with the heavy burden of responsibility of educating her young children, and not giving way to the sorrow she must have felt. I never heard her complain, or heard a word of self-pity, for either the loss of her husband or her parents. She went on working.

She often looked after young animals and came to visit us. We were friends, although we were both busy people, and didn't often meet. Diana went down from Langata to visit the *Hatari* film set. There was a large lion tied to a tree. She went over to talk to him when she heard that he was an animal she had reared as a cub. Suddenly the two girls she had been talking to heard her raised voice. To their horror they found that the lion was on top of Diana, and had mauled her.

'Get someone to help to get him off,' said Diana, practical as always. One of the girls ran off to get help, while the other bravely tried to push the lion off with a stick. Help arrived at last, but it was too late. Diana died soon after. The family and friends rallied round the children, who were fortunately almost grown up.

It was hard to imagine that Diana had gone. I had seen her only two days before her death. She told me of her plans to call on her friends on the *Hatari* set.

'When you come back, come and see us,' I said, not thinking that I would never see her again. I have to pass her house every time I visit Mervyn Cowie and his wife Val of National Parks. Wherever Diana is I hope she is with the animals she loved.

It is a theory with some people that if you are not afraid of animals you will not get hurt. Animals are less likely to hurt you if they know you do not fear them, but you can still get hurt if you do not take reasonable precautions with them. They may be frightened by some sudden noise and will automatically bite anybody or anything near to them; or an animal will kill for no apparent reason. Such was the case of Diana's tragic death. Certainly Diana didn't fear animals; and she was not a novice in the handling of them. Perhaps if the lion had been in its natural surroundings it would not have mauled her.

I know of a classic example of the fallacy of thinking because one doesn't fear an animal it will not harm one. A serviceman from Mackinnon Road saw his first wild elephant, got out of his car and offered it a bun. He was promptly killed. Obviously the man had only known elephants in zoos. Completely wild ones will react very differently, but it is impossible to generalise with animals.

Many servicemen who came to Africa became interested in the wild life of the country. At an R.A.F. station on the staging route from West Africa to Khartoum the airmen adopted a lion. Leo the lion became a treasured pet. When B.O.A.C. planes came in Leo would be the first to board them. Everyone knew Leo was docile and sweet-tempered. Leo had the freedom of the station, but was put in an enclosure at night.

One night a B.O.A.C. plane was expected to make a night landing and an airman went out to lay a flare path of gooseneck flares in preparation for the landing. Right in the middle of the runway sat Leo, watching the airman at work. The airman walked up to him, pushed him with his foot and told him to move. Leo got to his feet grudgingly and ambled off the runway. On completing his task the airman walked back to the guardroom to lodge a complaint about someone forgetting to lock Leo away in his night quarters.

In the guardroom he asked:

'Why was Leo left outside so late? Who was responsible for locking him up?'

'But Leo was locked up in his enclosure at five o'clock.' The airman, so it is said, fainted.

This story illustrates the point that if you are not afraid you won't be harmed by wild animals, and yet the man who offered the bun to the elephant didn't get away with it.

You can't make hard-and-fast rules about animals. Animals are as individualistic as people. There is a code of behaviour which we all sense in our contact with our fellow men. Animals also seem to have some rules too. But we still don't know many of the laws which govern their behaviour.

If you live in Africa you naturally know some of the hazards of infringing the animal code, but even then pure chance or some uncalculated circumstance can upset your plans.

We have on our staff a dark-haired tall girl called Diana McAvoy. Diana is one of those efficient dependable people who is more than the capable secretary that we engaged. She can face most emergencies, besides being a highly qualified secretary. Diana worked for two former Governors of Kenya. She is discreet and very loyal, as one would expect from someone who is used to diplomatic circles. There is really nothing more hateful for anyone in public life to be unable to relax at home in case their actions are twisted into tasty bits of gossip. There must be times in everybody's life when all goes wrong, the milk boils over, the roof leaks and you say something unprintable.

At weekends Diana often went picnicking. She would take her still camera and with a friend would spend a happy day at one of the many beauty spots where animals and birds abounded.

One Sunday Diana and a friend visited the Ngong Hills. The Ngong face our house. The other side of the Ngong is wild country. There must have been considerable volcanic activity many years ago, for the scenery is creased into valleys and hills. There is even a crater—Longonot. Armand and I have often flown across it on our way back from Lake Nakuru. It is wooded and buffalo can be found roaming under the trees. Diana and her friend saw a whole herd of buffalo just below where the car was parked. The buffalo were quite a distance from them, but out in the open and below. It was a perfect place to take a picture. Diana and her companion got out of the car. They wouldn't have to go very far on foot to get their picture. Both of them looked around before they proceeded further. They were absorbed in taking their pictures when they heard a noise behind them. Diana looked round. She saw a cow buffalo, followed by a calf, coming out of a small clump of bush. It really hadn't been big enough to give much cover. It is extraordinary how large animals can hide in such a small amount of cover and blend into the scenery. The buffalo looked at the two human beings and suddenly her head went down and she was in full charge. Diana started to run, hoping that the buffalo was only demonstrating, which sometimes happens with wild animals. They are apt to charge just to warn you off. Diana ran harder than she has ever run in her life, with her heart racing with excitement and exertion. With horror she realised that the pounding feet of the buffalo were not halting and it raced through her mind that the footsteps were coming ever nearer. She couldn't keep up with the speed of the buffalo and she could not run towards the herd either. The buffalo was just behind her. Diana knew that she only had seconds to live. She did the one thing which could save herself but which needed superhuman powers of courage in case it didn't work. She threw herself to the ground with split-second timing, for the buffalo caught her on her forehead as she fell. Diana's companion, completely unarmed, waved his arms at the buffalo and drove it off as it was about to gore her. Buffalo and calf joined the herd. Any animal with young will take offence, especially a wild one.

Diana's friend picked her up from the ground where she was bleeding and gashed. It was hard to see how badly she was injured. Diana, limping, was taken back to the car. She went straight to hospital. The first we heard of this adventure was when someone from the hospital telephoned us. 'Your secretary was attacked by a buffalo and she is in the European hospital.' All of the Denis staff, including ourselves, went to see her. I rightly guessed her room would be filled with flowers, so I stopped at the Jacaranda pharmacy in Kenyatta Avenue to buy some eau-de-Cologne which the Jacaranda pharmacy made themselves in Kenya. It was one of the most fragrant I have ever used and its odour was lasting. Just the kind of gift to cheer up someone who didn't feel very well.

Diana was sitting up in bed, wounded but cheerful, one eye was closed with an enormous black bruise surrounding it and a graze on her forehead. She was black and blue with bruises all over her. She had headaches for weeks afterwards, but luckily the X-rays showed no signs of other injuries.

I basked in Diana's reflected glory for quite a time. After all, it's not everyone who has had a secretary knocked down by a buffalo.

Perhaps one day things will so improve between man and animals that there will be more contact and less distrust on the part of the animal. In the days of the early explorers they walked through large herds of elephant without being molested. All this changed because of the predatory European's disregard for animal life. Man became an enemy and it is only in the twentieth century that he is winning back his status as a defender of the animals.

Many people have remarkable success in taming an individual animal. Lions, leopards, buffaloes and rhino have become the special pets of some people. Lions seem to be a particular favourite, especially in Kenya, where they are available. A girl called Mfupi kept five lions. Major Taberer, or 'Tabs', of National Parks had a lioness, Iola, who was almost human. More recently there were Elsa, the famous lioness of the Adamsons, and Norman Carr's lions. Several people have kept leopards and cheetahs. With both lions and leopards the owners usually assert stoutly that they have never had so much as a scratch from their pets. Usually they have conveniently forgotten that they have, because it is impossible to keep one of these beautiful creatures without becoming completely devoted to them.

There are one or two people in Kenya who become passionately attached to snakes. I would never harm a snake, but they always seem to be rather dull and limited pets. They don't seem to have the same personality as mammals. But perhaps that is because I have never kept a snake for long enough to get to know it properly.

There was one elderly lady in Nairobi who kept a python which she dearly loved. When people came to tea they were astonished to find its huge body slithering over the old lady's shoulder and into her lap. The old lady was fragile and dainty and didn't seem the type to have that kind of companion!

We have had our own irascible pets.

We had three bears which were the only ones in East Africa. Bears have kindly faces and seem harmless. Appearances are deceptive, however. What passes for kindness is really inscrutability. It is impossible to know what a bear has on its mind, that is why it is one of the most dangerous animals to handle.

Our three bears were from Asia and when we first adopted them they were the size of a fat fox terrier. Nothing could have been more appealing. Even in those days you had to be extremely careful when you were being photographed with them. They always smiled at you, and tried to grasp your hand. You would have thought how good-humoured they were if you hadn't been on intimate terms with them. The smile was nothing other than preparing to impale your hand on their teeth. We managed to find a good home for the twins in South Africa. The third bear we decided to keep because it seemed to have a nicer disposition than the other two. We intended to send to Asia for a lady bear when it grew big enough to want a wife.

Armand and I came back from a long safari with one unit and went off again with the Bartletts almost straight away. We went to Crescent Island, which is at Lake Naivasha. At that time it was like a miniature National Park. The owner of Crescent Island, Mr. Hanmer, took animals under his protection. He left for England and, unfortunately, when the animals lost their good friend they were hunted. Crescent Island could have been a wonderful tourist attraction.

In the days when Armand and I and the Bartletts went down to Crescent Island Mr. Hanmer was still in residence, and he invited us to stay on the island. We set up camp in surroundings which were strikingly beautiful. The lake had hills around it which were reflected in the water. At the time we were there the island was no longer an island, for its size fluctuated considerably with the level of the water, and that year Crescent Island was actually a peninsula. It was still relatively easy to protect the poachers or trigger-happy Europeans. We thought that our pets would enjoy a change of scenery too. It was not an arduous journey to Crescent Island, being mainly tarmac all the way.

Bruin the bear came with us. Armand and I used to give him a loaf of bread, well soaked in honey, when he was a baby, as a special treat. We had neglected to take a picture of this scene, which was on our list of scenes for photographing.

We left Langata in the Land Rover with poor Brucie Denis, our dog, chasing behind us. Tshikadi was cajoling Brucie to come back. Brucie always seemed to know when we were going on safari. We would have liked to take him with us, but dogs are often subject to quarantine regulations because of rabies. Another reason why we were not very keen on taking Brucie Denis was because he barked furiously whenever he saw another dog on the journey. In a confined space there is no noise to equal the penetrating qualities of Brucie's bark.

We arrived at Crescent Island and after greeting Mr. Hanmer

we drove off to the camping site, which was the other side of the peninsula. We then got our first glimpse of Bruin since returning from our last safari. He had grown astonishingly. Bears grow very quickly in comparison with other animals. We had known that they did, but we couldn't have believed our little fox-terrier-sized pet could have grown in such a short time into an animal heavier than Armand. He was all solid muscle, still retaining some of the lovable dog-like characteristics of his babyhood, but I noted with alarm that his eyes had not grown at the same rate as the rest of him. His eyes were small and mean-looking. I began to wonder whether we would enjoy the scenes we had to take. I couldn't imagine anyone in their senses offering Bruin a piece of bread soaked with honey. He looked as though he would much more enjoy a hand soaked with honey. At last we compromised. Des Bartlett produced the bread and the honey, and we decided to give it to Bruin on a sort of fishing-rod device. We found a pole in our equipment, tied some string on it and tied the other end of the string to the bread.

'Try and walk him back to his pen,' said Des.

This is exactly what we tried to do. We got some beautiful action pictures of Bruin taking the bread from the string. That part went well. It was just that he ate it so fast and had finished it before we could be supplied with another piece of bread. We were a good way from his pen and he had finished the bread. The ungrateful brute could only think that we were withholding his favourite titbit. He put his head down and started to amble towards us.

'Look out, Michaela!' shouted Armand.

We both ran. It was a good 300 yards to the only place of safety, which was in one of the vehicles. I ran off as fast as my legs could carry me, too frightened even to look back to see if Armand and the bear were following me. My lungs felt as though they would collapse. I managed to get to the car, tear open the door and leap inside.

Where was Armand?

He was still running, but in the opposite direction, with Bruin in close pursuit. Des was racing along behind the bear with another loaf of bread. It would have been an excruciatingly funny scene if the bear hadn't been dangerous. Des caught up with the runaway at a moment when Armand could not move another yard and Bruin's teeth were only inches away from his legs. Des waved the loaf invitingly under Bruin's nose and beckoned frantically behind him to his wife Jen to bring up one of the Land Rovers, which contained a very large cage on the back of it. I thought to myself it would take several days to get Bruin back into that cage and to transport him back to Langata. Luckily, when he finished off the loaf he gave us all a look of contempt and clambered up into the cage without any urging, curled himself up and went to sleep.

'I suppose you got some good footage, Des, at the beginning,' said Armand.

'The camera had to be reloaded just before the chase, and I had to leave everything to bring up the loaf.'

There is a difference between a baby animal and what it will be when it grows up. If one can bear the inconveience of a large pet, and alter one's way of life accordingly, it is rewarding. It is certainly a talking point, especially if visitors come to one's home at their own risk. Is that why some people keep snakes as pets?

Elizabeth and Derek Erskine are well-known people in Kenya. They were nearly always doing everything they could to help people. Derek Erskine had been in 'Legco',[1] and he had with his partner Duncan in the early days started a thriving grocer's business. He and Elizabeth built themselves one of those beautiful mansions which are such a feature of Kenya. Kenya was in many ways unique in having these lovely homes.

Elizabeth and Derek Erskine have been friends of mine for many years. The Erskines were, as I was myself, pioneers in the principles of multi-racialism! In the bad old days, when you could not invite your friends unless they were strictly European to fashionable hotels and clubs, the intellectuals of the three races of Kenya founded the United Kenya Club. The club's premises were originally in a disused railway godown. If the premises were not palatial, the club was, at least, rich in brains. A remarkable number of the members are today the top people in the country. Many of the old settlers of diehard, blimpish type accused the club of subversive activities.

The club was about the only place in those days where people of every race had a chance to get to know one another. There has certainly been considerable progress since then. Anyone, of any colour, can go anywhere he wishes in the Kenya of today. The only criterion is whether he can pay his bill.

Later the club was moved to a site on Hospital Hill Road. A new building was built and the members moved in. Every Wednesday

1 Kenya's Legislative Council.

the club invited a speaker to lunch to address the members. Many world-famous figures came to the club, including Ralph Bunche and Dag Hammarskjöld who spoke to us a few months before his tragic death.

The club did not stand still, for further ambitious plans were to be carried out. The building was to be enlarged and a residential section added, which was most imposing. The club had grown with the country. The Erskines had loyally supported the whole venture from nine months after its inception when the club's premises consisted of the railway dogown.

Nairobi grew up around the Erskines' home. They are possibly the only people I know who have a coffee plantation in the city of Nairobi. The Erskines kept horses and one day when I was invited to their house I found Elizabeth outside the grounds near the stables.

'Have you seen our ostriches, Michaela?' she asked me.

I hadn't.

They were as tall as hens, being only chicks, striped brown and yellow.

I didn't see the Erskines for some time. Elizabeth asked me when I saw her again whether Armand and I would be interested in adopting the ostriches.

'They scare the horses,' she explained.

It seemed strange that the adorable little chicks should frighten horses, but often small animals scare bigger ones. I was invited to the Erskine home again.

'Come and see the ostriches,' said Elizabeth. 'We have had to put them in a boma [enclosure]. They run after visitors.'

I was taken into the ostriches' enclosure and could hardly believe my eyes. Two enormous eight-and-a-half-foot birds towered above my hostess and myself.

'Are these the same birds?' I asked.

'Yes.'

'Now I understand why the horses are afraid of them.'

They behaved well with my hostess, but I could see they might disrupt one's social life. We discussed ways and means of getting the birds to Langata. It wouldn't be an easy task. Even as we discussed it a dreamy expression came over Elizabeth's face, and I could see she was torn by an inner conflict. Her pretty face, perennially youthful in spite of her grown-up children, told me clearer than words could that the journey we were discussing was a purely theoretical one. She was attached to the birds, and even if it needed a great deal of patience to put up with their sometimes tyrannical ways they were still her chicks.

I didn't press the Erskines about taking the ostriches to Langata. A way of life was worked out for them and their pets.

The ostriches were let out of their enclosure for three and a half hours a day. Then they were taken back to their enormous quarters until next morning.

When one of the gardeners swept up the leaves from the lawn the ostriches hovered behind him, opening and shutting their beaks in a snapping action, possibly eating minute insects. To anyone who did not know the birds it looked as though the gardener was in peril, but they were very friendly towards him because they saw him every day.

As the ostriches grew, the hedge had to be higher to keep them inside. All went well until one of the ostriches swallowed a bone which the dog had discarded on the lawn. (Ostriches will eat nearly anything and this is one of the dangers of keeping them, because they have no sense of self-preservation, and they will eat something which will not go down the gullet in their slender necks. I have even seen an ostrich make an abortive attempt to eat a tin of baked beans with the beans still in the tin.) Elizabeth arranged for a veterinary doctor to remove the bone. The ostrich did not survive the anaesthetic.

The other bird leapt over the four-foot-six-inch hedge and wandered off out of the Erskines' grounds on to the common land, which was between the Erskine Estate and the girls' school, looking for her sister. The Erskine household managed to persuade her to come back to the safety of her enclosure. She seemed to get used to being without her sister and has not wandered since.

Talking of unusual pets, I must mention Piggy Denis. A couple found, during the rains, three little wart-hog piglets in the roadway. When the rains come small animals are often found abandoned or lost by their mothers. The people who found the three baby wart-hogs tried to look after them, but they didn't have much success. Two of the piglets died. They decided they would find a home for the survivor. We were away on safari at the time, so they telephoned our other house, and Des and Jen adopted the little wart-hog piglet. She rapidly put on weight under their skilled care. Piggy, as she was named, grew rapidly. To many people wart-hogs are not the most beautiful of animals, but I fell completely in love with her.

I admired her white whiskers and the warts or protruberances which give the wart-hog its name. She had dainty little feet and a massive head. Her body had an uncorseted look, but her stomach and underneath her arms was of the smoothest skin. She was fond of rolling in the mud, and whenever she saw me she came to greet me, and it was fatal if she had been having her mud bath. I stroked her silky stomach, which provoked her into rolling over on her back, all four little hoofs raised in the air.

She had a remarkable vocal range, most expressive in her piggy emotions. Piggy had tremendous personality, and had very definite likes and dislikes. For some reason Piggy always charged Diana McAvoy, who worked for us. Diana could not cross the garden at our other house without carrying a stick in her hand to ward off attacks. We attributed these attacks to the fact that Diana was a dog owner, and Piggy was suspicious of other animals' scents.

Armand was also charged by Piggy, and was knocked flying. Perhaps she charged him because she didn't see him very often, whereas I went nearly every day to talk to her. I just couldn't keep away from her charm.

Soon after Piggy's adoption a neighbour told us that they could see a small animal down a deep hole in their garden. We managed to extricate the animal, and were surprised to discover that it was a baby hyena. Many people have reservations about the appearance and personality of that animal. I have always liked their looks, although Armand says their shape suggests that they are trying to avoid a kick in the behind. Their shoulders are noticeably lower than their hips, which gives them their strange gait and their slightly cringing look. Their eyes are magnificent, both large and lustrous. They can never quite bring themselves to look at you. Their jaws always look moist, as though they are drooling over some tasty morsel. Their teeth and jaws are extremely powerful. The normal food of hyenas in the wild is the bones from the carcasses which are left by lions and leopards. The hyena is not averse to eating baby animals. It rarely attacks an animal which is able to defend itself, which is probably why it has few friends. Even the most extreme hyena lover is revolted at the behaviour of hyenas when antelopes are giving birth. The hyenas follow the herds in large numbers, awaiting their opportunity to seize the newly born baby before the mother has recovered from giving birth. At such times the hyenas are grossly fat and squalid-looking, appearing intoxicated from the glut of easily gained meat.

Our own hyena looked respectable, but perhaps it is easy to look respectable when you have an easy life and are not forced to fend for yourself.

A hyena's fur is one of its good points and gives our own a cuddly appearance. He is covered with thick soft fur even on his paws. There are two types of hyena, the spotted and the striped. Ours is spotted, but when we first adopted him he was completely black, with very much shorter fur. He looked far more doglike than he does today. Hyenas are very emotional. Stinky, as the Bartletts call him, although I preferred the name Hy, had a short straight tail which expressed a range of emotion from excitement, when he flipped it almost to touch his backbone, to the emotion of fear, when it went right down and clung between his legs. He was passionately fond of handbags! One day during the taking of some still photographs he interrupted the photographic session when he ran off with my handbag. He was very annoyed when we took it from him, and burst into a clamour of protest.

Even when he was tiny he had the characteristic voice of a grown hyena. When I heard him call I used to imitate the sound and he answered me. Sometimes it was not my voice which performed this doleful duet but the voice of a hyena somewhere down in the valley.

I can never get over the sheer joy of living in a house where you can hear the sound of so many wild animals at night. Hyraxes, hyenas, lions and the occasional leopard, to say nothing of the frogs and cicadas!

12

The Witching Hour

I AM often asked what part does witchcraft play in modern Africa. My answer is that it still plays a large part. Even the most modern Africans in public life may patronise a famous witch-doctor. There is a celebrated witch-doctor called Kabwera. He lives ten miles on the Nairobi side of Malindi, on the coast. Very illustrious people, indeed, consult him. There is hardly an important African in Nairobi who does not know the name of Kabwera.

Around Dar-es-Salaam, in Tanganyika, is a large area of witchcraft-permeated territory. Being a witch is hazardous. A witch may be attacked and beaten to death by an angry mob. Occasionally the newspapers carry exotic items such as 'Witch-doctor demands talisman back from court.' The talisman was a human thumb! Young children have occasionally disappeared to be the *pièce de résistance* at a witches' banquet.

Belief in witchcraft is widespread in Africa, and it is not only amongst the Africans that the belief is held. I have heard many stories of witch-doctors' powers from people who were not credulous individuals. Undoubtedly auto-suggestion plays a part in the practice of magic, and most witch-doctors, if they are any good, are skilled psychologists. Many are herbalists. Not all witch-doctors use corpses or practise cannibalism to further their art.

I have known many witch-doctors because I am interested in psychic research, and it is always fascinating to have an interview with them and talk shop. Tshikadi tells me that I have the reputation of being a witch-doctor myself, and I have often wondered whether that is why I live happily and safely at Langata.

Our servants live in a house across the garden. Every night when they finish work, usually not later than eight o'clock, I wave good-bye to them from my kitchen window, watching to see they get safely home. They always appreciate this care, because we are not only in an area where wild animals abound, but occasionally suspicious characters may be on the prowl. We have an askari, or night watchman, but I still like to be sure that all is well with our people.

It was in the days when John was alive and well. He and Tshikadi were saying good-bye to me. I saw looking over John's shoulder a young man closely resembling him, but about six inches shorter and much younger. I asked John who the young man was and described him. From their expressions I could see that my servants were filled with awe.

'That is my brother,' said John. 'He died several years ago. He was exactly as you described him.'

Another incident which is inexplicable, but which helped my reputation, occurred with another servant. Tom (he was one of the successors to John after his death) was near his house. I was just going for a walk with Armand when I distinctly saw a man with a moustache, dressed in khaki clothes with an old brown felt hat on his head, walk purposefully into Tom's room. I had never quite trusted Tom and neither had Armand. He was inclined to do things without asking permission to do so. Such things as taking several buckets of hot water from the main house, leaving us no hot water for ourselves.

'Armand, a man went into Tom's room,' I said.

I ran to the house so that the man should not escape, and flung open the door. A well-dressed young African woman was sitting there. It was quite late, and it was obvious she was going to stay the night.

'Where is the man who just came in?' I demanded.

'Which man?'

Tom, thoroughly alarmed, came into the room, Armand following behind him.

'Where is the man?'

I described the man, giving every detail, because I had seen him very clearly, his height, his expression and the minutest detail of his clothes. The girl jumped up from the bed where she had been sitting and would have run out of the house if Tom hadn't gripped her wrist. They spoke quickly in their own language, then Tom turned to me and said in Kiswahili:

'You have described her father and she is afraid to stay here. Her father is dead.'

'Tell her,' I said to Tom, 'that her father's spirit will not hurt her, but you should not have guests staying in the house unless you ask permission first. I should always see anybody who stays here.'

At that time Tshikadi always told me when he was going to have a visitor, and took me across to the servants' house to introduce me. Our work-people may have friends and relations staying with them, and I am not against it, as long as I know that nothing is being done behind my back. It is for their safety as much as for ours. Terrorism would not have gone to such lengths if employers had taken more interest in their employees' private lives. Very few employers bothered to see just how many people slept in their servants' quarters.

Sometimes it was hard to believe what went on. Two or three years ago, in Nairobi, a lady had been exceedingly kind to her servants. She was well off and she had bought her servants land, a sewing machine, a radio and had helped them with the education of their children. One evening the police knocked on her door.

'We want to raid your servants' quarters,' said the policeman.

'Whatever for?'

'We believe they are holding oath-taking ceremonies.'

'I don't believe it, 'said the lady. 'My servants have been with me for years, and I am quite sure they would not even dream of such a thing. They have everything which they could conceivably want.'

The police officer, nevertheless, insisted on the raid. What he saw made an entertaining picture for the front page of the newspapers. A man sat on the floor stark naked, looking over his shoulder in amazement, obviously taken by surprise. An oath-taking ceremony had been in full swing and the lady's trusted servants were taking oaths at the time of the raid. She must have been a very sad woman after the news was broken to her. If servants are with you a long time they become part of your family, or so it is with me.

Many attempts have been made to link Mau-Mau with witchcraft. Undoubtedly Mau-Mau leaders have tried to incorporate some of the elements of witchcraft into their own ceremonies, just to impress the gullible peasants who will eat and drink *and* do the most filthy things, and pay a fee for the privilege of doing them.

In Kenya perhaps the largest and most influential group of witches live in Kamba country. There are both male and female witch-doctors. The female witch-doctors are very powerful. Witchcraft runs in certain families, not unlike our mediums of the Western world, who are nearly always descended from a long line of mediums. A mother must hand down her knowledge of witchcraft to all her daughters. This power was, in turn, given by her own mother. To deny or withhold such knowledge to a daughter is a sign of grave displeasure. A mother once refused to instruct her daughter in occult knowledge. The grandmother, when she heard of this deprivation, gave the grand-daughter the information. The witches have local variations as to when the novices are given the knowledge. Some are not given it by their mother until after the birth of a child. In some places female witches kill their first-born baby.

The initiate witch is distinguished from the other girls of her age group at circumcision. She is cut seven times by her mother, in seven different places. The places are the tongue, navel, genital organ, both buttocks, both breasts. Sometimes the wrists are cut instead of the breasts. After the seven cuts a short ceremony is held. Each tastes the other's blood and then they eat food together. It is then that the girl is told by her mother that after she has given birth to a child she will be shown how to use her power.

There are many strange objects carried in a witch's bag. The Wakamba witches possess a small container usually made from sisal fibre, the tail hairs of an animal and human hair. In this container is kept the powder called 'muthea'. The witch-doctor uses the muthea in various ways. If he or she wishes to do harm the witch-doctor blows this mixture in the direction of the intended victim, at the same time muttering curses.

Some witch-doctors may use an object made from three small seashells stuck to a piece of stick of the Kiandui plant. This is believed to cause ulcers. Animals' horns hollowed out contain various powders. Teeth and claws of animals, in particular the ant-eater, hair, and nails of corpses, miniature bows and arrows, owls' eggs usually of great age, dried frogs, elephants' excreta, marbles, stones, especially blue, are other ingredients of witchcraft.

When a wave of protest sweeps the Wakamba country a drive is started to stamp out witchcraft. A big pit is dug and the witches come forward and throw their witches' bags into it. The objects are then burned by the police.

The number of witches grows at a fast rate, especially since the introduction of modern medicines, when the witches' offspring are also subject to the same rules of overpopulation, caused by survival, as the rest of the world.

One day an old Mkamba going as far as our general store asked me for a lift in my car. He was carrying something which looked like an old-style carpet-bag. He was slim and tall, and had a fine face with chiselled features. I hadn't seen him before, but I gave him a lift and we chatted together. He had something almost aristocratic-looking about him. The old gentleman said:

'I have come here on a business trip and to visit my son. I live at Machakos.'

I couldn't think what kind of business he could be conducting, but as if in answer to my unspoken question he continued:

'I have a great deal of business in this part of the world. I wait until there are several jobs to do, and then I come down every few months. It is nice to see my grandchildren too.'

He told me about his grandchildren and how they all went to school. He asked me about myself and I told him what we did. I reached the garage and asked the Mkamba assistant to fill up my car with petrol, and check the oil and water. I noted that he looked at the car with considerable respect. 'Was I transporting a chief?' I wondered. I took the old man next door to the duka or general store and it wasn't until the next day that I saw the garage assistant.

'Do you know who you were transporting yesterday?' he asked me.

I shook my head.

'He is a very famous witch-doctor. One of the best, and he comes from the village next to my own.'

There is a famous witch-doctor who lives at Molo. Some friends told me about him. One of their servants had lost his wrist watch. It disappeared in highly suspicious circumstances. It could only have been stolen by one of the other servants. The police were called, but they were unable to pinpoint the actual criminal. My friends called in the witch-doctor. They had heard a great deal about him. They were most disappointed when they saw him. He arrived on a bicycle in an old army overcoat, shoeless, with army trousers, and bicycle clips round his ankles. He was most unprepossessing. How could he have achieved his enormous reputation? Anyway, my friends decided to try him out.

He listened to their complaint.

'It will cost you a hundred shillings if you want me to find the thief.'

My friends decided that it would be most unwise to have a thief in the house and that the money would be well spent, but would he be able to deliver? There was quick consultation between husband and wife. They agreed to pay. Besides, they were curious to find out how he would conduct his enquiries. When the fee was paid the witch-doctor unstrapped the bag which was attached to the carrier of his bicycle.

'Is there somewhere I can change?' he asked my friend.

She suggested he should go to the kitchen. The witch-doctor locked himself in and before he closed the door told her to assemble all the servants and to form them in a circle outside the house. This she did. After half an hour the witch-doctor emerged. A very different man, indeed, from the one who had locked himself in the kitchen. He was resplendent in feathers and paint. He wore a skin apron and carried a rattle. The only reminder of his former garb were the bicycle clips round his ankles, which had rattling amulets tied to them.

The witch-doctor moved into the centre of the circle. He started to chant and move his head from side to side. Then he appeared to grow in stature, even to my friends from their vantage point outside the circle. His eyes rolled back to show only the whites for a second or two. He seemed completely entranced. He danced slowly backwards, in a circle within a circle. He then moved forward to a man in the group. It was almost as if he were no longer in a trance, for suddenly his voice came quite naturally, and quietly, and he had only one request to make.

'Hold out your hand.'

He put some powder into the outstretched hand of the man in front of him. He then moved forward to each man in turn. He waited then for five minutes.

'Hold out your hand again,' he said to the men.

He had reached the third man when the next-door man but one keeled over in a fit.

'There is your guilty man,' said the witch-doctor. 'Carry him to bed and in the morning he will give you back the wrist watch.'

No one could say how it had been done, not even my friend. They could only assume it was some kind of auto-suggestion from the thief, who had an unswerving faith in the power of the witch-doctor.

Besides witch-doctors in Africa there are many prophets.

The District Commissioner in a certain district was surprised to find one day an enormous crowd gathering. They all carried buckets, and one man and his wife were carrying a foot-bath.

'Do they expect it to rain?' he thought to himself.

He called his assistant.

'What's happening outside?' he said. 'Send one of your constables and see if he can find out what it's all about.'

From his window he watched the crowd. The constable, neat in his navy-blue jersey, was talking animatedly. The watching man saw several of the crowd point to the sky and everyone was looking upwards. A tousle-headed woman pranced forward. She was shouting in a high-pitched voice, her skinny arms gesturing. The constable came back to the office of the administrator, where he sat with his colleague and assistant.

'This woman who is dancing,' said the constable, 'has told the people that ten-shilling notes will rain from the sky in another half-hour.'

The administrator jumped up from his seat.

'What are we waiting here for? Bring out all the forty-four-gallon drums you can get hold of. We are wasting our time in government service.'

The constable smiled.

'Everyone will be very disappointed, sir,' he said.

The dancing woman had disappeared by this time. The administrator sent out the constable again to see whether he could locate her. He didn't want the prophetess to come to grief if her prophecies were not fulfilled.

The crowd was getting even bigger. Some people had brought food with them. One or two had transistor radios with them. It is one of the fascinating aspects of Africa that the twentieth century rubs shoulders with the fifteenth, and somehow nothing seems out of place.

The excitement of the crowd mounted as zero hour approached. There was no sign that the heavens would open and that the ten-shilling notes would shower down, unless the large black cloud which was forming could be considered as being loaded with the promised money. Zero hour arrived. After ten minutes the mood of the crowd changed to dejection, and on the fringe of the crowd little groups started to shout threatening slogans. As is usual with a mob, it is very easy to turn its head. Suddenly from quiet dejection it became a screaming, howling monster bent on venting its disappointment on the false prophet and her disciples. The administrator was reaching for the phone to get help when nature intervened. There was a sudden dramatic burst of thunder and a torrential downpour. It is hard to retain one's fury when it is cold and wet.

The crowd dispersed helter-skelter, running in all directions with their buckets and receptacles. The next day all the animosity was forgotten.

False seers and seeresses can always cover their failures by saying that their instructions were not carried out faithfully. It is not Africa alone which has the monopoly of these prophets, for it was not so long ago that a whole gathering of Europeans sat on a hill-top, awaiting the end of the world, which was supposed to take place at a precise time that day.

'But do the witch-doctors believe in their own powers?' asked Armand.

'I am sure they do. They would be no good if they didn't.'

At one time Armand and I lived for a few months in Paris. We had an apartment on the Rue Tronche—which runs between Printemps and Madeleine. This street for some reason was well liked by the gypsies. They were dressed in traditional gypsy costume. Long skirts, blouses with full sleeves and bandanas round their heads. They were always stopping people on the street and pleading, whining and cajoling them into having their fortunes told.

Armand was looking out of the window one day when he saw a large crowd of gypsies with someone in the centre. He decided to investigate. He went down in the elevator the two floors to street-level. He crossed the road and, being much taller than anyone else in the crowd, could see over their heads to the heart of the crowd. I was in the middle of the group reading a gypsy's palm for her. As I talked she nodded her head in agreement. The other gypsies clamoured to have their hands read when I had finished. After that whenever they saw me they would hasten to consult me.

'Obviously they believe in palm reading,' said Armand.

The witch-doctors in Nairobi vary in the size of their practices, just as any other doctors do. There is also another important category. The same kind of person as Armand's lawyer's son in America.

Armand asked him what the boy was doing, and the lawyer answered:

'He is a psychiatrist, but,' he added, 'he is no ordinary psychiatrist, in fact he is a psychiatrist for psychiatrists.'

So there are witch-doctors for witch-doctors!

A witch-doctor near a small country town which we often visited in Kenya, because nearby was some splendid bird life, consulted me. He asked the porter at the hotel whether he could speak to me. The porter, looking thoroughly frightened (did he think I had offended the witch-doctor?), said:

'There is a man outside who wants to speak to you.'

I thought perhaps the visitor had brought in an animal to be adopted by us. The gentleman outside was very well dressed, although I thought it was a mistake, sartorially, to wear a bright red sweater with yellow corduroy pants.

The young man said, 'My father wants to see you.'

'Why?' I asked. 'What can I do for him?'

He lowered his voice. 'It is very important.'

'Why doesn't he come to the hotel with you?' I asked.

'He doesn't want to be seen. You see,' said the son, 'I am a witch-doctor and my father is too. A much better witch-doctor than I. He keeps on having a very bad dream. It worries him very much.'

'Can he not cure himself?' I wanted to know.

'Nothing has been able to help him. He wakes up screaming whenever he has it.'

'What makes you think I will be able to help him?'

'It is well known in Nairobi that you can talk to spirits.'

It was news to me and I wondered who had been reading *Psychic News*.

'I'll try to help.' The young man at my side in my car was as colourful as a macaw. He directed me along the road. I wondered what I had let myself in for, when we turned on to a track which was filled with pot-holes. I drove with great care, not wishing to have the long walk back to the hotel if I did some damage to the car.

We passed several huts until we came to a much larger one. Outside it sat two sturdy African women dressed in handsome cottons. The man pointed.

'That is my mother and my aunt.'

I stopped the car and ran out to open the door for him, as the handle was rather stiff. He spoke to the two women in his own language. He continued in Kiswahili.

'Come inside and wait for him.'

I went into the house. There was a card-table with a gaily embroidered tablecloth on it. On the table were some carefully arranged, beautifully clean cups and saucers. There was also, surprisingly, a photograph of an African soldier in uniform.

'That is my father's brother,' said the young man, as he saw me looking. 'He was in Burma in the big war.'

The hut got darker as someone blocked the entrance with his body. I looked up to see an elderly man entering. I got up to pay my respects to him, and he motioned me to sit down on one of the two chairs with which the house was furnished.

'Does your father speak Kiswahili?' I asked the son.

'Hallo, how are you?' said the witch-doctor in English.

I answered him in the same language, but it was obvious from his expression he had exhausted his English vocabulary on me.

'Your son tells me you do not sleep well at night. What is it that you see when you sleep?'

'I see myself in a small wooden room. The walls seem to move in on me and I know I am going to be crushed,' replied the old man.

I sympathised with him. I suffer very much from claustrophobia myself.

'When did you start having these dreams?' I asked.

The old man sat and thought carefully before he answered.

'It was when the mother of the mother of the girl outside came to visit us. She often used to look after me a long time ago when she lived in this village.'

'She must be an old woman,' I thought to myself. I was almost certain that the clue could be found in the childhood of the witch-doctor, in something that was connected with the old lady. I would have to be very careful in my interrogation in case the patient and his family thought she had bewitched him.

Someone ran off to get the old lady, who came back bent and wrinkled and smelling very strongly of beer, although it was quite early in the day. After placing her in a chair I sat down solemnly. The witch-doctor had conjured up five or six more chairs, and the hut was rapidly filling up with spectators to see what I was going to do. I asked the son to act as my interpreter.

'Does she remember your father as a small boy?' I asked.

The question was repeated, and it was answered by the old lady and several other people who had managed to insert themselves into the rapidly filling hut.

The old lady, I thought, looked rather apprehensive, and I tried to put her at ease—a doubly difficult job when all we said had to be put through the interpreter. She, it was obvious, had also considered the possibility of my trying to blame her. In my own mind I thought it highly unlikely that it would be her fault if the witch-doctor had a bad dream, but it might easily be connected with that period of his life, when she had been around every day. The sight of her again might easily trigger off some mechanism in the mind, recalling a painful episode long since forgotten. Had not a similar long-forgotten incident given me my pathological fear of water?

When I was two years old my mother and grandmother had taken me to the beach. Mother and daughter installed themselves in deck-chairs with magazines and chocolates.

The fact that my grandmother was a pessimist of fanatical dimensions probably saved my life. In the midst of a magazine romance she suddenly screamed not only to my mother but to the whole beach, 'Where's the child?' and then to my poor mother, 'You wicked woman, you have no right to have a child in your care!'

My mother and grandmother set off to try to find me, with several sympathisers. I was nowhere in sight. By this time my mother was also thoroughly alarmed.

Then a schoolboy pointed towards the water's edge.

'What's that sticking up over there?'

The grown-ups looked. My mother ran without a word to the water's edge, her motherly instinct instantly telling her that her child was indeed over there and in dire danger. It was fortunate for me that her reflexes were fast. She saved my life.

Some children had dug a deep hole in the sand, which they had filled with sea water. They had most probably been called for tea by nanny or mother, and left the hole.

I presume that I wandered off from my mother's side, because I have no recollection of the incident. I fell head first into the hole, with my two little legs sticking up, and the walls of the hole fitting snugly round my body, my arms pinned to my sides. My mother dragged me out of the hole only just in time. I was a very peculiar colour, but I was still breathing.

From that time onwards I have never quite trusted the water. The thought of water covering my head is especially terrifying.

I could never account for this unreasoning fear until one day my mother asked me whether I remembered the incident. I didn't. But I am sure that it is buried deep in my subconscious. Because the terror was so great it was the best way for my mind at that age to cope with such an experience. Nevertheless the lesson had been learned. Be careful of water.

To return to the old lady. 'When this man was a little boy did you often see him and his mother?'

'Yes.'

'Was he ever in danger?'

The old lady tried to remember. She mentioned one or two incidents.

'Did he ever get shut in anywhere?'

'He got shut into a schoolmaster's cupboard a long time ago. He was there for a long time. The schoolmaster's dog scratched at the outside of the cupboard. We opened the door and took him out. We thought he had finished dying. He stayed with the schoolmaster and his wife that day and came back to stay with his mother two days after. He was quite better.'

'Why was he shut in the cupboard?'

'He was only a small boy. He went inside the cupboard thinking it was a little room, and the wind blew the door shut. We left the room to go into the garden.'

'And then?'

'We missed him, but didn't think of looking in the room with the cupboard.'

The old lady tut-tutted to herself as she thought of the near tragedy all those years ago.

'Did you hear what the old lady said?' I asked the witch-doctor.

'Yes, it is a terrible thing. But why don't I remember it?'

I didn't think I could satisfactorily explain the workings of the subconscious, but I tried. The witch-doctor seemed to understand my explanation, but the rest of the crowd looked blank.

I took a coin out of my handbag. I held it in my hand. I commanded the people to sing. After some discussion as to who should start, a woman's penetrating soprano soared upwards to the thatched roof. The others raised their voices in harmony. Surely this is one of the most unique gifts the African has, to create such stirring harmony?

I closed my eyes and whispered to myself, 'Go, bad dream, go.' I really meant what I was whispering. I moved over to the witch-doctor. I danced slowly in front of him. I made a couple of passes in his face and then blew in it. I touched the top of his head and went through movements of drawing out an invisible object. I then ran out of the hut and threw the 'object' into the fire which was smouldering just outside.

There was a great ululation and a renewed burst of singing. I pressed the coin into the witch-doctor's hand. It had a hole in the middle, as our East African ten-cent pieces have. The witch-doctor produced a cord from his pocket and threaded it through the coin. He hung it round his neck and solemnly shook my hand.

Which would keep his bad dream at bay? My explanation of the forgotten which haunted him, or my talisman?

Since a child I have been what people call psychic. For many years I had no idea that such a word existed. When I was tiny I used to see people who had died. I thought everybody could see them. I remember how astonished, and at the same time shy, about it I was when I found my companions could not see the people. I only knew they were dead because I had once been playing with a small girl. She was three or thereabouts and with her was a little boy of three. I wanted to include him in the game, but she couldn't see him. Her aunts came in in at that moment.

'Why can't we play with the little boy?' I asked her.

'What little boy?'

'The little boy over there,' I said, quite surprised that she didn't see him either.

'What does he look like?'

'He has dark hair and is wearing a yellow shirt and grey trousers. He has hurt his arm. He is pointing to it. The cut is just there.' I drew a line along my arm. Even as a small child I could see that the lady had turned white. I wondered why she looked so ill.

She started to cry and ran from the room. I was even more surprised, as I thought at that time that only children cried, and I had never seen a grown-up burst into tears.

I went on with the game with my friend. We went into the room where the lady was sitting with the little girl's mother. She was talking to her sister and hadn't seen us come in.

'But it was unmistakable, she described him exactly.'

'But surely Doris told her.'

'Doris never met Freddie' said the aunt. 'Don't you remember that he died when we were living in Manchester? Even you didn't know about the cut on his arm, did you?'

Doris's mother shook her head in wonder. They saw us then and stopped talking about it, but I remember that I thought there must be something strange about the little boy I had seen and why didn't the others see him? After that, similar incidents used to happen, but I usually kept quiet about them!

13
How do you do this Magic?

WITCH-DOCTORS have their enemies. Some Churches are jealous of their power, and would be happy to see them and their arts disappear and be forgotten. I myself have nothing against witch-doctors as long as their ingredients are vegetarian and their practices do not inflict cruelty on animals or human beings.

Why not register witch-doctors? Fraudulent people could not then pretend to be witch-doctors when they are not.

A rich African was sitting in his house one day. There was a knock at the door. The rich man's wife opened it. Outside stood a well-dressed man. 'I want to speak to your bwana.' The rich man got up from his armchair.

'What is it?' he asked.

'I have a business proposition. I have power to make money multiply tenfold. It is a magic power I have inherited.'

The rich man listened. It sounded incredible, too good to be true. He thought to himself, 'I'll make a test with a small sum.'

'How do you do this magic?'

His visitor said, 'I cannot tell you exactly, but I can only show you with some actual money.'

The rich African made an appointment with him to meet on a waste piece of ground. That evening he told his wife.

'I shall be back in two hours. If anyone wants to know where I am say you don't know.'

The other man was already waiting at the rendezvous.

'Are you going to try this magic?'

'Yes,' said the rich man. 'Here is ten shillings.'

The sorcerer took the note and from his pocket he removed a little plastic container. He said some magic words, and dug a hole in the ground with the panga he carried, then he put the note into the plastic container and put the money into the hole. He covered up the money and stamped on the ground seven times with his foot. 'Come back here at the same time tomorrow evening,' he said.

He and the rich man left the waste ground and each went their separate ways. The rich man felt mildly excited.

'I should have done it with five shillings instead of ten,' he thought to himself.

The following evening he was back again waiting for the sorcerer. The man was not there. The rich man was in two minds whether he should dig up the plastic container, or perhaps the sorcerer had already done so?

Just as he had almost made up his mind that he had been robbed of his ten shillings he saw the sorcerer approaching. The man squatted down on his haunches beside him. The man carefully dug with his panga in the spot where they had buried the money, and produced the plastic container. It looked thicker than the day before. He snatched the container from the other man and opened it. Sure enough, there was 110*s*. The sorcerer got up.

'You can give me ten shillings,' he said to the rich man, 'that is my fee for multiplying your money.'

He made as if to go. The rich man clutched his arm.

'Can you perform this miracle as many times as you want?' he asked.

The sorcerer nodded.

'Will you meet me tomorrow?' asked the rich man. 'I will give you more money.'

'Meet me here tomorrow and I will do this magic again.'

The rich man could barely wait until the morning when the banks opened. He was delirious with excitement. He went to his bank as the doors were opened, and drew out 5,000*s*. in ten-shilling notes. It made a bulky package.

That evening the sorcerer was waiting for him. The money was handed over to him and he stuck it into a plastic container. It barely fitted in, but when it was covered up to the sorcerer's satisfaction he dropped it into the hole again, and went through the same performance as he had done with the ten-shilling note.

'Come back tomorrow at the same time,' he told his client. The rich man was there the next evening. The sorcerer hadn't arrived, but, remembering his first experience with the ten shillings, he was not unduly alarmed. He waited for half an hour, then an hour, then an hour and a half. It was a deserted place and suddenly he felt unaccountably frightened. A rat scuttled from a pile of rubbish into the thick grass near some abandoned machinery. He could bear it no longer. With his hands he dug at the place where the money had been buried. The earth came up quite easily because it had been loosened when they had interred the package the previous night. As he dug deeper the earth became hard. He had excavated the loose earth, and there was no sign of the money they had put in, let alone any multiplication of the original amount. The rich man rubbed his hands together to try to get some of the dirt off, and picked his way carefully over the waste ground back to the road.

He went back to his house and told his brother what had happened. His wife overheard what he was saying and as she was a friend of mine she told me about it.

'Why doesn't he go to the police?' I asked her.

'He is afraid of looking foolish,' she replied.

A month or two later I read in the newspapers an account of court proceedings against a self-styled sorcerer. The elements of the case were almost identical with that which had befallen my friend's husband. The man was sentenced for his crime.

If witch-doctors were registered, things of this sort could not happen.

An organisation has been formed of those who wish to register a society for the abolition of witchcraft. This seems to be going too far and where does one draw the line? It would be wrong to forbid mediums to practise. If a careful analysis was made of witch-doctors there would be several categories. Some would prove to be skilled herbalists whose art would be well worth studying. Others would be found who had undoubted psychic powers, more like our spiritualist mediums.

Kenya has not only its witch-doctors to represent the mystic side of life, but it also has several spiritualist groups amongst the Europeans and Asians.

I used to sit every Sunday evening with a group of Brahmins. The séance was held at the home of Mr. Jamnadas. Mr. Jamnadas read the two famous publications for spiritualists, *Psychic News* and *Two Worlds*. There was an account of one of my psychic experiences in one of these publications. When Mr. Jamnadas realised I was in Kenya he telephoned me. We had quite a long talk on the telephone. He sounded a very nice man. At that time I was burdened with a colossal amount of work. Although I was interested in the circle of Mr. Jamnadas, and felt honoured that he should invite me to attend it, I just couldn't spare the time. A month or so later I was doing my hair. My thoughts were very far from anything of a spiritualistic nature. I was suddenly aware that an Indian lady was standing slightly to the left and in front of me. She directed me to call Mr. Jamnadas straight away and go to his séance. I called Mr. Jamnadas and arranged to go the following Sunday. I had never met him.

He met me on the threshold of his house. It was a beautiful house, which was built Asian fashion, with a courtyard inside the entrance and with rooms leading into this centre. There was a staircase on one side. Mr. Jamnadas held the séance in his room which was upstairs.

He had several sons and they and their wives lived in the other rooms. The family met in the large dining-room for meals. There was a reception room downstairs for formal occasions.

Before I went upstairs, and after I had introduced myself to Mr. Jamnadas, who was tall and slim, I told him why I had called him. I described the Indian lady.

'Would you recognise her photograph?' he said to me.

'Yes.'

Upstairs I pointed straight to a photograph. 'That is the lady who came in and told me that I should get into touch with you.'

'That is my wife,' he said.

I often saw her when I went to the Sunday séances. I knew she had some trouble with her leg, for she told me so.

One day in the middle of the week she urged me to telephone Mr. Jamnadas. 'There is an anniversary.' I didn't ring him. Partly because I was very busy and secondly because, although I see these apparitions and have some communication with them, I am a sceptic.

That Sunday I asked Mr. Jamnadas about the anniversary and the day on which his dead wife had appeared to me.

'I got the urge to call you in the middle of the week.'

'I nearly called you on that day,' said Mr. Jamnadas. 'It was an anniversary. A very important one for us. It was the birthday of my first son. I almost called you to come over and celebrate with us.'

One of the Brahmins gave trance addresses and I often saw scenes; several people used to come to the séance and listen outside the circle. I sat in the middle with the brahmans, some four or five of us altogether. There were flowers in the room and incense was burned. Promptly at a certain time a red bulb was put into the electric light socket so as to dim the light, and we would clasp hands and Hindu prayers were chanted.

But it was not only during the circle itself that the results used to come, but often before or after the séance. All the people who came were strangers to me. I prefer that it should be so, because there is nothing then forgotten which you might have known, and which comes to the surface when you are in a self-hypnotised trance.

I described minutely the young man who had been killed when he had ridden down a steep street on a bicycle and had crashed into a vegetable stall. There were some Sikhs who instantly recognised the scene as that of a relation's death. All the details were correct, except that he had been on a motor-cycle instead of a bicycle, as I had seen it.

One day a distinguished-looking Indian gentleman who was passing through Nairobi came to the circle.

I saw an Indian lady. A name was spoken into my ear several times which I tried to push out because it was the name of someone I always try to forget. After the séance I described the lady, and gave the name, slightly mispronouncing it because I could not quite bring myself to say it.

'You have described my wife in the clothes in which she died and also you have her name almost correctly,' said the gentleman.

She had the name of the person whom I wanted to forget.

There were many other incidents. Perhaps the most remarkable was when another visitor from India, whom, of course, I knew nothing about, attended. The room was darkened—the séance commenced.

Afterwards, when the normal lighting was resumed, I turned to the stranger and said:

'You will probably think this is idiotic, but I saw Gandhi standing beside you, and he was holding in his hand a wide gold ring with a diamond set in the middle. I don't understand why I should see this, but I know it is something connected with you and no other person in the room.'

I didn't even know whether the man knew Gandhi. He said

something to Mr. Jamnadas in Gujurati and then he turned to me and said:

'I was a very close friend of Gandhi.'

One of the Jamnadas household left the room and then came back holding something in his hand. He opened his hand and there was the ring, wide, gold and with a diamond in the centre, just as I had described it.

'I left it here with Mr. Jamnadas' family because I am going on safari tomorrow,' said the visitor. 'As it is one of my most treasured possessions, I didn't want to risk losing it when I was on safari.'

I am often asked if Armand takes an interest in psychic research.

Yes, he does, but not in an active manner. He is just merely interested. He is not mediumistic, but his mother was.

Armand's mother and I instantly liked one another, which is rare with mother and daughter-in-law! It was almost as though we recognised something in ourselves which bound us closely together. I loved Maman very much. She had a tremendous sense of humour, and a lively mind. Also, Mother-in-law had many psychic experiences.

My sister-in-law as a small girl was swinging in the playground of her school and fell off the swing. The heavy wooden seat swung forward and hit her on the head as she sat on the ground. It knocked her unconscious. A teacher was sent to tell mother-in-law about it.

My mother-in-law was dressed in her outdoor clothes, and was running up and down in front of the house trying to get a cab. When the carriage drove up to the house my mother-in-law ran to the schoolmistress before she could even alight.

'Is she all right?' she said. 'Take me to her at once.' She knew that Angele had had an accident and that she was unconscious.

Armand and I together experienced a remarkable psychic phenomenon which at times became rather a nuisance. As I have explained, our house is built with the living-room upstairs, and the bedroom and workrooms downstairs. It is a spacious house.

Often we have been in bed and heard footsteps above. They then go downstairs and up again. As there are so many burglaries in our area (there were as many as four in one month in our road alone) we have to investigate. Armand and I get up, and room by room we search the whole house. There is absolutely no sign of any living thing. Ginger, the cat, and the dogs are in the room with us, so we know it is not our animals' footsteps. Anyway, the footsteps are not those of an animal, they are quite definitely and distinctly human, but there is no one there.

This has happened very often and we simply daren't risk not investigating it in case the noises are caused by burglars.

One week we heard the footsteps, and about three nights later, just as we were in bed, we began to talk about the mysterious visitor, and then about psychic phenomena generally. I told Armand how there had been some psychic phenomena, similar to the activities of poltergeists, when I was very young. As we were discussing the noises I used to hear, the throwing about of china and the thumps and crashings, there was a roar through the house almost like that of an express train going through a tunnel.

Armand and I (we had not put out the light yet) looked at each other in awe.

'Michaela, you never do things by halves, not even poltergeists. Maybe you had better not talk about it. It seems as though you still can conjure them up. I've never heard such an appalling row. It is likely to give us both insomnia for life.'

Armand looked at his watch. 'A quarter past eleven, that must be your zero hour for psychic phenomena.'

The next morning we read in the newspapers that there had been an earthquake at precisely a quarter past eleven! So much for poltergeists at Langata.

More people are becoming interested in psychic research. I am even told that there are serious scientific investigations being carried on in Russia.[1] That there should be some recognition of extrasensory perception is a sign of progress. Psychic phenomena has been so well documented, and its occurrence all over the world has been so widespread, that it is no longer permissible to dismiss it.

Those people who have seen or experienced it are often first-class scientists who would have no earthly reason for inventing the episodes. They are interesting enough people without having to make themselves more so by fabricating evidence. There are certain areas where psychic phenomena are more prevalent. Scotland is one such place and Africa is another.

When I first arrived in Africa I had an absolute conviction that I had arrived home, even though I had never set my foot on African soil until I stepped from the plane.

Armand and I have a considerable fan mail. Many of the letters

1 Work is also going on in America, England and other countries.

concern psychic matters. I had a request from one lady to consult a witch-doctor about her son. By the same mail a parcel arrived from the same lady. I tore it open and inside was a schoolboy's cap. With it was a note which said:

'Please take this cap to a good witch-doctor and let me know his opinion about my son.'

People write for talismans and I have had several palm-prints sent to me to give a reading of people's hands. I always stress that I don't believe in it, but Armand explains to people who want their hand read by me:

'Although Michaela doesn't believe in her own powers, she is always terribly accurate, and I advise you to be careful if you have any secrets.'

The hand seems to act as a focus for one's thoughts. Perhaps it channels the psychic faculty towards its subject, and reveals something of them. It might even be a sort of psychometry, the art of holding an article and then having a series of pictures or impressions about the owner of it.

I had no idea that I could psychometerise articles, but a long time ago a spiritualist friend asked me to hold a little gold watch. I immediately told her its whole story. She knew quite a lot about the origin of the watch and its former owner. There was quite a terrifying association attached to the watch which I knew nothing about. I described in the greatest detail all the people involved. My friend recognised the people I described, and the houses and scenes which I saw. After that, whenever I met a group of spiritualists they usually gave me something to hold, to see what impressions I got from it. I have no theories as to what causes these series of vivid vignettes. Why should one person be able to paint and another one not? There were also theories on why the artist should be gifted, including the hereditary factor. The same undoubtedly applies to mediumship.

I was browsing through some newspaper cuttings of the East African Newspaper Group. They and the *East African Standard* kindly permitted me to use their library. I have always had the highest opinion of our newspapers in Kenya. The feature articles, as well as the news coverage, are of the highest calibre.

At one time I used to collect newspaper cuttings of particular interest to me, but I found that I was getting swamped out with newspaper cuttings. There was really so much worthwhile material to keep that there was just not enough space to keep it all in an ordinary house. I also found that the secretary I had at that time became so engrossed in the job of pasting the clippings into the scrap-books that her other secretarial chores got neglected.

One day I was looking for something else when the photograph which illustrated an article caught my eye. The cutting was headed '*Sunday Nation*, 10th June 1962'. I started to read the article. I recognised the style as that of Margery McGrindell. I found out later that she had indeed written it, and from her and the editor of the *Sunday Nation* I have obtained their kind permission to allow me to reproduce the article—here it is.

'It was a dull-looking flattish circular piece of mutton fat jade about three inches in diameter, and of two interlocked animals.

The jade was acquired in 1946 when a young married couple were furnishing their Hong Kong house.

She bought something else and the shopkeeper insisted she should buy the jade piece as well, which to keep him quiet she did, for seven dollars fifty.

She didn't bother to display it. It simply lay around in her bedroom.

Some time later the woman and her household intended to rest in the hot afternoon. Her small son and ayah were in the next room to her, on the third-floor bedroom. On first and ground floors the servants rested. The heavy front door was locked and bolted, as were two iron gates beyond it.

Finding the heat unbearable, the woman undressed, and, standing before her dressing-table, she was surprised to see, in the mirror, her bedroom door slowly and quietly opening. Swinging round, she was horrified to find a very old Chinese man. He was an old coolie. He wore a faded blue-grey cotton shirt with sleeves just below the elbow, and dark blue trousers extending to his calves. His white beard was then wispy and long.

The naked woman was too appalled to move, but the man paid her no attention. He glanced quickly round the bedroom and examined the mantelpiece. He touched nothing.

As he turned his back on the woman she regained her sense, grabbed a dressing-gown and rushed into the child's room, from where she sent the startled ayah for the servants. But her room proved empty. Vainly the servants searched the house. The front door was still locked and bolted.

Rickshaw coolies at their stand in front of the house were questioned. No one had seen the iron gates open or anyone enter.

A year later the couple left Hong Kong for China, from where they were evacuated with a minimum of belongings. Between this time and 1950 they packed and re-packed suitcases in India, South Africa, England and Europe. Finally they came to Kenya.

One evening the woman turned out a few small boxes and discovered the jade. At the sight of this she decided it was best to furnish their Nairobi house in Chinese style. She intended to concentrate on acquiring Chinese antiques. She placed the jade ornament on the lounge table.

Through her interest in these antiques she heard of an overseas visitor with similar interests staying in Kenya, and invited him to the house.

"Where did you get this?" he asked avidly, picking up the jade piece as soon as he entered the lounge.

He would have liked to have it, especially as the woman did not value it. But for her instantaneous dislike and distrust of the man, this woman says, she would willingly have parted with her ornament.

Throughout the evening the visitor tried to win over the woman, and on rising to depart slid his hand over the jade. But the hostess grabbed his hand.

"A damned good try, wasn't it?" she remarked, tactfully laughing off the incident.

But the man's action roused her interest in the ornament. Especially when he persistently telephoned and later visited the house again to acquire it.

She had the ornament taken to the British Museum and received the following letter:

> "The jade ring is not at all easy to date. It is archaic in style, but I would doubt if it is earlier than Ming, although I admit it might be as early as Tong. As you may know, there is practically no date material for comparison with pieces of this time. . . .
>
> Signed BASIL GREY
>
> Keeper, Department of Oriental Antiquities,
> British Museum."

Thus the letter established definite antiquity and value of the piece.

Then a few years later came the incident of the psychic Karen resident. She went to our woman's house for a séance and immediately her attention was attracted to the jade ornament. Holding it thoughtfully, she advised the owner not to part with it.

The stone was very old and valuable she said. It had passed through many hands during its existence, and had been stolen from its rightful owners on several occasions. The present owners must watch it carefully. Already there had been one attempt to take it from them and another thief would try also.

The Karen woman was well known for her ability at psychic automatic writing, where messages are received presumably from spiritualist mediums or persons who have died.

The medium fell later into a trance.

On her pad she illustrated Chinese houses, costumes and horsemen. Intrigued, the owner of the house read through reference books in the Han dynasty in 206 B.C. The horsemen and their clothes she found complied with accounts and illustrations of the Mongol invasion of north China under Kubla Khan in A.D. 1260.

There were other scenes which the jade owner was able to connect with Chinese history, though it took her extensive research to do so.

The Karen medium had not been to China, and claimed to know nothing of its history. But most remarkable, together with the medium's statement that an attempt had already been made to steal the jade, was her description of one of its previous owners from whom the stone also once had been stolen.

This was an old man, a poor man, she could see his coolie hat, his faded old blue grey shirt and dark blue cotton trousers, his beard was long, white and wispy.'

I sat thoughtfully at the desk. The woman in the story was Vanda Bishop, wife of Air Commodore Bishop, and the medium? It was I.

Margery had not used our names because I had been out of the country on one of our filming expeditions. They had wanted to go to press, and they had not had time to get in touch with me to seek my permission. Naturally, I would have given it.

14
Magazine Widow

IT IS strange that big events are sometimes unheralded. If I had only known that a casual meeting at a party in London would be responsible for making me a magazine widow! Armand and I had always been together. That unheralded meeting at a friend's house doomed us to long partings. Armand continually went on business trips without me.

One of the business interests in which I was not included was the chief editorship of a magazine. This was particularly irksome, as it had been my idea to have a magazine. Strange, also, that the dangers of editorship should be considered more hazardous than all the other dangerous jobs I had undertaken with Armand in the past!

Was this going to be the pattern of our life from now on? Would I for ever have an absentee husband? When friends asked me where Armand was, half the time I didn't even know his address, for he was for two days in one place, three in another, twelve hours in another and so on. I was acutely embarrassed at the way things had turned out.

Once someone was rude enough to say, 'Are you and Armand still together?'

'No, but I am a magazine widow.' I made a joke of it. It was the only thing I could do.

After its successful launching in England the magazine was going to be launched in Australia. Armand would be away for some time. Armand said good-bye to me and I was left alone at Langata. It didn't worry me much except I missed him. I was not a nervous person and in spite of the number of burglaries in our road I slept like a log.

The Bartletts in our other house were on safari. My neighbour opposite, an African politician, was also on safari, but the fact of not having any close neighbours did not disturb me. I was perfectly able to look after myself. The Bartletts paid one of their brief visits to Nairobi and I was very happy that they were there, for another misfortune occurred.

One night I suddenly awakened and the room was going round. I felt desperately sick. I staggered out to the bathroom and my legs would hardly carry me there. I came back to bed and my head was aching so much I literally couldn't keep it on the pillow. I could barely see. The house was bolted and barred. I felt so terrible I wouldn't have been surprised to find that I was dying.

My one fear was that the Bartletts would decide to go off on safari early in the morning, and that the dogs and cats would be locked in the house and starve to death, if I really was dying. I forced myself out of bed, hanging on to the walls in case I fell. I managed to stagger to the phone. It was in the middle of the night, but I felt if I left it another minute it might be too late. I telephoned the Bartletts. After a long interval Des answered the phone.

'Des,' I said, 'I feel very ill. Please don't go on safari unless you see the dogs and Ginger are let out.'

'I am coming straight away,' said Des.

My legs were buckling under me by this time, but I managed to unlock the door and I got straight into bed. Des kindly made me a cup of tea, which I drank without milk or sugar. The very thought of anything solid filled me with nausea.

The next day we called the doctor and I was ordered straight to hospital, where I stayed for nearly a week. I felt as weak as a kitten. When I came back I was completely drained of strength. All I wanted to do was sleep. I got a tremendous welcome from the animals.

I got back into the routine of the household and quickly recovered. I still don't know what my mysterious illness was, although the doctor thought it might have been one of the strange 'influenzas'. I am sure that many new diseases are constantly evolving because of the suppression of their natural enemies, various small antibodies which are destroyed by antibiotics.

I made a quick business trip to England, then returned to Kenya alone.

I had some good news to cheer me up. Armand was coming back to Kenya for two and a half weeks. I spent three or four days at my sewing machine, and having the house painted to welcome him. It was almost like a honeymoon to have him back again. I put out of my mind the fact that it was only for two and a half weeks, but this idyllic period inevitably came to an end.

I said good-bye to Armand at the airport and returned to my solitary existence.

The time would pass quickly because I have many interests.

I was in Nairobi on my weekly shopping expedition when I noticed a man approaching. He had for many years been a great admirer of mine. Unhappily, now that he knew I was a magazine widow his attentions had become more pressing, as he thought his chances had improved. In fact it was quite embarrassing for me. I was in a main street and realised that the admirer had seen me. I pretended I had not seen him and fled. I dashed into a side street and promptly tripped over the kerb, falling flat. I put out my hand to break my fall. A red-hot pain seared my hand. I leapt up and ran into the nearest shop, which happened to be 'Tropicals', a pet-shop kept by some friends of ours, the Matthewses. I hid behind their tropical fish tanks, the fish weaving in front of my face as my admirer came quickly past the shop. I was thankful he didn't see me. The Matthewses were very concerned about my hand. They washed the dirt off and insisted that I should have a hot cup of tea, which made me feel right, although I still felt shaky.

I went to an auction, where I had promised to bid for an article for Phil. I didn't get it, unfortunately. I drove on to the supermarket to buy my week's supplies. I took out my cheque-book at the cash desk. I couldn't hold the pen. My fingers were absolutely nerveless. It was an odd sensation to will oneself to hold something, and find the message from the brain was not obeyed.

I managed to scrawl something with my left hand.

'If the bank queries the cheque get them to call me at my house,' I suggested to the assistant, who kindly filled in the amounts for me.

'You'd better go and see a doctor right away,' she advised me.

It was lunchtime. I telephoned my doctor, but she was not in her surgery. With difficulty I drove to the hospital. There was bound to be someone on duty in the Casualty Department there.

The doctor was expected in a quarter of an hour, so I sat and waited. As I sat in the waiting-room I had second thoughts about seeing the doctor, and would have fled if the nursing sister had allowed me. Inevitably I heard snatches of conversation between the nursing sisters.

'It's a suspected ruptured kidney,' 'Send him down to Surgery,' etc. Perhaps I was making a mountain out of a molehill with my hand. I would be overcome with shame if it was, after all, only imagination. Anyway, I waited. A young pretty woman doctor came in to see me. She examined my hand and ordered an X-ray. Having pictures taken of me was part of my job, but this was hardly a photograph which I could send to fans.

Yes, my wrist was broken and for the first time in my life I had a limb in plaster.

'Do you think you can drive yourself?'

'Yes, I think so. The people haven't come back from lunch yet and the streets will be relatively quiet.'

I hadn't realised how much I used my hand in talking, and what a menace I was now I had a dangerous weapon on one wrist. Not only that, I hadn't realised what a nuisance it was to take a bath with one limb held aloft. Naturally it was my right wrist. In the mornings I chose what I would put on for the day, only to discover that I couldn't get my arm through the armhole. I discovered that there were only three garments I could wear in my whole wardrobe.

I would never have imagined that I could write with my left hand. It is extraordinary how we can adapt ourselves. Within three days I could write rather shakily but no one else could read it!

I even managed to sew with my left hand.

Many of my pursuits soil my hands, gardening is one of them. I met a friend whom I hadn't seen for a long time, and to our mutual amusement we found we both had hands in plaster.

'How long have you had it on?' I asked her. Hers looked snowy white, and mine looked as though I had been burrowing through the earth like a mole rat.

'Eight weeks,' she said.

'How did you keep the cast so clean? Do you keep it in cellophane at home?'

My friend laughed.

'I'll tell you my beauty secret,' she said. 'I put white shoe-cleaner on it.'

I immediately bought two tubes of it.

At this time I knew Armand's address for the next week and I was writing him a letter every day. I was thankful I had learnt to type. I would not have been able to write any long letter with my left hand, but I found that I could type, especially if I used my right elbow for the space bar.

It was quite painful at night, but otherwise it did not incapacitate me too much. I even went to a big dance. I found my picture on the front page of the newspaper next day, twisting energetically and making the uhuru sign with fingers which were barely visible in the top of the caste.

Strangely enough, the most difficult of all tasks was one of the most prosaic. That was to eat my boiled egg in the mornings.

I decided I really couldn't manage without a secretary. I have had various secretaries, three of the best being Betty Jones, Audrey Reid and now Sheila Tuckwell. These three come into the category of the perfect secretaries. Betty left Langata to go to Embu with her husband. Audrey was obliged to return to England where her husband was going on an officers' training course, but Sheila at that time was unhappily very much in the future.

I put an advertisement in the newspaper and was inundated with replies. One dear lady begged me to take her.

'Salary is no object,' she said.

'What is your shorthand speed?' I asked her on the telephone.

'Shorthand . . . ?' Her voice faltered. 'I don't do shorthand.'

'What is your typing speed?' I asked.

'Will I be expected to type?'

'I am terribly sorry,' I said. 'I need a qualified secretary.' I nearly added—and one who has brains.

Another lady came to see me, who nearly cried when I told her that living thirty miles away from Langata would prove difficult for her. She was a great fan and I had the utmost difficulty in persuading her not to buy a car especially for the job, or to have her move house nearer.

Many international bodies met in Nairobi.

I attended the International Union for the Conservation of Nature conference. I was permitted to speak, and from the reaction of the delegates I knew I had contributed something worth while. I was helping my adopted country of Kenya and helping also to promote

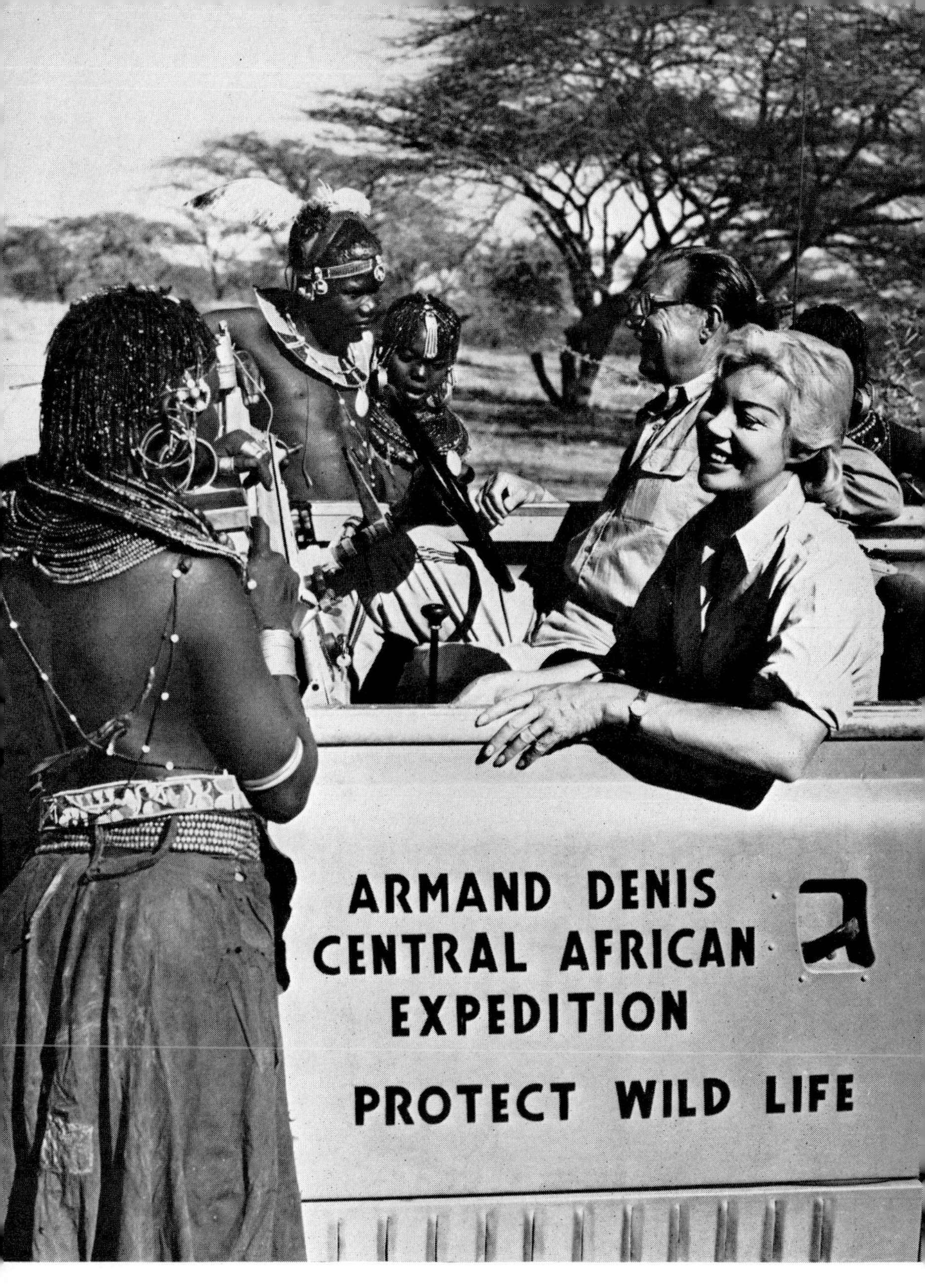

29 One of the Sukhs speaks Kiswahili and asks where we live

30 Masai woman and child

31 The elegant coiffure the young Masai warriors (Morani) is attended to b one another

32 Ila-Tonga woman smokes her pipe and nurses her baby. Ila-Tonga are the people who were evacuated from Zambezi to higher ground when Kariba was built

(*over*) 33 Our car drives past and elephant mother ushers her baby into thick bush

34 The old lady is reputed to be over ninety and was rescued from slavery many years ago by the British

35 Field Marshal Mwariama makes his first public appearance from the forest

36 Young Njemps baby-sitter shares a joke with me

the conservation of natural resources, which is a world problem. What more fulfilling thing in life could there be? I knew, also, that I was on the threshold of reaching out for something worth while, and far more important than my personal preoccupations.

At the conference I met friends both old and new. Mr. Asibey from Ghana was there. It was good to see him again, for he started his career as a forester. His minister also attended the conference. I thought how splendid the two Ghanaians looked in their national costumes. Dr. Vincent and Len Stuart were also friends we had met at other times. Len Stuart was from Southern Rhodesia. There were people from nearly every large country. Ian MacPhail, of the World Wild Life Fund, and his talented wife Michel, who is a famous musician, were there; their son Ian attended the conference.

Many of the delegates were pioneering in their countries the idea of the conservation of natural resources and wild life. Such a conference was vital to them in focussing their efforts. Not only did they gain moral support from the assembly but much useful advice from experts. To me it was completely fascinating to see so many specialists in one room.

I got to know the Russian delegates and was fascinated to hear about the wild life in Russia and how it was being conserved.

Such a conference emphasised the importance of experts of every nation getting together. No artificial barriers should be created by politics. Basically the world has the same problems. Overpopulation with its consequent abuse of natural resources makes it imperative that the men who know some of the problems should be able to exchange ideas.

There was only one sad feature in the conference and that was that the South African delegates had not been allowed to attend. The brains assembled in the City Hall conference room at Nairobi had nothing to do with ethnic background or creed. It gave the lie to any justification for racialist policy. South Africa had given freely of its experience in the scientific field. Science and the arts should be above politics.

I was delighted to find that I followed all the discussions, some of them highly technical, without any trouble. I felt I learned more in attending the conference that day than I had learned for many years. Some of the eminent scientists who recognised my great interest promised to send me scientific papers. What astounded me was that most people assumed I had some kind of scientific background myself.

'You *must* have been to a university, Michaela,' one doctor said to me. I was as flattered as if he had mistaken me for Madame Curie!

One of my greatest friends is Muriel, Lady Dowding. Muriel is a born leader of public opinion. She is beautiful and dedicated to the cause of animal welfare. She is not a passive lover of animals and neither is her husband Lord Dowding, the great hero of World War II, the much-respected chief of Fighter Command. Both these two fine people have fought selflessly for animal welfare.

Lady Dowding was concerned about the way cosmetics, if kept for any length of time, became rancid. She investigated their components and discovered to her horror that many contained ingredients made from animal derivatives. In many cases the ingredients had been obtained, with extreme brutality, from animals. For example, I quote Dr. Harry R. Lillie, who has been on whaling ships:

> 'We are in an era in which man has earned the reputation of being the only selfish destructively cruel animal the world has ever known. And of the widespread suffering he inflicts in his exploitation of his defenceless fellow creatures for money, one of the most degraded industries of all is whaling. It is carried on for the production of margarine, soap, lubricants and cosmetics, for all of which there are ample vegetable sources that could be used.
>
> The whales, warm-blooded, up to over ninety feet long and weighing over 100 tons, are the most majestic of animals. With explosive harpoons it may take over an hour of the most incredible suffering to tear and blast the life out of one of these magnificent inoffensive creatures, and we are deliberately wiping out the lives of 50,000 of them every year.
>
> Are you still indifferent? Then try to imagine a horse with explosive spears driven into its stomach and made to drag a heavy butcher's lorry through the streets of one of our cities while it pours blood over the roadway, until, an hour or so later, it collapses. You may then have a slight idea of what a whale goes through.
>
> With an International Commission supervising the industry from headquarters in London, we in Britain stand indicted for the callous neglect of our obligations over the years—for our

failure to take adequate care of the creatures living on this planet with us and dependent on us for their welfare. We have failed to set the example and to insist on an end to cruel standards of behaviour.

Retribution is already on the way for mankind. Our materialistic golden age of the infliction of suffering on others is in its twilight. But there may still be time to make some amends.'

Lady Dowding was so concerned about this situation that she founded a society called Beauty Without Cruelty. Several of her friends joined it and I was greatly honoured when they asked me to serve on their committee.

Beauty Without Cruelty stands against the wearing of furs. Animals suffer a terrible and slow death in the cruel traps set for them. Many an animal has gnawed through its own foot in its agony to try to escape, tearing at the sinews and self-inflicting hideous wounds. The picture of an animal in a trap with its cheeks sunken in and its teeth bared through starvation is a haunting one.

I was wearing a handsome leopard nylon coat in a big London department store. The shop assistant eyed it enviously, and finally could not contain commenting on it.

'What a beautiful coat,' she said, 'but then I suppose that as you live in Africa you can obtain all the leopard skins you want.'

I shook my head and said, 'This is nylon leopard.'

The girl was astonished and blurted out, 'Why, can't you afford a real fur coat?'

'The cost is too high but not for me,' I answered.

Luckily, I had in my handbag one of the pamphlets with photographs of trapped animals. I produced this and showed it to the girl. She went white and looked quite sick. She faltered.

'I had no idea that anything so horrible could be permitted. I will never wear a fur coat again.'

15

Michaela's Diary

AFTER anxious months of waiting Armand returned to Kenya. Before he left we had to discuss some business questions. I hated to bring business up during his regrettably short visit, but it had to be done. First and foremost I asked Armand if he would object to my having my own programme called 'Michaela's Diary'. There was someone waiting to finance this project, and on my brief stay in London I had already started looking for staff.

I thought that as he was doing three programmes of his own, and was now going to spend several months out of Kenya, it would be a good thing for me to be busy. I didn't want to retire. Armand was dead against my doing programmes by myself. He said it would hurt 'On Safari'. I agreed I wouldn't go ahead with my plans. My first loyalty was to our joint programme.

It was then that I made the discovery that Armand was more important than my career.

Armand departed and was fêted everywhere. He had a wonderful time, although it must have been exhausting. His letters to me at this time read like a royal tour. There were whole series of personal appearances, radio and TV broadcasts and newspaper interviews. Armand was in his element. He sounded so happy that I felt very happy for him. He had no idea how long he was going to be in each place. I wrote very frequently, and was much alarmed when his letters to me stated that he had no news from Langata. I started to send copies of my mail to two or three addresses. Eventually he got the letters.

I went on with my gardening and looking after the house,

attending my committees and writing (yes, I do write my own books and articles). I was perfectly happy, especially now I knew that Armand was doing a wonderful job of promoting his magazine.

I am not the kind of woman who gets bored or sick of her own company; there were always too many things to do. My happy state of mind was suddenly shattered. People stopped me in the streets of Nairobi to say 'We are sorry to hear you are leaving Kenya.'

'Leaving?' I said. 'Never, unless the post office folds up.'

'Why the post office?'

'Because my manuscripts have to get safely to the publisher and the TV films also have to reach the labs, but why do you say I am leaving Kenya?'

'It is in the newspaper. Your husband is going to buy a house in western Ireland.'

'It is the first I have heard of it.'

I thought either Armand had been misquoted or my informants had misread the newspapers. The next week I was inundated with letters from people who wanted to sell us a house in western Ireland.

I was really alarmed. Did Armand intend to sell the house over my head? Did he intend that I should sit outside in the roadway with all my beautiful antique furniture around me?

What was maddening was the fact that I could not get in contact with Armand. I am passionately attached to my house and garden and even more passionately attached to Kenya. I decided to ignore the rumours.

Armand would certainly find some way of letting me know of such a drastic step, even if he did it by carrier pigeon. I still have not got to the bottom of the mystery of the Irish rumours.

A month later everyone was asking me when we were going to move to Switzerland. 'Armand has a house there. Don't you know?'

There were many stories as to why Armand and I, for the first time in our lives, were not travelling together. One was that Armand had left. Another was that I had left Armand. Another was that we were not married.

When I was shopping a woman edged up to me and said that she wanted to hear the worst.

Our staff at Langata were hard at work. The business interests of Armand Denis Productions were expanding in all directions at once. Armand's firm was now going to supply pictures for photographic books under his name. He had made a deal with some Americans to supply film for programmes in the States. He had *Animals* magazine and he had fallen in love with being an author. His first book had been published under the title *On Safari*. I was very touched that he had dedicated it to me. He wrote on my copy: 'To Michaela, brave as a lion. With love, Armand.' When he was away I often read his book. It seemed to bring him nearer to me.

I met Cynthia and Syd Downey. They had a sad event to report. There was a leopard on the prowl again in Langata. Leopards often attack and devour dogs. The leopard was active in our little valley. The Downeys' house was further up the valley and they had lost a cat. A leopard had killed and eaten it. The Downeys were very upset about it. It was a nice old cat which had been in the Downey household for many years. I always locked the cats up very carefully at night. Kitty-Kat, our beautiful white Persian, usually stayed in the house with Ginger. It was she who had been Jacky Jackal's companion. Kitty-Kat was a large, gorgeously beautiful Persian, with long snow-white fur.

She was also highly intelligent.

I called all the cats in one evening togive them their food. It was half past five. Dogs and cats are fed in a certain order. I called and called. There was no answer from Kitty-Kat. She was a talkative cat and whenever she heard her name she answered me. Kitty-Kat, unhappily, went off fairly far from the house. One of her favourite places was near a look-out Armand had built overlooking our beautiful Ngong Hills. Kitty-Kat used to sit on the wall. Often she ventured even further away from the house, and on my walks with the dogs I had even found her halfway down to the river.

When there was no answer from Kitty-Kat I feared that she might be in a snare. Pet animals are often nearly choked to death in these ghastly weapons of torture, which can be bought for a few pence. A slip noose is made in a piece of wire or clothes-line and any animals which are unfortunate enough to pass that way can be slowly strangled, or have their legs cut to the bone, or even amputated. Dogs or cats have been known to lie for days in agony, and when found the murderous piece of wire is embedded inches deep in their flesh, and the wound is usually festering by then.

It was getting dark, and still I called, and there was silence.

There was no moonlight that night. When the moon is full our valley is lit in pale blue colours. Moonlight nights are the traditional nights for dancing in Africa. For then the people can see what they are doing, and the spectators can enjoy as much as the dancers. But that night, as twilight turned into night, a black velvety blanket descended.

I knew that I could not rest unless I looked for my pet straight away. It was a risky procedure. Not only is it the most likely time to walk into a leopard or a lion, or even tread on a snake, but if anyone is up to something illegal, then such a dark night is ideal for them.

I had no gun in the house. In the old days when I was alone I slept with a revolver under my bed. I had never fired it, but Frank McRae, who kept the garage up the road, had explained its mechanism. One day during my ill-fated trip to England I had opened the newspaper, and there on the front page was a small news item to say that Armand had paid a fine for forgetting to renew the licence of the gun. Armand gave the gun in to the police. I was therefore without a weapon.

I couldn't spend time worrying about whether or not I should go, I was going then and there. If Kitty-Kat was in a snare the sooner I searched for her the more chance she would have of being rescued. I put on my thick safari walking shoes, took a stout walking stick, one of my favourites, given to me by my gardener, and pocketed my torch. I set off into the black chasm which was the valley on such a night. A voice spoke behind me.

'You mustn't go alone,' said Tshikadi. 'It is dangerous.'

'Thank you. You are a good friend.'

Tshikadi knew the danger as well as I did myself. I felt a great surge of gratitude. Truly my servants were far closer than servants, or even than friends. A brother would have done the same.

We went down the steep path in inky darkness, the feeble finger of torchlight barely poking a hole in the opaque darkness. I had never ventured down to the river even after six o'clock. There were rustles in the undergrowth which we passed, but no one could know whether they were made by a large or small animal. It might have been the noise made by a small rodent not much bigger than a mouse, or it could have been the soft-footed tread of a leopard. Every time I heard such a rustle I flashed the torch to see if it was Kitty-Kat, too weak perhaps to answer. From time to time I called her name.

We walked halfway down to the river and then along the straight path which Kitty-Kat used. There was no answering sound, only our echo. We turned back again, greatly saddened. Tshikadi knew how much I loved my cat. There was something special about Kitty-Kat, because she had been the wild foundling, and she had become more affectionate than any of my other cats.

That night I fell asleep in a state of darkest depression. The next morning I asked Kamunia, Ngure, Tshikadi and Jamesie to look for Kitty-Kat. It was Kamunia who came to me with the news.

'I have found something.'

'What is it? Is she in a snare?'

'There is nothing left only white fur.'

'Take me to it,' I asked him.

Together we retraced the route I had taken the previous night with Tshikadi. There in the long grass by the path, barely five yards away from where we had ended our search, were several patches of white fur. I touched it, hardly believing the sensation I felt in my fingers, and trying to conjure back Kitty-Kat. It was no use—she had gone from this earth for ever. I searched to see if there was any more of her body left, but there was nothing.

The leopard may well have been only five yards away from us when we had gone on our search, and, catlike, had sat quietly aloof as we called and searched. If Tshikadi and I had gone any further we could have stumbled into it.

I grieved for several days about the loss of Kitty-Kat. That evening the plates for the animals' food were put out and someone had put Kitty-Kat's plate with the others. It was hard for us to realise that our friendly cat was gone.

I was working at top pressure during this time in writing this book. I had given myself very little time to finish it, because I had to leave Kenya on the night of the 12th, the night of uhuru. I was, therefore, delivering the book two weeks ahead of the date-line. For relaxation I was busy on my beloved house.

At one time we had a mongoosery in the garden. This structure had started off as an enclosure, with a stone wall some four foot high. It was quite long and wide, as all our animal enclosures are, and Armand and Des had built a stone edifice which looked something like an artificial anthill. The mongooses had long since departed. When Minnie died I had never really fallen in love, completely, with another mongoose. I admired them all, but it was almost an unthinkable act of infidelity to fall in love so heavily with another. I decided that it would make an ideal aviary for my parrot and our tame crow.

It became a tall cage with a doorway. I planted red Mexican ground orchids around it, striped grass as tall as an elephant at one corner, giant honeysuckle and other flowering plants. I had a sort of dovecote made to give the crow and parrot shelter. A little pool was made for them to paddle in and to use as drinking water. You would have thought that it was a perfect paradise for birds. But the parrot and crow thought otherwise.

Perhaps the parrot had been attacked by some mysterious ailment, but it became ill and died. I took the crow to our other large aviary where it could have company. We tried to let it go, but it didn't want to leave these comfortable quarters. There were trees in this aviary, and any inmates had the illusion of freedom but complete safety.

The mongoosery aviary was now empty. I decided it would make a perfect place for a shade house. Ngure and Kamunia, my clever gardeners, helped me with my plan. We stoned the ground, and round the walls made deep irregular beds of earth, held in place with boulders. We dug out one or two stones from the floor, and replaced them with ferns, begonias, African violets and many other plants both indigenous and exotic whose names I didn't even know. The pseudo anthill we hollowed out in places and planted in the rocks plants which cascaded down their sides. Creepers grew over the top of it and palm trees grew inside.

Phil, my friend, had bought in an auction a lovely wrought-iron plant holder consisting of two shelves with a delicate filigree of iron leaves. Phil decided that this piece of garden furniture was too large for her balcony. I bought it from her and it was absolutely perfect in my shade house. Or should I have called it my 'conservatory'? It was hard to know what to call this blessed spot.

I bought two wrought-iron chairs and put some tall legs on a long narrow coffee-table also of wrought iron, which I had never used and had intended to auction. At very small cost I had made a perfect outdoor writing-room completely cat and dog proof, and having the advantage of giving me constant inspiration in my work. If I got stuck for words I had only to look out towards the Ngong

Hills in the background and my ornamental pool in the foreground. It was a perfect arrangement.

I also had my lunch there every day. As I am a vegetarian and nearly always have salad for lunch there were no problems of serving hot food. Passers-by might have wondered why Michaela Denis was sitting in a cage, but they would not have wondered for long, for I was artfully planting a traveller's palm, and a gigantic aloe in the one place where spectators from the road could glimpse me.

My other piece of building had been more difficult, although technically it was simpler. Our house had two very large garages on the ground floor. Armand had taken one of these as a workroom for himself. The other garage was even larger. It was intended for our safari vehicles—the Land Rovers. In all the time the house has been built the Land Rovers have occupied their garage less than six months. For the last ten years or so our safari vehicles have always been kept in the grounds in the vicinity of the other house. My own garage was near our servants' house.

I had wanted for a long time to take possession of this lovely, challenging space. Armand said he wanted it as a workshop when I asked him for it. For another few years the unused room had contained a screwdriver, three sets of walkie-talkie sets, bought from Army Surplus, which didn't work, and innumerable and sometimes unidentifiable junk.

When Vanda's husband died I bought her Chinese collection of antique furniture. I had an uncontrollable compulsion to do so. I had often been there for séances at her house and it seemed like a desecration that the pieces should be parted one from another. They were steeped in some kind of personality of their own, almost like animate objects. I had nowhere to put the furniture. My house was completely furnished.

'May I put them in your garage?' I asked Armand.

'If you must,' he shrugged.

I put them in, fitting the priceless objects into what was then a rat's paradise. Rats scuttled across the floor and built their nests in the only built-in cupboard in the room. When we were away Des and Simon, our assistants, exterminated thirty-seven healthy happy rats which were eating their way through several old magazines. They knew if they waited until I came back I would want the rats escorted off the premises, where they would probably plan a return the next day.

I bought several other Chinese objects and put them into the garage. Then Armand went away. Before he left I said:

'May I tidy up the garage?'

'I wish you would,' said Armand.

I engaged myself a Kikuyu workman.

All the completely useless things were sent to the auction. Spares for cars which long since had been sold were sent off to the commercial district of Nairobi for sale. The walkie-talkies were sent off to the workshop in our other house, and I had constructed two cupboards up against the garage doors. I put hardboard over peep-holes made in the doors. We had some very nice windows, for Armand had never quite made up his mind whether this place should not be a room! I designed pelmets with a Chinese pattern, and painted them black and gold. The walls I painted white, and the concrete floor I painted black, and highly polished it. It looked really sumptuous.

I put in a Chinese lantern with carved betasselled dragons, and celestial beings painted on the silk panels. I then arranged the carved black wood furniture. I had one magnificent cabinet which had been bought from the Petit Trianon (the Nairobi one). Many years ago two Frenchmen built a replica of the Petit Trianon at Muthaiga, a fashionable suburb of Nairobi. This was the kind of exciting thing which happened in Kenya. One could not imagine many countries where people would be so inspired, or so daring, as to attempt to copy such a masterpiece.

The marble had been imported at a staggering cost. The building had risen and for many years the Frenchmen lived in royal splendour. Then one of the friends died. The survivor sold up all the superb antiques. The building was purchased and then presented to the nation by the Sorsbies, whose public spiritedness will go down in the history of Kenya. The Petit Trianon was renamed the Sorsbie Gallery, and was used to encourage local artists to exhibit their work. The Chinese cabinet had been bought by Vanda. Now it stood in my Chinese room. It was in good company.

The fact that the room looked like a garage from the outside added to the piquant character of it. Inside the room was so authentically Chinese that one could imagine oneself in China.

I looked forward to the time when I should take Armand by the hand and say:

'I want to show you something in the garage!' . . .

I had kept my promise not to make any structural alterations in the house. One couldn't call paint and two built-in cupboards and pelmets structural alterations! The screwdriver was solemnly put into one of the built-in cupboards. I looked forward to building Armand a workshop. I was already planning it if he would let me.

After a hard day's work I usually slept very well. Ginger, the cat, decided that he didn't always want to sleep in the bedroom with me and the three dogs. One night he knocked a vase over. I didn't even awaken. I had often wondered what I would do if there was an attack on the house, or if someone tried to break and enter.

The dogs had sporadic barking bouts with canine friends who lived a few miles away, but this didn't seriously disturb me. At about three o'clock one morning the dogs started to bark and I woke at once. I put on the light, and knew immediately there was an intruder. Luckily it was a cold night, otherwise I wouldn't have had a stitch on. Instantly I leapt from the bed and grabbed the policeman's truncheon. I put on my shoes, went into the hallway and flung open the front door. The dogs and I poured out of the house like Victoria Falls! The impetus of our exit carried us halfway across the garden. Just by my garage stood a man. The dogs surrounded him instantly and I was just going to attack when he called:

'I am from Night Security. Please forgive me, I have come to the wrong house.'

The poor man didn't sound too happy. I thought he certainly had a hazardous job. Not only could you disturb a burglar, but if you came to the wrong house you were always likely to find yourself in difficulties with the house owner.

Night Security was a firm which employed a large number of askaris (police or watchmen). Every night the organisers took the askaris in Volkswagen buses to the houses which they had been hired to watch. The services of these watchmen could be hired by the night or for any period. It was a perfect arrangement for people who were going on holiday, or if husbands had jobs which took them away for the night. Twice during the night, at varying times, a car would call at each house where the Night Security askaris were on duty, to see that they were on the job. The Night Security firm had shown great enterprise in providing the public with a service so sorely needed.

We had some very good rains just before uruhu. It was almost as though it was a lucky sign for the future of the country. In Asia it is always considered fortunate if there is rain at a wedding. I was in a fever of planting, which competed with the building and the book.

Armand wrote to me from Hong Kong to tell me that my sister-in-law's husband had died. His letter arrived at the same time as a letter from my sister-in-law. I have always been immensely fond of her, and regarded her as a sister. I wrote to Armand straight away to ask if I should invite her to stay with me, but I was too late, because she had already been invited to Buenos Aires by her daughter. Angele had come out to stay with us over a year ago. She was one of the nicest guests imaginable. She was tremendously fond of gardening, and was always looking round for things to do to help us. She resembled my mother in one way in that she was always immensely grateful for even the smallest thing which one did for her. Gratitude is perhaps one of the most endearing virtues. Angele was one of the most unselfish people one could ever meet, and it was a pleasure to please her.

We were sitting on our upstairs balcony, overlooking the valley, just before lunch one day. Opposite our house the land which was supposed to be Masai Reserve has had an influx of ex-Mau-Mau detainees. The handsome, indigenous forest has been ruthlessly chopped by tree poachers. As either side of the river bank slopes steeply, there are grave possibilities of the land eroding into a gully. That would inevitably be followed by the disappearance of the magic quality of the valley.

I have tried to protect the other side of the river in every way possible. Armand and I even tried bribing the Africans by offering to pay their children's school fees if they would stop destroying the land. Unhappily, we did not realise that politics were involved. The Masai elders wanted nothing to do with the ex-detainees, and were adamant about either leasing or allowing us to buy the other side of the bank.

From time to time I have been instrumental in stopping illegal cultivation at the bottom of the valley. Arrests have been made. It is against the law to put a plantation in a place where water supplies are endangered.

To the left, on the other side of the river, was a 'shamba of mealies' (garden of corn on the cob). It had been established three years ago when we had been on safari, and had remained, with the addition of a small hut, hidden from the people above, on the opposite bank.

My sister-in-law Angele knew how much I loved our valley.

'Look, Michaela. There is a man on the other side in the very act of chopping down trees.' There was also another man digging the ground, which was raw and ugly-looking.

Furiously, I called the Provincial Commissioner on the telephone. By good fortune I got him immediately. He promised to come straight away.

'May I come to your house to see it from your side?' he asked.

'Certainly. You can borrow our field-glasses and perhaps your men will be able to identify these vandals if they try to disappear before you can question them.'

The Provincial Commissioner arrived and I took him upstairs.

'Very poor corn,' murmured the Provincial Commissioner, peering through the glasses.

'The result of cultivating on a steep slope. The run-off in the rainy season has to be seen to be believed,' I said indignantly. Despoliation always leaves me in a state of anger.

'You would hardly think they would bother to continue to plant for such a miserable crop.'

The Provincial Commissioner and his men left. They had to make quite a long journey to reach the other side of the valley. There was no direct route for a car, and they had to retrace their way back to the road which led past the park. After some time we at length saw the Provincial Commissioner's Land Rover on the other side of the valley. His men got out and moved stealthily on their quarry. The men in the valley went on working, unsuspectingly. The raiding party reached them before they were even aware they were under observation. The police fanned out while two stalwarts guarded the labourers. From the hut more people emerged.

To our astonishment, Angele and I saw the men carrying large bundles on long green stalks. There were many more men under arrest than we could have believed had been hidden in the shamba. Under the scrutiny of the police guards we could see the men who had been preparing the new ground working in the established plantation. They seemed to be weeding, for they left the corn untouched.

'What can they be doing?' asked Armand, who had come to watch with us.

We had not long to wait to find out.

The Provincial Commissioner's Land Rover, plus a reinforcement which had arrived on the scene, moved off loaded with prisoners. An hour afterwards the Provincial Commissioner called us. Armand answered the phone.

'You won't be worried by those people for some time to come. I doubt whether they will be ruining the ground any more. The corn was just a cover-up for a gigantic field of bhangi. It was being grown between the rows of mealies.'

Bhangi is a drug which is also known as Indian hemp, or Phagga, in South Africa. Its addicts become highly dangerous and might turn into homicidal lunatics. One tribe is particularly addicted to it. There is a quarry which is hidden in another depression in the land, and it was for these quarrymen that the illegal crop was grown.

I often wondered whether I was in too much of the minority to awaken Africa to the danger it faced in losing its tree cover. It is a well-known fact that on the borders of the Sahara Desert certain places had at one time had trees on the now bleak-looking hills. One or two of these spaces were even cultivated only a generation or two ago. The desert encroached, due to the crass stupidity of man. There is no end to the thoughtless waste which has gone on for centuries in this wonderful world of ours.

Our climate deteriorates yearly because of the chopping of the trees. One day my path crossed that of Chief Njonjo and Lieutenant-Colonel La Fontaine. Both were as ardent champions of the trees as one could wish to find. I had long wanted to meet Chief Njonjo. It was my friend Beatrice Muchura who, when she heard that I wished to meet the Chief, arranged a meeting. The reason why I was so eager to meet him was because he was the chief 'Man of the Trees' in Kenya. Many years ago he had met Richard St. Barbe Baker. The Chief believed as firmly as St. Barbe Baker himself in the role trees played in conserving the earth, especially in the tropics. It was not surprising to find this outstanding Kikuyu holding such ideas. He was a highly intelligent man. A natural leader amongst men, and was besides a great patriot.

The Chief invited me to be a member of his council of The Men of the Trees.

I promptly accepted.

Colonel La Fontaine and the Chief merged the two societies dedicated to arousing the love of trees in the Kenyan people. Colonel La Fontaine was chairman of the Arbors Society of Kenya. As the aims of the two societies were identical, they wisely decided to amalgamate. Colonel La Fontaine was another extraordinary person. He gave an impression of youthfulness, although I knew he had been awarded the Military Cross in Tanganyika in the 1914–18 war. One of the blessings of living in the twentieth century is that we have active older people.

16

Uhuru

THE DAYS sped towards uhuru. It was decided that 12th December 1963 should be the all-important day. It was reassuring to find that our erstwhile politicians were turning into statesmen. The biggest statesman of them all was Bwana Kenyatta himself, but then he had always been a statesman.

I have many African friends. I found that they were even nicer to me, and to other Europeans, than they had ever been. I maintain that Africans are tremendously polite. If there are any bad-mannered ones they have usually learnt this from people of other races. Some of the finest gentlemen I know are those who live in isolated places. Their natural courtesy has been unadulterated by foreign ways.

Elation was in the air. Those Europeans who would not, or could not, fit in to the changed pattern of life had already left or were leaving before the big day. Those who stayed did so because they had faith in the country.

When people asked what I thought about the position of the immigrants in Kenya I pointed out that we were fortunate in this country in having a far larger preponderance of educated people than in the other territories.

The country was like a pregnant woman. The pregnancy had dragged on with many misgivings, and with many hopes, according to the point of view. Some said that the infant child, the Kenya nation, would be a wise and lovely thing, others said it would be a monster, uncontrolled and evil. The trappings for the impending confinement were in evidence everywhere. The New Stanley Hotel, which stands in the heart of Nairobi, had for many years faced the statue of Lord Delamere, a pioneer from Europe, who had done much to write the twentieth-century history of Kenya.

The statue of Delamere was for many people as familiar a landmark as Mount Kenya itself. The statue was a handsome one, and Peter Scott's mother had every right to be proud of it. But now it was not quite in keeping with the new infant shortly to be born. The son of that Delamere, the present Lord Delamere, made a happy suggestion that the statue should be removed to Kenya's Sorsbie Art Gallery.

In place of the statue was a large disc constructed right in the centre of the roundabout. It was not until two or three days before *The Day* that the purpose of the disc became apparent. A sparkling fountain was set right in the heart of the disc. Its crystal water sprayed up towards the sky.

Water is the symbol of life itself, its purity cleanses and brings harmony to soul and body. No more fitting or more mystical decoration could have been chosen. There were flowers everywhere. It was surprising how quickly the city garbed itself in festive clothes. The visitors who come to Kenya always remark on the flowers and flowering trees which grace the city. This garden landscaping is the work and vision of Peter Greensmith, who on this occasion excelled himself. Purple petria cascaded from giant urns in the centre of the streets. Oblong caskets about eight foot long displayed tropical plants in full flower and of every hue. A welcome sight for the state visitors who had come from the northern winter.

The rains had been late, but as though nature was combining in welcoming young Kenya, the clouds gathered, and libations from above poured on the hungry earth. The grass which had been yellow and dried up was overnight lush and green, adding its emerald to the other jewel colours.

The flag which had been designed for Kenya was a striped one of black, red and green, with thin bands of white dividing the main colours. At the centre was a shield and crossed spears.

Every building, large and small, decorated its façade with the national colours, and there were many striking displays. The people, too, wore emblems on their lapels. The money collected went to the Kenya National Fund for the poor, and the needy were not forgotten in the celebrations. Some people went even further, and were not content with a lapel pin, but wore shirts, hats and even dresses made from material with a white background, sprayed with Kenya flags.

On my way to town one morning I passed the neat barracks of the Kenya African Rifles, with its gleaming white posts and expanded metal fencing. The barracks were also the home of a camel. My secretary had seen it one day walking down to the dam by itself to have a drink. She could hardly believe her eyes, as camels are to be found very much further north than Nairobi. There was a crowd of men digging furiously just past the barracks, and fencing in a vast expanse of nothing. The gusto and goodwill which they were displaying on this mysterious task aroused my curiosity, and all the way to town I wondered about it. It was not until a few days later that I noticed the builder's board announcing that this site was for the Uhuru Stadium.

It didn't seem possible that it would be ready in time, but not only was construction going on at the site but the whole web of small roads, with the stadium at its centre, appeared as if a giant spider had been working day and night. Electricians installed miles of lights along roadways and around the stadium itself.

One company supplied 800,000 feet of Dexion to build the enormous edifice which would house a quarter of a million spectators at the great event. It took three months to complete the building, with the help of two European engineers, the Dalgety Construction team and 145 Africans hired for the job.

The stadium looked hollow, like a desiccated insect, a mere skeleton. It was hard to visualise what it would look like on the great night. On that never-to-be-forgotten 12th December, when it was clothed in visitors, it looked fleshy and prosperous and no longer emaciated. The Duke of Edinburgh had been appointed the Queen's emissary.

Just before the great day I sat with an African couple watching television. With us were two Europeans. My two African friends were loyalist Kikuyu—that is, they had not been convicted of Mau-Mau activities. The Europeans were fans of long standing who had asked to meet me. They were elderly and I have a very soft spot in my heart for older people. Although I was very busy, I made the effort of trying to see them.

We sat after dinner watching the television news. On the twenty-three-inch screen flashed a face, which caught our conversation. We gazed at it spellbound. It was the face of Field Marshal

Mwariama of the Mau-Mau. His long hair hung well below his shoulders. His eyes were large, unblinking. They had a gimlet quality which stared through to the other side of one's head. Not only did his remarkable eyes dominate, but he was also extremely tall. He had a very powerful thumb, which is always an indication of strong character. He was reputed to have more than 5,000 Mau-Mau adherents in the Meru District. It would be hard to imagine the degree of the terror that the words Mau-Mau provoked unless you had lived through those suspenseful days. To many it would be a chilling thought to have these people in the midst of the twentieth-century young nation of Kenya. Yet without these people's efforts could the same results have been achieved? Field Marshal Mwariama had come down from the Mount Kenya Forest to pledge his loyalty to the Prime Minister, Mr. Jomo Kenyatta, at his home in Gatundu.

I now remembered that the Prime Minister had promised an amnesty to the forest fighters, as Mau-Mau was now called, and to the already imprisoned adherents. There was a whole deputation of people with the Field Marshal. One name which was famous to the Emergency police forces was that of Marshal General Acholi. The Mkamba, Marshal Kabui, from Kandundo, was also in the party. He was the chief forest gunsmith, and samples of his work were presented to the Prime Minister. Marshal Generals Salimu and Kivamba and Marshal Kaiugi made up the six leaders in the deputation.

My friends from Britain looked anxiously at my African guests. I could read what was in their minds as plainly as if they had expressed it in words. What would happen to the loyalist Kikuyu when the Mau-Mau came out of hiding?

I thought it was appropriate to speak about it. 'There is one very good quality in the African character which those in Europe could well emulate. Africans are remarkably forgiving. They do not usually harbour grudges, as do other races. I have often been astounded by the way Africans will completely forgive, and apparently forget, injuries fancied or otherwise.'

My Kikuyu friends smiled gratefully. Perhaps they had also overlooked this most important characteristic. I saw the husband surreptitiously take his wife's hand and give it a small reassuring squeeze.

I hoped that there would be no deviation from this admirable

African trait. If we could start anew, putting animosity behind us, we had, all of us, everything to gain.

Armand was away, and I dreaded he would want me to meet him at some rendezvous far away from Kenya. At first it had been suggested that I should meet him on the 6th of December, and the great day itself was set for the 12th.

I knew that if I could not persuade him to alter this date I would have to disobey him for the first time in our marriage.

Fortunately I was able to persuade him to alter his plans for our meeting, which was complicated by the fact that the plane to Israel, where he wanted to meet me, left Nairobi once weekly. Armand suggested I should meet him on the night of the 12th. It was almost like being Cinderella. And like Cinderella I contemplated arriving on the plane in my festive uhuru clothes, changing on the plane itself into my workday wear. I had another reprieve. Armand, to my delight, altered his plans again. He was going to London and it was arranged I should meet him on the 20th in Israel instead. Still later, and after the great day, Armand cabled to say he was coming back home, and we would have the long-awaited reunion in Kenya.

The birthday of Kenya was a festive but also historic occasion. I wanted to savour the full joy and excitement of it all, and it seemed an anticlimax to leave it in the middle. I was grateful that our plans had permitted me to experience the significant, never-to-be-repeated, events in the country which I loved with so much devotion.

Day by day the planes brought important visitors and disgorged them at Nairobi. Mrs. Indira Gandhi, the daughter of Mr. Nehru, was representing India. It was not the first time that this charming and graceful lady had been to East Africa.

There were all sorts of exciting functions. The uhuru art exhibition of African paintings, alive and vital, making the unrepresentative daubs of so-called modern art look pathetic in comparison. There were two official balls, the state and civic, at which many international stars, including Harry Belafonte, Miriam Makeba and Kenya's own Sal Davies, who had left Kenya to study law and returned as a famous entertainer, added to the gaiety, tirelessly giving their time and talent.

The Governor gave a garden party and there were dozens of other functions besides. But it was not only the distinguished visitors who gave the occasion its particular air of enchantment, it was Kenya's own sons and daughters who wandered in the delightfully decorated city, seeing the sights. People from the country in their traditional dress, gaily coloured and beaded, and young urban men and women in new Sunday-best-type clothes, eagerly crowded the streets and highways. It was exactly as though the whole of Kenya was celebrating one gigantic birthday, which indeed it was: the birth of Kenya.

Some gloomy people forecast that there might be a few drunken parties, but nothing could be further from the truth. Bwana Kenyatta had appealed to his followers not to overindulge. I did not see a single drunken person in the streets. One could not say the same thing for New Year in Paris, London or New York. I felt very proud to live in Kenya and to associate myself with its people. It was the Prime Minister's extraordinary personality which made this miracle of self-control possible. He was truly both father and teacher.

The culminating excitement was the ceremony to be held in the Uhuru Stadium at midnight, when the Union Jack would be ceremonially lowered and Kenya's flag raised. The flag-raising ceremony must surely be the proudest moment not only of a people but of the Prime Minister, the Hon. Mr. Jomo Kenyatta. He had given many years of his life and sacrificed and suffered for this precious moment of history.

There was a rehearsal on Monday of that week. The big day was to be Wednesday. A dress rehearsal was abolutely necessary in view of the enormous crowds expected and the complexity of the ceremony, which would go on from eight till twelve. When the rehearsal was under way it poured, disrupting everything. The Prime Minister rose to the occasion and restored everybody's good spirits by an impromptu speech.

The weather permitted a last-minute rehearsal the following day. Then at last the 12th.

I gave the whole household two days off and a gift of money. My people cooked the dogs' food for me, and prepared my salad for two days, so that I should have the minimum of work to do, a piece of consideration which was very touching. I told them that I did not want them to do the smallest amount of work, and I myself would throw away the rubbish, make the beds and do anything else that was necessary.

The garden party was from four o'clock to six o'clock, and the celebrations at the Uhuru Stadium started at eight. It would be impossible to get home in time to change in view of the heavy traffic which was expected. I decided to take my short evening dress with me and change at the United Kenya Club. The garden party was the most international Kenya had ever seen. The Governor, Mr. MacDonald, and his wife were dearly loved in the comparatively short time they had spent in Kenya. One somehow thought of them as Kenyans. The Duke of Edinburgh was in fine form, his famous repartee being much in evidence. One of the visitors was dressed in monkey skins. The Duke stopped to chat with him. The man said he had a farm.

'What, a monkey farm?' said the Duke, and then passed on to talk to another visitor.

The Prime Minister walked beside the Duke and the Governor, mingling with the crowd. The Prime Minister has very remarkable eyes. They are hazel in colour and hypnotic. He has great psychic power, as any psychic person would confirm.

After the garden party I went to the United Kenya Club, quickly changed and ate a hasty meal. I left the club and drove to the Princess Elizabeth Highway—the main road out of Nairobi. I couldn't believe what I saw in this familiar street. The cars were bumper to bumper on the three-lane highway. It was utterly impossible to move more than a few yards at a time, with at least ten minutes' wait in between each move. Luckily the time passed pleasantly, as everyone waved and talked to each other. I had many friends because of our television programmes playing in Kenya.

After having a conversation with one carload of people, whether Asians, Africans or Europeans, their lane would suddenly become mobile again. You would wave good-bye to them, and after ten minutes of waiting think they were parked at the stadium, but then the car in front would start moving, and you would find yourself passing them. It was very dark, but the headlights from the cars illuminated the people walking on the pavements—thousands of people were walking. They had been asked not to attempt to come to the stadium on bicycles, and indeed it would have been utterly impossible for them to do so.

The police were magnificent. They were courteous and helpful in this traffic policeman's nightmare. The enormous crowd, although good-humoured, was determined to reach the stadium as fast as possible. Everyone had tickets, which were issued free to those who had applied for them, and an early arrival hoped not to miss anything. It was stated on the tickets that all cars should be parked at eight o'clock. Only a small proportion of the crowd could have managed to comply with this request.

I walked across the grass to the stadium. My secretary had prudently suggested that I should wear flat-heeled shoes. I had my high-heeled shoes, and a lovely little silver mesh handbag, a torch and a hairbrush in a K.L.M. bag, which I slung over my shoulder. I managed to reach the stadium in spite of putting my leg into a muddy puddle up to the knee. A kind Asian family pulled me out as I wallowed around like a hippopotamus trying to keep my balance. I have never seen a more extraordinary sight than the Uhuru Stadium on the big night. There was a sea of faces all looking towards the centre of the arena. In the centre was the biggest ngoma (dance) I have ever seen in my life. No one can ever have seen, or is likely to see, such a sight ever again in Kenya. The arena itself was colossal in size.

There were several groups of different tribal dancers in every part of it. These dance teams had been chosen months before as the best representative dancers of their tribes. There were Giriama from the coast, in their short full skirts, which reminded one of the ballet. There were Kikuyu loaded with their decorative ear-rings; Turkana resplendent in ostrich feathers; Arabs doing traditional sword dances and a large group of Indian folk dancers, who had started the proceedings just as it began to rain, and valiantly carried on as the people took their seats. There were Masai tall and striking in their red-ochre-coloured paint, and long red pigtails. I could never see them without thinking of the splendours of ancient Egypt.

There were several groups of dancers playing drums. The pulsating throb of the drums is the very heartbeat of Africa. It filled the air and must have been audible for many miles. The complexity of the steps, the perfect rhythm and the authentically traditional dress of the dancers were purely African. How happy to see that the Africans had not forgotten their cultural heritage! Perhaps the beautiful dances and costumes with which I had fallen in love when I first came to Africa would not disappear. As Kenya arose to take its place amongst the other nations, pride in its own originality would remain.

There were signs, already, that a modern costume would evolve which would displace European clothes. I had for many years been advocating that African womanhood should adopt a costume suited to the climate.

'What would you suggest, Michaela?' asked one of my African friends, who knew that I had been a dress designer many years ago.

'I would suggest that it should have one bared shoulder, giving a diagonal line, with the material fastened on the other shoulder. This is the most beautiful line for a woman. It is reminiscent of many African traditional dresses—the Kikuyu, for instance. It is also not unlike the line of a sari. I would myself be happy to wear such a costume.'[1]

The men were also beginning to experiment with various Kenya-type robes.

The rain pelted down, but I had brought my Japanese umbrella, and sat in the middle, between an Asian and an African girl, sharing this small piece of cover. As I put down my umbrella I felt behind my feet for my K.L.M. bag. There was nothing behind my feet at all, just space! I got on hands and knees and peered between my seat and the next row of seats, to discover there was a sheer drop of thirty feet to the ground. I had forgotten the skeleton nature of the edifice on which we sat.

'What are you looking for?' asked the people around me. I told them, and everyone was immediately concerned.

'Go down and see if the police have found it,' suggested my neighbour. I reached ground level and asked one of the organisers whether anything had been handed in.

'Not to my knowledge,' he said, 'but after the show is over you will have more chance of making a search.' I returned to my seat.

When the excitement was at fever-pitch the Prime Minister entered the arena in his white Lincoln. He stood up for all to see him clearly, waving his white fly-whisk in the African ceremonial manner. The Duke of Edinburgh arrived ten minutes later in the uniform of an Admiral of the Fleet. Other notables arrived to take their place in the state enclosure.

There was an unrehearsed piece of excitement when Mr. Milton Obote's outriders and car went off the road and landed in thick mud. The wheels of the heavy limousine dug deeper and deeper in the quagmire. Mr. Milton Obote had only a short walk to reach the

1 A well-known fashion designer of Nairobi, Sheila Bellows, created a stunning garment for a national costume. Although we had not met at that time, she had designed it with one bared shoulder. I met her later, and wore her attractive version of Kenya national dress, on television.

dais. It took three-quarters of an hour to liberate the car from the clutches of the mud. Two figures walked across the great arena, those of the Prime Minister and the Governor General, Mr. MacDonald. A dramatic sight by very contrast to the crowded arena a few minutes before.

At one minute to midnight the large stadium was plunged into darkness to spare the feelings of the British, who might be saddened to see their flag slowly descend the flagpole.

In that one minute a lifetime was lived. It was birth but also death. The death of a whole way of life, which had its good aspects as well as its bad. It was the familiar life and now it had seconds only to live. It was phoenix-like. The new Kenya would rise on the pyre of the old one. Out of the ashes of the old would come the new Kenya. It would be made from the same components as its forbear. It would evolve, we hoped, to something new and finer. If it was a strong child it would do so, but if the infant was weak it would be seduced into folly, and who could tell the result?

The huge audience was obviously having the same thoughts, for there was not a single sound. The very silence was impressive. Oppressive with emotion. The strains of 'God Save the Queen' were played solemnly. A spotlight revealed another flag going upwards. It was the flag of Kenya. The Kenya nation was born.

The solemnity was instantly banished and from thousands of throats came the cry '*Uhuru!*' Simultaneously the strains of the new anthem burst into the new day, still dark as night. Dazzling colour spilled into the sky. A firework display so magnificent that even I enjoyed it! I am not a great lover of fireworks, having once been burned by one on my foot many years ago during another great festive occasion. The fireworks had unusual sound-effects other than the usual bang, bang! Some made whistly noises and one or two sounded as though they were also saying 'Uhuru!' The crowds left the stands, but I remained behind to search for the bag.

I was heartbroken, especially because of the silver mesh bag which had a history:

In London on a short business trip I hired a competent secretary from my friend Stella Fisher, who runs a secretarial bureau. My secretary went out shopping for me. I was so overwhelmed with work I did not have time for shopping. My secretary arrived with the purchase.

'Do you like it, Michaela?' she asked.

'I think it is the most beautiful evening bag I have ever seen.' She was delighted.

'I knew it was exactly what you should have as soon as I saw it.'

It was, of course, very expensive. If I had gone shopping by myself I would have spent two or three pounds on an evening bag, no more. I couldn't spoil her pleasure by sending it back to the shop to change it. I also felt slightly less guilty if I kept it, as someone else had bought it, not I.

An American voice broke in on my thoughts.

'Can I help?'

I looked up to see two very good-looking young men and a girl. I told them what had happened.

'Hold my camera,' the man who had spoken to me first said.

Dave Borkenhagen, with typical American energy, went first to the police, and then to the lost-property office, and afterwards climbed through the meccano-like structure of the stand to search for my K.L.M. bag. I called to him to let him know approximately where to search. Nothing could be found.

The nuisance value of losing all one's keys was frightful and I dreaded the next few days. I was fortunate in having a special kind of starter in the Buick which could be operated without a key, if you knew how.

'Let me take you to your car,' I suggested to my newly found friends.

'No, it is too far. You will have difficulty in driving there because the roads are still crowded.'

'Why not come back home with me and have something to eat, and wait until the crowds have dispersed?'

'Can we telephone from your house to find hotel accommodation? We want to stay somewhere where the car will be safe, without unloading everything.'

'I know the perfect place for you,' I said.

'Is it far?'

'It's at Langata, at my house. I have a guest house and your car will be perfectly safe in the grounds.'

'We can't give you so much trouble.'

I wouldn't listen to his protestations and those of his two friends, but took them back home.

We left behind us a whole army of police still on duty who were seeing that people got home safely. Amongst the many situations with which they coped were the five babies born in the stadium and the people who lost their cars.

I managed to persuade Mary and Jack Merselis and Paul Borkenhagen to stay for three days.

The week after uhuru gave everything which happened enormous significance. This was especially so in connection with the Prime Minister. A Prime Minister of any country is an important person. When a Prime Minister is also a leader of a liberation movement his words and deeds are magnified. He has a peculiar relationship to his people which is as a father, hero and teacher. Such a man is His Excellency Jomo Kenyatta.

It is strange that many of the greatest problems which bedevil mankind are unrecognised. If the long-range effect of deforestation could be brought home to the public there would be as much alarm on a large scale as a threat of nuclear war. In the end deforestation will be as deadly to mankind. His Excellency Jomo Kenyatta is one of the far-sighted individuals who recognises this threat to mankind and is in a position of being able to do something about it.

On 13th December the Royal College in Nairobi bestowed on Mr. Kenyatta an honorary degree, after which the opportunity was taken to plant a tree. The chosen tree was a *Mugumu ficus hochstetteri*. The mugumu has long been revered as a sacred tree.

Before the arrival of the Prime Minister there was a sudden sharp shower. The guests who were invited to see the ceremony ran for cover. The rain ceased and the Prime Minister arrived. It was a dramatic moment as the Prime Minister left the dais and walked in the company of Chief Njonjo and Colonel La Fontaine, the chief supporters of the Men of the Trees, to the site where the mugumu tree would stand. There was a hole in the ground and the tree stood with a bole of earth around its roots. The Prime Minister ceremonially shovelled in the soil.

He addressed the crowd around him.

'The tree is a symbol of life. I would like to see every Kenyan plant at least one or two trees every year. We would save our country from turning into desert. Trees help to preserve the earth from erosion.'

I could visualise many generations of students of the Royal College finding a perfect meeting place in the shade of the mugumu. This single tree would symbolise to those who come after us that a great man of wisdom had pointed the way to save the land.

My last day together with my three friends was followed, after the tree-planting ceremony, by the Royal College cocktail party. They invited me to dinner at the 'Chopsticks', a Chinese restaurant which sold mouth-watering food, and was patient enough to serve me vegetarian dishes. Then they took me to the concert given by Miriam Makeba and Harry Belafonte at the National Theatre.

I waved good-bye to them the next morning feeling sad and hoping our paths might cross again.

I went back into the house still feeling rather flat. I would cheer myself up by going to town under the pretext of getting my supplies of yoghurt.

Before I turned into the main road I saw a very, very old woman in Kikuyu tribal dress. Her back was bent and she was as frail as a butterfly's wing. She was obviously going to walk to Nairobi. I stopped the car, jumped out and spoke to her.

'Where are you going, Mama?' I asked her.

'I am going to Nairobi.'

'Come, I will take you there.'

I opened the door for her. The bent and wrinkled old lady was overwhelmed with gratitude, and in fact she started to sing a little song for me.

She said, 'You are my child and you have helped your mother who is old.'

I in turn said, 'You are my mother and it is my pleasure to help you.'

When I got out of the car I took her and the small hand-woven bag she carried and handed her down to the pavement. She blessed me and we hugged one another before I left her. I longed to be able to do something for all the old people, who have so rightly earned our love and respect by having lived a selfless and useful lifetime. Everyone should do honour to all these innumerable nameless old people, who are not the generals and princes, but who are the very life-blood of the future.

When I got home I told Tshikadi and the other servants about the old lady, wondering if they knew her. They didn't recognise my description. She must have been visiting one of her children and was going back home. Tshikadi said, 'You did a very good deed to stop and help the old lady and God will bless you.'

The very next day there was a telephone call from the police.

'We have your bag which you lost at the Uhuru Stadium.

Will you come along and identify it and see if everything is intact?'

I couldn't believe my ears. I am sure if I had lost the same bag in any other city the chances are remote that I would see it again.

It was my bag. Inspector John, at the Kingsway Police Station, told me that he always watched our programmes on television and enjoyed them. It made me feel more than ever that we were part of Kenya, for although our programmes go out to thirty countries it is most important to have a following at home.

EPILOGUE

Harambee

PROBLEMS are not automatically solved by political independence as many of the more naive East Africans had imagined. But still there was hope. Bwana Kenyatta had shown us the way. He had been speaking and he had used the word *Harambee*, which spread through every level of society in Kenya. He must have been inspired in no ordinary manner to use just that word. Harambee is hard to translate. It has something of the element of 'Do it yourself', 'Help yourself' or 'Push together'. When men carry heavy burdens or move some heavy object slung on poles they will put their shoulders to the common task and together they will chant 'Harambee'. They tense their muscles for a superhuman effort and on the last syllable they lift and push. So are large burdens dealt with and so may our problems be dealt with too.

'Harambee, Harambee, Harambee.'